SPECIAL AGENT

SPECIAL AGENT

MY LIFE ON THE FRONT LINES OF THE FBI

CANDICE DELONG
AND ELISA PETRINI

HEADLINE

Published in 2001
by HEADLINE BOOK PUBLISHING

Published in the United States of America in 2001
by Hyperion, an imprint of Buena Vista Books Inc.

10 9 8 7 6 5 4 3 2 1

DeLong, Candice
    Special agent: on the front lines of the FBI
    1.DeLong, Candice
    2.Federal Bureau of Investigation – Officials and employees
    3.Policewomen – United States – Biography
    I.Title
    363.2'082'092

ISBN 0 7472 3248 2

Printed and bound in Great Britain by
Mackays of Chatham PLC, Chatham, Kent

Text design by Casey Hampton

HEADLINE BOOK PUBLISHING
A division of Hodder Headline
338 Euston Road
London NW1 3BH

www.headline.co.uk
www.hodderheadline.com

He who strives for freedom every day
To him may we grant redemption

—GOETHE

This book is dedicated to the thirty-three brave men and women of the
Federal Bureau of Investigation who have been killed in the line of duty
as the direct result of an adversarial action, and to their families. The
brave sacrifice of their lives, for the good of all, will never be forgotten.

Edwin C. Shanahan, 27 years old when killed on 10/11/25 in
Chicago, Illinois

Paul E. Reynolds, 29 years old when killed on 8/9/29 near Phoenix,
Arizona

Raymond J. Caffrey, 30 years old when killed on 6/17/33 in Kansas
City, Missouri

W. Carter Baum, 29 years old when killed on 4/22/34 near Bohemia
Lodge, Wisconsin

Herman E. Hollis, 31 years old when killed on 11/27/34 near
Barrington, Illinois

Samuel E. Cowley, 34 years old when killed on 11/28/34 near
Barrington, Illinois

Nelson B. Klein, 37 years old when killed on 8/16/35 in College
Corner, Indiana

Wimberly W. Baker, 27 years old when killed on 4/17/37 in Topeka, Kansas

Truett E. Rowe, 33 years old when killed on 6/1/37 in Gallup, New Mexico

William R. Ramsey, 34 years old when killed on 5/3/38 near Penfield, Illinois

Hubert J. Treacy, Jr., 29 years old when killed on 3/13/42 in Abingdon, Virginia

Joseph J. Brock, 44 years old when killed on 7/26/52 in New York, New York

John Brady Murphy, 35 years old when killed on 9/26/53 in Milwaukee, Wisconsin

Richard Purcell Horan, 34 years old when killed on 4/18/57 in Suffield, Connecticut

Terry R. Anderson, 42 years old when killed on 5/17/66 near Shade Gap, Pennsylvania

Douglas M. Price, 27 years old when killed on 4/25/68 in San Antonio, Texas

Anthony Palmisano, 26 years old when killed on 1/8/69 in Washington, D.C.

Edwin R. Woodriffe, 27 years old when killed on 1/8/69 in Washington, D.C.

Gregory W. Spinelli, 24 years old when killed on 3/15/73 in Charlotte, North Carolina

Jack R. Coler, 28 years old when killed on 6/26/75 at Pine Ridge, South Dakota

Ronald A. Williams, 27 years old when killed on 6/26/75 at Pine Ridge, South Dakota

Johnnie L. Oliver, 35 years old when killed on 8/9/79 in Cleveland, Ohio

Charles W. Elmore, 34 years old when killed on 8/9/79 in El Centro, California

Jarad R. Porter, 44 years old when killed on 8/9/79 in El Centro, California

Robin L. Ahrens, 33 years old when killed on 10/5/85 in Phoenix, Arizona

Jerry L. Dove, 30 years old when killed on 4/11/86 in Miami, Florida

Benjamin P. Grogan, 53 years old when killed on 4/11/86 in Miami, Florida

L. Douglas Abram, 48 years old when killed on 1/19/90 in St. Louis County, Missouri

John L. Bailey, 47 years old when killed on 6/25/90 in Las Vegas, Nevada

Martha Dixon Martinez, 35 years old when killed on 11/22/94 in Washington, D.C.

Michael J. Miller, 40 years old when killed on 11/22/94 in Washington, D.C.

William Christian, Jr., 48 years old when killed on 5/29/95 in Greenbelt, Maryland

Charles L. Reed, 45 years old when killed on 3/22/96 in Philadelphia, Pennsylvania

CONTENTS

ACKNOWLEDGMENTS

I am grateful to the following people for their help with this book: Retired Special Agents of the Federal Bureau of Investigation Rick Hahn, Roy Lane, Jr., Gordon McNeill, Gerry Miller, Tom Norris, Michael D. Wilson, and to the many others who requested that I not mention their names; to K. D. Sullivan and Ann Longknife of *Creative Solutions*; to David Lombard-Koy, for true friendship; and to Kathy Dunlap Haibach, for always being there.

I also very much appreciate the help of former Assistant United States Attorney Jeremy Margolis; retired Special Agents of the Illinois State Police Ed Cisowski and Tom Schumpp; Special Agents of the Drug Enforcement Administration Rick Barrett and Dave Tibbets; Abdul Mabud of the Bureau of Alcohol, Tobacco, and Firearms; Sheriff Tom Templeton of LaSalle County, Illinois; Chief John Milner and Commander Ray Bradford of the Elmhurst, Illinois, Police Department; and I honor the memory of the late Gary Konzak, former chief of the LaGrange, Illinois, Police Department, and the late Edward Hegarty of the Federal Bureau of Investigation.

I am thankful to Ken Follett, who saw the potential in my story, encouraged me from the beginning, and opened the right doors; to my agent, Elaine Koster, who made the dream come true; to my writer,

Elisa Petrini, for getting my voice on paper; and to Martha Levin at Hyperion for believing in this book.

Finally, I am eternally grateful to my parents, Ken and Geraldine Rosing, for raising me in an environment where anything was possible, and to my brothers, Wayne, Keith, and Glenn Rosing, for keeping me on my toes rather than on a pedestal. I am especially thankful to my son, Seth Rosing DeLong, my grounding rod, whose encouragement, support, coaching, and gentle nagging made this book happen.

Elisa Petrini would like to thank Candice DeLong for the glimpse into a fascinating world of intrigue and adventure—it has been thrilling to walk even a mere block or two in Candice's shoes!—as well as Seth DeLong, Rick Hahn, and the many others in law enforcement who have contributed time and memories. I am grateful to Deborah Schneider for the referral to Elaine Koster, our intrepid agent on this book; to Elaine, for pulling the project together, running interference, and offering tireless support; and to Martha Levin and all the hardworking folks at Hyperion. I am also indebted to Stuart Applebaum, for his invaluable goading and unfailingly wise advice; to Lisa Drew, for books and good counsel; to Denise Stinson and Craig Nelson, for daily encouragement; and to Alan Hubbell and Ann-Marie Komiensky; as well as to dear, sustaining friends and colleagues: Jody Rein, Susan Goodman, Jim Landis, Leslie Meredith, Ellen Levine, Ilene Bellovin, Susan Kamil, Mary Evans, Sheila Weller, Gina Barnett, and Joseph and Dvorah Telushkin, along with my longtime mainstays Todd Miller and Pat Hanafee. Finally, I would like to acknowledge my parents, Mario Petrini and Valeria Colombatto Brown, Aunt Alma Petrini, and Grandfather Joseph Colombatto, and especially, my sister Andrea Petrini, for her priceless gifts of time.

PREFACE

In the year 2000, I reached my twentieth anniversary in the FBI and became eligible for retirement. Most agents retire after twenty years or at age fifty, while they still feel young enough to shift gears, rather than work straight through to the mandatory retirement age of fifty-seven. For me, the date alone suggested completion—it seemed only fitting, at the close of the millennium, to wind up a phase of life. Then, too, most agents harbor certain ambitions: to catch a Class A fugitive, to capture a dangerous terrorist or killer, and to rescue a child from an abductor. I had done all three.

As I talked to my family and friends about retiring, I came to realize that my fairly typical life in the FBI sounded rather extraordinary to those outside law enforcement. Female special agents were well represented in fiction, but no one could recall a memoir by a woman who came in, as I did, in the years shortly after J. Edgar Hoover's death. So, on the eve of my retirement, I was persuaded to record these stories and gained, as agents must, the blessing of the Bureau (to ensure that no sensitive information related to national security or pending cases is revealed). After my retirement, when I would no longer be perceived as a Bureau spokesperson but as a private citizen, I would be allowed to discuss them publicly.

Some of the people cited in this book who are still active or retired FBI personnel could not be located or have requested anonymity, so I have assigned them pseudonyms, referred to them by nicknames or first names, and in some cases, altered their descriptions to preserve their professional privacy. Other names, places, and physical characteristics have been changed to protect the identities of victims. Finally, I have changed names and descriptions, often inventing nicknames, to avoid embarrassing some who might deserve to feel chagrin. It's enough that they know who they are. Pseudonyms are designated with an asterisk (*) at first mention throughout the book.

On my wall, I now have the commemorative plaque that the Bureau prepares for every agent who retires. PRESENTED TO SPECIAL AGENT CANDICE DELONG, it reads, and bears my credentials, along with my ten- and twenty-year pins, above my dates of service: 1980–2000. This book is a repository of the memories that it symbolizes, the satisfactions and the regrets.

—*Candice Rosing DeLong*
Spring 2001

SPECIAL AGENT

PROLOGUE

The call came at four 'clock in the morning. It was Tom, my squad-mate on the San Francisco Child Abduction Task Force, who had a hot tip from the Nevada FBI. "Candice," he told me, "a guy's passing through town with a kidnapped boy. Wanna get in on the bust?"

"Hell, yes," I said, instantly awake. It's rare to get a chance to thwart a kidnapping in progress and to recover the victim alive. In more than 90 percent of non-custody-related abductions, the child is molested and then quickly released. But each year, of the 200 to 300 children who go missing for more than twenty-four hours, fewer than 50 percent ever make it home.

This child, Joshua,* was the eleven-year-old son of a single mother, who had let her friend Michael treat him to a week at the beach. Having raised my own son alone, I can certainly understand how welcome such an offer might sound. But it's not at all uncommon for pedophiles to befriend or even marry women just to get at their children. There's actually a special law enforcement term for it—the stepdaddy syndrome. Others may enter adult relationships as a cover for their true predilec-tions. The notorious John Wayne Gacy, for example, a divorced father of two, married his second wife the same year he embarked on a rampage of abduction and torture that would claim the lives of thirty-three teen-age boys. He buried most of them in the crawl space beneath the house where he lived with his wife, her children, and his mother-in-law, who would often complain of the odor of "dead rats."

Frighteningly, a full quarter of the annual tally of sex-related murders have victims under the age of seventeen. Indeed, according to the Department of Justice, children under seventeen suffer a shocking proportion—78 percent—of the sexual assaults resulting in imprisonment. Over 85 percent of their abusers are people they know and trust—people like Michael, a family "friend" for several years, who had kidnapped Joshua.

On the day he was to come home, Joshua called his mother to ask permission to stay longer. She said no—and then her son disappeared. The local FBI office managed to determine that the abductor had bought two bus tickets to Oakland, California, across the Bay Bridge from me. I went to meet Tom and the rest of the team at the Oakland Greyhound station.

"No luck yet," I was told. It was possible that we had missed the abductor and child, for at least one bus had already come in that night. At 9 A.M., Ray Cummings,* supervisor of the Oakland violent crime squad, suggested that we split up and also stake out the Amtrak station, in case they tried to catch the early-morning train. Its destination was San Diego, just ten miles from Mexico. Once they made it across the border, they would probably be lost to us forever.

The train left at 9:30, so we sped right over. Ray's direction proved right, for there on the platform, ready to board, was a man with a young boy who matched the description of the missing child. As soon as we approached, the guy tried to bolt, with the boy tight in his clutches. A chorus of shouts rang out: "Hold it right there!" "FBI!"

As the team grabbed him and tried to wrestle him into handcuffs, I reached through the jostling arms and pried the boy from his grasp. "You're okay, honey," I said soothingly. He was crying and shaking with terror.

Then, all of a sudden, the suspect pitched forward, gasping and gagging, and collapsed, croaking out, "I'm having a heart attack."

I'll just bet you are, I thought.

Leaving Joshua in the care of one of my squadmates, I pushed through the crowd that had started to ring the suspect. "Don't worry," I said, dropping down beside him. "I'm a nurse."

I checked his pupils and his breathing and slid my fingers to his throat to find his pulse. Like a mother examining a child for signs of fever, I laid my palm on his forehead and his cheeks. My suspicion was correct. "He's faking," I told the squad hovering over us.

They yanked him to his feet and cuffed his hands behind him. Sobbing out loud now, Joshua screamed, "Leave him alone! He's my friend!"

That didn't surprise me. The reaction was classic—the outrage of a child seduced by the promise of love. Unlike psychopaths, who get sexual or sadistic or vengeful thrills from their power over the weak, pedophiles have erotic feelings for children and try to woo them with gifts and affection. The lonely child of a mother run ragged by trying to care for her family and to make ends meet may be all too vulnerable to the lavish attentions of another adult. Then, when the adult who has so insidiously won his love awakens his sexuality, the child will be torn apart by confusion and guilt. The psychic damage pedophiles do children, with their seductions and betrayals, is profound.

Over the next eight hours, I would learn the harrowing details of Joshua's ongoing abuse and recent "vacation." At first he kept fidgeting and stonewalling me, reluctant to betray his "friend." Finally he admitted, "Michael said I should never tell the cops about anything. He said you would hurt us and take me away."

"You know, I have a son named Seth who looks just like you," I told him. "Do I seem like someone who would hurt you?"

He acknowledged that I didn't.

"Besides," I went on, "nobody's going to hurt you because you've done nothing wrong. Adults who like children in the wrong way will say things like that to fool them."

I kept using the words *children* and *child* to emphasize to Joshua that whatever had gone on, he wasn't responsible, even if—being eleven and so immature that he looked nine—he wanted to think he was a man. He had suffered enough emotional torment to overwhelm a grown man. I wanted to give him permission to feel victimized.

But Joshua insisted that Michael was his friend and wanted to show me his gifts to prove it. When he unzipped his duffel bag, I saw a crack pipe sticking out of a tangle of clothes. "What's that thing?" I asked.

He pulled it out and then let a little of the story leak. Fed only cookies and soda pop by his kidnapper—and plied with crack cocaine, presumably to numb him into submission—in a single week he had dropped from eighty to a haggard seventy pounds. Still, Joshua thought that getting to smoke crack was "cool." "And look what he bought me, Agent Candy," he said, digging out some CDs. "He loves me more than my mother—and I hate her."

This kind of brainwashing is typical too. Pedophiles try to boost their odds of success and reduce their risk of exposure by alienating their young victims from their families.

"That's what bad adults do," I told him. "They buy presents—they'll try anything to get what they want. They tell lies and make promises to make children think they love them. But your mother is the one who loves you more than anything. She's the one who called so we would rescue you. That's how much your mother loves you."

I reiterated, "And no matter what a bad adult might say, nothing bad that happens is ever the child's fault. The adult is the one—the only one—who is wrong."

Clearly, love had little to do with the abductor's plans. He had told Joshua that they were headed for Mexico, where he would "buy" a little girl and take the two of them to the Netherlands. They would make a video to send Joshua's mother, explaining that he was never coming back. That the Netherlands figured in the scheme suggested that they'd be making other videos too, for shooting child pornography films there is relatively easy. After that, I had no doubt, two children would be useless, disposable baggage to a man on the run.

I also felt certain that Joshua had been sexually abused. We had discovered that his abductor was wanted in Texas for parole violations following two prior child-molesting convictions. It appalled me that such scum had been allowed to ooze back onto the streets. Yet abusers all too commonly are. Child molesters rarely do serious time, even though they murder children's innocence.

But it is very hard for any eleven-year-old boy to talk about sex, never mind one who has been abused by a man. I tried to give Joshua neutral language to express what had been done to him. "Were you ever touched in the 'bathing suit area'?" I asked. "That's what some adults will do to children."

Little by little I chipped away at his resistance. When Joshua finally opened up, it was like a boil had been lanced, and what came out made me want to cry. In a rush, he described the acts he had been forced to perform, some of which Michael had captured on video. A search of Michael's duffel bag would turn up these homemade sex tapes. For over a year, Michael had been, in Joshua's words, "violating" him, just as he had done with his older brother in the past.

I kept reaffirming that the abuse wasn't his fault, that any wrongdoing was Michael's. "He's the one who could go to jail, not you," I stressed.

The idea of Michael behind bars seemed to comfort Joshua immensely. I still remember how his shoulders relaxed, as if he were shedding a burden, and how his face softened. I was watching a brittle young man ease up and become a sweet little boy again—the child he deserved to be. He clung to me for solace, and I just held him and let him cry. He then fell fast asleep, sitting in a chair.

Joshua was still too upset to talk to his mother, who was irate when she reached me at home that night. "Look," I had to say, "do you know that your boyfriend beats your sons with a belt? And that your great pal Michael has sexually abused both of them? He's been doing it to Joshua for over a year."

"What?" she said, incredulous.

"That's right, your older son too. He's going to need some therapy."

At that she broke down in tears.

"Give Joshua some time," I told her more gently. "For now, let's just be thankful that he's alive."

I could well imagine the anguish and terrible guilt she had to be feeling. Fortunately, it took only a few days for Joshua to come around, and then he grew very anxious to see her. That made me feel good—and so did the compliment that Ray Cummings was kind enough to pay me: "I've never seen anyone turn a kid around that fast."

I couldn't take all the credit, however. I had been applying some of the principles I'd learned from Ken Lanning at the FBI Academy, one of the world's leading authorities on child victimization.

If Joshua's turnaround seemed fast, our case against Michael unfolded in slow motion. Though we had caught him dead to rights, he feigned mental illness and was held in a psychiatric facility for evaluation—a rather common dodge among sex offenders. John Wayne Gacy tried to claim that he wasn't responsible for his crimes because he had multiple personality disorder. As John Douglas, one of the FBI's legendary profilers, jokes in his book *Mindhunter*, "I'll let the innocent personalities go as long as I can lock up the guilty one."

Finally, Michael was found mentally fit and, two years after his arrest, pled guilty in court. I sat next to Joshua that day, and he could now say of his former "friend": "I hate him, Agent Candy." He would be sentenced—thanks to his sex videos of Joshua, the cocaine found in Joshua's bloodstream, and other violations tacked on to the abduction charges— to thirty years in prison. The prosecutor told me that it was the heaviest sentence he'd ever seen imposed on a child abductor whose victim was alive. Imagine how a jury would have walloped him!

Michael will be eligible for parole after twenty-five years. Since he was forty-three at the time of his arrest, he will then be sixty-eight years old. If you think that age will render him less of a threat, think again. While the average age at arrest of all violent offenders, according to government statistics, is twenty-nine, sex offenders skew older. About 7 percent of rapists and 12 percent of those convicted of sexual assault (a broader category encompassing sex acts, such as sodomy, apart from frank intercourse) are over fifty. I know of one man—99 percent of all sex crimes are committed by men—who was convicted of sexual assault when he was a hundred years old.

Joshua's story doesn't have a happy ending—at least not yet. Sexual abuse victims require intensive psychotherapy, which the federal government will underwrite for as long as they need it. But many continue to suffer such backlash effects as extreme aggression or a lifelong sense of stigmatization. The victims' families are traumatized as well, especially when the offender is a close relative, as is the case roughly 45 percent of the time when the victim is under the age of eleven. Some victims must be treated for diseases they contract as a result of the abuse, including AIDS. Tragically, unless they get help, about a third will perpetuate the cycle of violation by becoming child molesters themselves.

In my twenty years in the FBI, I've had the chance to bear witness to history. I came in on one of the early waves of women storming what had been an unassailable male bastion for more than fifty years. Back then women represented less than 4 percent of a total agent force of 8,000. Today we're still a minority but a much more significant one— 15 percent of the total 11,500 agents—1,700 strong.

But women were just one of the great sea changes transforming the Bureau at the time I entered. It was the dawn of the art/science of profiling, the most systematic analysis of crimes and their perpetrators ever attempted in history. I was lucky enough to train under the masters at the Bureau's celebrated Behavioral Science Unit and could now and then dream that I was helping to advance the field—as when John Douglas, the father of the discipline, praised one of my profiles as "making his job easier" and when the great Roy Hazelwood, the preeminent authority on all aspects of sexual criminality, from rape, sadism, and murder to autoerotic asphyxiation, pronounced a peculiar case of mine "one for the books." That made me feel proud—like I was making a contribution.

I have helped snare serial rapists and killers, bird-dogged dangerous terrorists, and stood on the front lines as the infamous Unabomber was brought to justice—wearing my son Seth's jacket! I had been tracking the Unabomber for months, and on that day, I left a message on Seth's machine, saying, "It's over now," breaking into tears of relief. When I heard he'd saved that tape and when I saw the walls of his apartment papered with news stories on our mission—and in each, our captive, Ted Kaczynski, had the ski parka I'd "borrowed" from Seth draped over his shoulders—I cried again.

But the single most gratifying achievement of my entire career was rescuing Joshua and returning him to his mother's arms. He asked me to bring him home; so I was there at the airport when she reached out to him in remorse, sorrow, sympathy, reassurance—and above all, joy—

and he stepped into the protection and comfort of her embrace. They had a long road ahead to repair their shattered lives, but they were ready now to take the first step.

The controversial cases—the Wacos, the Ruby Ridges—are the ones that make the news, but in that moment I thought, "This is what I wish the public could see. This is why I joined the Bureau. This is what we do, protect and serve."

For ultimately, it's not the high-profile or even the high-adrenaline cases that have made my life in the FBI so satisfying. It's been just as much the day-to-day feeling that I am part of a safety net—as if the Bureau were a big shark fence protecting the world from the dangers and predators of the deep.

1

DARK EYES

I was working as a nurse when I first got the notion of joining the FBI. Not your average bedside/medical surgical nurse but head nurse in a maximum-security psychiatric unit at University Hospital* in Chicago. So I had to laugh when one of my instructors at Quantico, seeing me avert my eyes at the skull-sawing-open point of an autopsy movie, declared that I'd make a poor FBI agent. It was a pretty natural human reflex to look away, but to him it meant that I couldn't "handle stress" (code for being squeamish, like a girl).

I could have told him plenty about stress. I almost said, "You're an idiot," but luckily I didn't. As it was he wrote me up for being insolent, just for laughing.

On a maximum-security psych ward, you live under constant stress, with your antennae always up, ready to fly into action at the sound of a thump, a shout, or the drumming of running footsteps. When you have violent patients, you must be hyperattuned, ever watchful as their moods escalate, day by day, waiting for the inevitable explosion to come. I did a stretch like that for five years once, without a break, though today many hospitals require psych ward personnel to rotate off such units periodically for the sake of their own sanity. But back then, psychiatric nursing was what I believed I was born to do.

• • •

When I was young a close friend of mine suffered from a crippling depression, and I saw how devastating the demons of the mind can be. My idealism was ignited, and I resolved that when I got older I would help those living under the scourge of mental illness—in what capacity, I wasn't sure. Like most girls of the immediate postwar generation, I assumed that my options were limited.

My mother, Geraldine, worked in a bank until she met my father, Ken Rosing, a building contractor. He had first spotted her by the pool table at the Hasty Pudding Club, when he was a Harvard student and she was a USO volunteer. After a whirlwind two-month courtship they wed and, at the time of my father's death, had been devoted to each other for fifty-five years. They raised four children on a three-acre spread near Phoenix. I grew up on the back of a horse. Then, when I was fourteen, my family moved to San Francisco, trading the wide-open spaces for the confines of an apartment in Pacific Heights. But I loved the city, and being the only girl, I was lucky enough to get my own room. The boys had to share.

My oldest brother, Wayne, was an amateur astronomer and had a home telescope lab, where he taught me to grind mirrors. He would go on to become a computer engineer, helping to usher Apple into its boom years. But he continued to build telescopes, and now—professionally, as an avocation—he creates high-powered devices and installs them all over the world.

My brother Keith, two years younger than Wayne, introduced me to the Invisible Man and Invisible Woman, clear plastic models of the human body filled with brightly colored organs. We had a game, competing to see who could name all the different parts of anatomical systems the fastest—respiratory, digestive, endocrine, the bones of the skeleton. Keith would go on to become a doctor, one of the first physicians to be board certified in emergency medicine. Somewhere in our DNA there must be a gene promoting the love of risk and crisis.

I am two years younger than Keith, and two years after me, Glenn came along. He is the computer systems specialist for the Milwaukee

FBI. He has been tremendously supportive, frequently calling during my training at Quantico to give me encouragement and to tell me how proud of me he was. We always shared as kids, and now as adults both working for the FBI, we have even more to talk about.

Compared to my brothers, I was an underachiever, a late bloomer. I enrolled in a three-year nursing program right out of high school, then got married when I was nineteen. Six years later, my only son, Seth, was born. I had met my husband, then living in Champaign-Urbana, Illinois, when he was spending a summer visiting his family in California. He was standing at a gas pump, filling his car, when I tried to roll, literally, into the station. My car had run out of gas—on an incline luckily, so I could push it myself most of the way—and had lurched to a halt on the street right by the station. I told him my predicament, asking him to help me roll it the rest of the way to the pumps. He let out a beautiful laugh—he had such a fine alto tenor voice that he had trained to sing opera—and I fell in love.

Moving to Champaign-Urbana with my new groom, I enrolled at the university to get a bachelor of science degree in nursing. Out of curiosity I took a criminology course, not realizing that its "highlights" would include regular presentations of slides featuring violent deaths. Half the campus, it seemed, would turn out for these freak shows, to shiver and laugh at the grisly images. That made me sick. There was one terrible picture that I can still see in my mind—the headless torso of a coed, dressed in a plaid skirt, sweater set, and saddle shoes. The class tried to guess whether we were looking at a homicide, a suicide, or a misadventure. Almost no one got the correct answer—it was a suicide. A psych patient out of the hospital on a pass, she had thrown herself under the shrieking blade of a sawmill. "Aha!" everybody laughed, as I sat paralyzed with horror. I was studying to be a psych nurse but now thought seriously about abandoning my lifelong ambition. I was certain I could never stand it if I lost a patient that way.

Here I am, thirty years later, having spent my career steeped in gore, untimely death, and human suffering. Gruesome crime scene photos have been my stock in trade.

•   •   •

But I stuck with psych nursing. Surprisingly, I had been the only student in my class of thirty, back at the small nursing college, who was at all inspired by the psychiatric specialization. Many of the others thought the psych rotation was "stupid," a "waste of time," not "real" nursing at all. Others were terrified that they'd be walking into a snakepit, where they'd risk being injured or killed. It's true that in the late 1940s and early 1950s, all too many state hospitals resembled the institution in *One Flew over the Cuckoo's Nest*. But this was 1970 and we were doing our training in a much more humane setting, the small locked psych ward of a general hospital, under an instructor so revered that the staff called her Dr. Nurse.

For my first day of clinical practice I dressed carefully, I still remember, in a plaid suit and a gold sweater—psych nurses wear street clothes instead of whites, so the patients feel more like clients than incarcerees—eager to make a good impression on the patient assigned to be my very own. He was nowhere to be found, however, so I wound up disappointedly sitting in the dayroom, where a kindly man around my father's age approached me. We made small talk and he confided that he had entered the hospital because he needed a "safe environment" in which to "deal with some things." I felt so proud—already a patient was feeling comfortable enough to open up to me.

I was determined to continue to draw him out, so I went along when the man suggested that I come to his room, where there was something he wanted to retrieve. He kicked the door shut, and as he fumbled in the closet, I settled onto the bedside chair. "You're not like the others," he said, "I like talking to you."

I allowed myself a small private smile of pride.

"I like talking to you because you are interested in me and what I have to say, not just in telling me to do something."

"Telling you to do something . . . ," I echoed, as we had been taught. Reflecting a patient's thoughts so he could hear them out loud was supposed to help him develop new insights.

"Yeah, always telling me what to do, wanting things . . ." He moved away from the closet, pacing back and forth in front of the door as his agitation built. "Always clawing at me. Nothing is ever good enough . . ."

Great, I thought, *he's emotionally engaged.* I was oblivious to the fact that I was effectively trapped in the room. I then popped the classic therapeutic question, "How does that make you feel?"

"Feel? I feel like they're always watching. They'll never leave me alone. They're always wanting something, I can feel their eyes—"

"Whose eyes?" I interrupted.

"My wife's, of course! She's always pushing me, pushing—she can never be happy . . . I don't want to hurt them, I love them, my son and my little girl . . ."

By now he was crying and shaking, and just then, the door opened. Dr. Nurse said firmly, "Candy, I need to see you at the nursing station."

"Don't go," the man begged, clutching desperately at my hands. I tried to reassure him: "We can help you here, don't worry, things will get better for you . . . ," as Dr. Nurse gently tugged me away.

In the hall she asked, "Do you know why that man's in here?"

"Well, he seemed like a paranoiac," I began, warming to my role as junior diagnostician.

"You might say that," Dr. Nurse replied. "Paranoid enough to think his family was trying to kill him, so he killed them first. While they were sleeping, he bludgeoned his son and his three-year-old baby girl with a golf club, and then he stabbed his wife to death. He is what's known as a 'family annihilator.' "

Sadly he was just the first of many family annihilators I would encounter in my years on maximum-security wards and, later on, as a field profiler for the FBI.

The encounter didn't scare me. More than anything, it fueled my commitment to the work I was convinced was my calling. I resolved that day that to come to understand how such terrifying delusions could grip the mind and what happened in that horrific moment before such savage impulses were unleashed. Barely out of my teens, I was fired with passion, determined to help other sufferers—so many of the homicidally insane patients I came to know were the products of profound physical and mental brutality—before they reached the point of murder. Thirty years later, through the art/science of profiling, I'm still grappling with the same mysteries, though from a different point of view—with an eye to saving potential future victims of violence.

But I wasn't so naïve as to miss learning some important lessons from my mistake: That was the last time I ever got myself cornered alone in a room with a patient; and I now knew better than to press a psychotic person to "get in touch with his feelings." A patient in such a state needs to be watched and reassured that the voices in his head or feelings that are overwhelming him aren't real, until medication can bring him some relief. "Insights" fan the flames of terrifying delusions, but I've even seen psychotherapists badger patients to express feelings that the lucid parts of their minds are struggling to contain—and for good reason. I used to call that the "these hands" syndrome—a hubristic belief, flying in the face of patients' needs and cues, not to mention plain common sense, in one's own ability to effect healing.

I finished my studies and became a registered nurse (RN) specializing in psychiatry. My patients ran the gamut from the troubled, people who needed a brief stint in the hospital to get over some emotional speed bump in life, to those afflicted with anorexia nervosa, manic and chronic depression, and schizophrenia with full-blown auditory and visual hallucinations. Few of them were homicidal, of course—the majority of the "criminally" ill on the wards were garden-variety mentally disordered sex offenders. Nor was the strangest patient I ever saw a killer. Rather, she was a tiny, plump, elderly woman with a sweet round face, clear blue eyes, and snow-white hair tied up in a soft bun. In her cotton floral print housedress, she looked like Norman Rockwell's idea of the perfect granny.

In fact she was a great-grandmother, an octogenarian living with her middle-aged daughter and son-in-law, who one day, all of a sudden, got combative, throwing glasses of water and spitting at anyone who crossed her path. Her shocked family called their family physician, who advised them to take her to the emergency room, thinking that perhaps she had hit her head or was having some kind of bizarre seizure. That was easier said than done. No one could quell her ferocity long enough to get her into the car. So they called the paramedics, and eventually it took three trained men to wrestle the 100-pound woman into the ambulance. In the ER, fighting like a demon, she had to be clapped into four-way leather restraints to protect the staff.

When exhaustive testing yielded no physical key to her condition, she was admitted to the psych ward, where she began to wreak havoc. Not because of her wild flailing—we were used to that—but because of the roars coming out of her mouth. She was bellowing the most vividly obscene, almost kaleidoscopically inventive vulgarities any of us had ever heard. When I first met her, she greeted me with a vehement burst: "Eat shit, you ugly pussy-eater slut, fuck you, you cocksucker bitch whore"—that was just the warm-up—followed by a beatific smile. Then she spat at me, with her daughter standing by, mortified. I was choking, trying not to laugh.

Nothing I studied at St. Joseph's College of Nursing ever prepared me for this!

Her problem, of course, was not really funny. The poor woman's verbal assaults went on around the clock, for days. She never even slept. Every few seconds a barrage of obscenities would spew from her mouth, like an eruption of Old Faithful. The profanities might come in sentences or in an alphabetical list, or sometimes just in a torrent like one long, screamed curse. We had to confine the patient to her room so that her howls wouldn't disturb the others and for her own protection, lest some already agitated patient be provoked enough by her imprecations to attack. It was hard enough for us to withstand her abuse. She was under twenty-four-hour observation, which meant that staff members had to take turns being shut in with her and subjected to her hour-upon-hour litany of vulgarities. We would draw straws to pick each shift's sacrificial lamb. When we were finally able to get her sedated enough to sleep (a little-by-little process that took a few days), a blessed calm descended on the ward, as if a twister had just passed through it.

Then, just as suddenly as it began, the storm passed. After a few days of heavy sedation, when she slept most of the time, she started to have lucid moments, and by the end of that week she had stopped swearing altogether. Ten hellish days after being admitted to the hospital, she went home, completely restored to her old sweet self, with no memory of the episode whatsoever.

What had happened to this poor woman? No one ever found out. She had no detectable brain tumor, no evidence of neurological or mental illness of any kind, no identifiable stressor in her life that might have precipitated some kind of psychotic break—nothing. There is a disorder, Tourette's syndrome, that is known to produce bouts of uncontrollable cursing, but not for days on end without letup; and it doesn't just pop up unheralded by other symptoms and then vanish. The woman's daughter told us that she had never in her life heard her mother utter so much as the word "darn." The mysteries of the human brain continue to confound us. Who will ever know which crossed wires or misfiring circuits turned a kindly old lady into the inexhaustible smutmouth I called the Cursing Granny?

I wish all of my cases had such happy endings. But in the various hospitals where I worked, most psych patients had more serious afflictions, some resulting in homicide or suicide. One who still haunts me was a young man named Bobby,* who killed his mother. He had been admitted to the locked psych unit for observation, pending a hearing to decide whether or not he was mentally fit to stand trial.

Such patients can be very challenging for the nursing staff. Most of us were mothers, after all, and Bobby didn't seem particularly (even reassuringly) "crazy." On the surface he seemed like a son any of us might have—a baby-faced, quiet, reserved and even shy young man. Most of the female staff was scared of him and avoided contact whenever possible, but while I retained a healthy dose of fear myself, my heart went out to him. I also wanted to understand what could drive someone to kill the one person in the world on whom he is most dependent for love, care, and support.

I knew that Bobby's mother was not a totally "innocent" victim. She abused Bobby physically, emotionally, and even sexually from the time that he could crawl. But no one deserved the kind of death she suffered; and the vast majority of abused children do not become murderers (instead, too often, they go on to perpetuate the cycle of abuse with their own children). What differentiates those who do?

I tried to reach out to Bobby by playing games with him: Gin

Rummy, Crazy Eights, and Go Fish. Psych nurses have to be well versed in card games, for they can be neutral ground on which to interact with a patient, a way to connect. Then too, when patients are lucid, they get terribly bored on the wards. For weeks Bobby said nothing of substance either to me or to his psychiatrist. Then one day we had a breakthrough, and he offered me an explanation of his violent act: "I couldn't help it. She made me do it. She needed to leave me be but she never would. I couldn't take it anymore. It just happened, but I don't remember anything about it. She still loves me, I'm sure . . ."

Many killers blame the victims of the murders they commit, and it's not uncommon for them to deny any recollection of such a horrific event in their lives. (For violent offenders of a different kind, the ones I would come across later, as a profiler, reliving their actions was an integral part of the crime.) What unnerved me as much as anything Bobby said was his delivery. He spoke in a monotone, with no voice inflections, and with no display of emotion at all—as matter-of-factly as if he were ordering pancakes for breakfast.

That was as close as anyone got to Bobby. He remained beyond reach, through numerous sessions with his psychiatrist and with me, continuing to maintain: "She made me do it, but I don't remember."

Finally he stopped talking about it altogether. I think he was afraid to speak of it anymore, half-believing that if he didn't, he could convince himself that it never happened or make it magically go away. He was found "sane" by the court panel, meaning that he knew what he did was wrong at the time that he did it. He was tried for the murder of his mother and found guilty—juries tend to be afraid of defendants who have killed their parents, whatever the reason—and was sentenced to a stint in a "psychiatric" prison. Since he was a juvenile at the time of the crime, the state would hold him only until he reached twenty-one. At that time, he would be released, presumably cured.

But would he be cured? Radical change is possible, of course, and patients who want it badly and get decent treatment can recover. But those who are sentenced to psychiatric hospitals by the courts, forced into treatment because their demons have pushed them to brutal murders—never mind the true predators who kidnap, sadistically rape and torture, as well as kill—I don't think so.

In 1973 a man by the name of Edmund Kemper placed a call from a pay phone in Pueblo, Colorado, to the Santa Cruz, California, police to announce: "You guys must be looking for me." As it turns out, they *were* looking for him. They wanted to tell him the sad news of his mother's death. She and a friend had been savagely murdered in her home on Easter Sunday, the week before. But before the officer could extend his condolences, Kemper countered with some news of his own: He had beaten his mother to death with a hammer, decapitated her, and raped the corpse; then invited the friend over for dinner to decapitate her too. As if to ensure that he would have the final word, he excised his mother's larynx and shoved it down the garbage disposal, which ejected it, to his frustration: "Even when she was dead, she was still bitching at me!"

These were not crimes of passion but well-planned murders capping off a yearlong killing spree. Nor was this Kemper's first brush with the law. At the age of fourteen, he had shot his grandparents in cold blood, stabbing his grandmother's body with a kitchen knife, for good measure, to punish his mother, who was off on her honeymoon with her second husband.

He was sent to the Atascadero State Hospital for the criminally insane in California, where he was a model patient, though some therapists recognized his calm exterior for the façade it was. Nonetheless, when he turned twenty-one, he was released. Was he "cured"? By his own admission, "I appeared serene on the outside, but I was raging on the inside."

He had returned to live with his mother, who had mercilessly emotionally abused him his entire life. It was only a couple of years before he kicked off a new murderous rampage by stabbing two coeds, who were roommates, to death, suffocating a third, and then shooting three more. Each time, before disposing of the remains he brought the victim's body to his mother's house for dissection; and he buried one young woman's head in the backyard, facing his mother's room, because she expected everyone "to look up to her." Finally he recognized that it was intense hatred of his mother that was driving him to kill. As he later told a reporter, "Because of the way she raises her son, six young women are dead."

So he butchered her, along with her friend, and when the police were exasperatingly slow to come after him, turned himself in. Thank God! He was found guilty on eight counts of first-degree murder, becoming the only twice-convicted serial killer in California history.

These events occurred while I was a young psychiatric nurse, and being acutely conscious of the dilemma hospitals face when violent patients come up for release, I followed them in the media very closely. I still recall a newsclip that chilled me then and rather graphically illustrates the limitations of psychiatric prognostications. It said, in essence, that during his year of killing six young women, Kemper was required to appear before a board of psychiatrists and psychologists who would determine whether or not the record of his previous crime, of killing his grandparents when he was fourteen, should be sealed. Kemper wanted to become a police officer someday, and if he were to achieve that status, the record of his double homicide would have to be sealed. (Personally, I cannot believe that this request was even given consideration.) After interviewing him for a few hours, the board of five learned men decided that his murder record should be sealed because he was now "reformed." They decided that his unfortunate past should not haunt his bright future, insofar as he had been "cured" and was in no way a danger to society. In fact, they said, his motorcycle was more of a danger to society than he was.

While Kemper sat before this board answering the good doctors' questions, the headless torso of a young coed whom he had recently murdered was stashed in the trunk of his car in the parking lot. So much for predicting human behavior.

How likely is it that the methods of psychological evaluation have vastly improved in the twenty years since Edmund Kemper bamboozled his examiners? Not very likely at all, judging by my case files at the FBI.

Kemper obviously falls into the predatory category of killers, certainly "sick"—and like a striking proportion of those behind bars, the product of extreme childhood abuse—but unquestionably sane. Many such murderers (and serial rapists), who carefully plan, enjoy, and even boast of their violent acts, seem so "normal" that they easily gain the trust of naïve victims and later the confidence of naïve mental health professionals. But even those who common sense tells us may warrant caution will slip through the net.

One of the most violent patients I ever encountered was a paranoid schizophrenic named Steven,* whose bulk alone made him a force to be reckoned with. He came from what was by all accounts a "normal" home, with no history of abuse. I first met him when his father, a short, slight, elderly man, brought him to the hospital for the fourth time in two years. The father was exhausted with trying to care for his son and cope with his debilitating illness, and he apologized to me for Steven's behavior when I admitted him to the unit.

"You don't wear glasses, do you?" he asked. Part of Steven's delusional system centered on eyeglasses, for the voices in his head told him that people who wore glasses were evil and out to hurt him. He would snatch them off people's faces, and though he was myopic himself, he refused to wear glasses for fear of becoming evil too. If he took his medication religiously, Steven could function outside the hospital, often for as long as a year. Despite the drugs, he was too profoundly ill to hold a job, for the intensity of his suspicions made it impossible for him to concentrate on even the most menial tasks. Eventually his fears would overtake him, and he would wind up back in the hospital to get rebalanced on his mental tightrope.

When Steven was in the grip of paranoia, he was very difficult to manage. It could take a few weeks of antipsychotic medication and confinement to quiet the voices that tormented him. This time his internal alarms told him that he was in danger in the hospital, and he grew increasingly hostile and menacing to the staff. Then came the day when I heard yelling and screaming down the hall and saw a stampede of frantic nurses and attendants rush past. Steven was trying to escape!

Though the ward was locked, a huge, driven man can find a way to break through any barrier. The year before we had lost a patient named Ron,* a professional man in his forties who was hospitalized in the throes of a sudden, severe attack of paranoia. Almost as massive as Steven, Ron grabbed a weighty medical scale (like the kind found in a doctor's office), swung it around his head like a baseball bat, and beat off the four men and three women who were trying to restrain him. As one mental health worker lay unconscious, Ron snatched his set of keys and bolted for the exit. He made it outside to Michigan Avenue, where he spotted a Chicago policeman directing noontime traffic. Ron tried to seize his gun and in the ensuing scuffle was shot dead.

With trembling hands, I quickly readied a syringe full of tranquilizing drugs, as one of the other nurses grabbed a pillowcase containing four leather wrist and ankle restraints. Trying to inject a thrashing and frenzied patient, even with big men struggling to hold him down, is one of the most difficult tasks a psych nurse is called upon to do. It can be risky for the patient, since a shot in the wrong spot may do irreparable and painful nerve damage, and perilous, obviously, for the 115-pound nurse fighting to stay astride a bucking, punch-throwing, obscenity-screaming patient twice her size. It's one of those jobs that never gets easier. Fortunately I managed to get Steven shot full of tranquilizers, and the staff was able to constrain him for another ten minutes till they kicked in. It took seven people to get Steven under control, and the tussle left all of us drenched with sweat, completely worn out.

Back in his room, Steven was secured to the bedframe with padded leather restraints on all four limbs. If that sounds inhumane, consider the alternative: a "rubber" room, where Steven would effectively be locked in isolation, probably too disoriented to eat or care for himself, and shaken up/disrupted every few hours by the seven-person battle royal it would take to get another dose of drugs into him. As it was, in "four-ways," he had checkup visits from the staff every fifteen minutes, had physical contact when he was turned and repositioned every two hours, and could be spoon-fed by another human being. He received frequent doses of antipsychotic medication until finally his delusions were quelled, which took about a week.

One night during that time, I came to Steven's room with an attendant, Mark, to check on him. He was awake, though it was after midnight, and more lucid and serene than I had ever seen him. I greeted him warmly, and he asked me for a cup of water, begging me to free one of his arms so he could hold it himself. Staffing was light on the graveyard shift, so there weren't enough of us to tackle Steven if he decided to make a break for it. I turned him down.

I filled a cup with ice water from the bedside pitcher, then as I raised it to his lips, I found myself looking deeply into his eyes for the first time. Other staff members who had cared for him on his previous visits had talked about his "Steven eyes," and I saw them now—impenetrably black eyes with no discernible iris, utterly devoid of emotion or humanity, like the eyes of a shark. Being drawn into those eyes was like peering into the abyss. I was slightly unnerved, which he recognized, so he jerked his head forward in a spastic motion, seizing the plastic cup between his teeth, and flung it in my face. That snapped me back to reality. Luckily I wasn't close enough for him to bite off my nose. He started screaming, "You fucking bitch, I'm going to kill you, Candy." My heart almost stopped when he shouted my name. "You better pray that I never get out of these things."

Then, all of a sudden, his voice grew eerily calm. "Don't think that you can ever be safe," he crooned at me. "No matter where you try to hide, I will find you, Candy, you miserable bitch. I don't care how long it takes . . . No matter where you run I will find you. I could cut your head off. Or do you want me to tear your heart out? I'll do it while your heart is still beating. How's your husband going to feel when he finds you dead, with no heart? You want that, Candy?"

He started laughing. I felt sick, but knowing that replying or showing fear would just feed the fire, I stayed calm, even impassive, as all my senses came alive in the body's automatic "flight" response. I could feel every hair on my skin.

Since then I have risked my life many times—it's my job—and sometimes even thrive on the adrenaline rush you get from danger. But the darkness—the only word I can think of to describe the toxic charge in the air and the bottomless, pitiless depth of Steven's eyes—of that moment scared me more than any other confrontation in my life.

Before long, Steven's demons succumbed to the medication and he grew less psychotic, more integrated and organized in his thinking. He was then discharged into the care of his family, no doubt to begin the cycle again. He wasn't readmitted to that ward in the time I worked there, and I lost track of him, though I think I may have caught a glimpse of him across two lanes of traffic on a busy Chicago street.

I did, however, see his father again. Fourteen years later, I was at an

FBI seminar on "Advanced Criminal Profiling," where a guest-lecturing medical examiner was showing autopsy slides. As the gruesome images beamed onto the screen, one after another, he pointed out wound patterns, and so on, that figured in each victim's untimely demise. He never mentioned and probably didn't even know his subjects' names. One image showed a man with such vicious stab wounds over his chest and neck that his head was almost severed from his body. But his face was unobscured enough that I could recognize him, and I still remember involuntarily shaking my head, as if to cast the image away. The medical examiner explained that the elderly victim had been killed by his son, who was a paranoid schizophrenic. The image on the screen was Steven's father.

What a tragedy!

But how could it have been averted? Society makes little enough provision for those who are known to be a danger to others—the Kemper case being just one egregious example—never mind those who may just have the potential. Our knowledge of the biochemical and psychodynamic roots of violence has barely scratched the surface. Modern psychotropic drugs are a double-edged sword, bringing relief and functionality to so many who might otherwise live in an internal world of torment, but also fooling us (or letting the legal system or the insurance companies fool us) into believing that the profoundly ill, including the violent, are fully able to lead "normal" lives on medication. Our diagnostic measures are still too crude and the treatments themselves too unreliable to sustain the illusion that such people can get "well."

We can barely help those who are primarily a danger to themselves because they are dysfunctional—look at the legions who roam the streets of every major American city, many of whom have the medication that can allegedly allow them to live in the world, but not the psychosocial supports—intractably addicted, or chronically depressed. I lost three patients in my years of nursing, two to "suicide by cop"—provoking policemen to shoot them while committing minor infractions, which is a surprisingly common way for people who lack the nerve to end it all— and one in a fire that she set with a cigarette after drinking to the point of passing out. I had begged her to readmit herself for alcoholism treatment but she was too depressed to make the effort to get clean—she just couldn't make herself care enough. But because she wasn't frankly, acutely suicidal, there was no way I could hold her in the hospital.

Every medical professional loses patients, which is heartbreaking, but in psychiatry, especially, when there is no X ray or blood test you can look to as physical evidence of the progression of disease that ultimately conquered your best efforts, it can feel devastating. You must set boundaries, of course, but the very nature of mental illness keeps you enmeshed in your patients' emotional lives. I gave birth to my son Seth while I was a nurse, and the entire ward was involved in my pregnancy and excited about the impending arrival of "our" baby. How could it be otherwise?

Then there are the patients you never lose, for whom the hospital has a revolving door. You spend months patching them up with a combination of therapy and medication until they reach an acceptable level of "wellness," then you release them. Often you send them right back into the challenging environments, whether families or communities, that promoted their illnesses to begin with—and back they bounce to the hospital, typically worse for the wear. But where else can they go?

The very best nurses remain idealistic, but their goals change—to comforting and relieving psychic pain rather than expecting to help patients get well. It can be very hard not to get disillusioned.

These were the kind of thoughts that were preoccupying me by my ninth year in psychiatric nursing. I was pushing thirty and beginning to have what in retrospect seems like an inevitable crisis of faith. My nine-year marriage had dissolved, my son had turned four and was showing signs of craving independence, and I had to completely reorient myself in the world. So I was highly susceptible to recruitment into the FBI.

Funnily enough, the guy who brought me in had no idea that he was recruiting me!

2

THE PROVING GROUND

At age twenty-eight, after ending nine years of marriage, I knew embarrassingly little about meeting men or dating, so it was lucky that Clay Carlson* found me. It was 1978, the height of the disco craze, and since I loved to dance, some fellow nurses from University took me out to a club for my birthday. I was bouncing all over the dance floor that night when Clay moved in and got in synch with my rhythm. When the song ended, he told me, "Little girl, you need to be reined in."

"Oh, yeah?" I said. "And you're the man to do it?"

He found the challenge charming, and I thought he was attractive too, in a macho/sensitive sort of way, being six foot three, a brawny couple hundred pounds, with green eyes and reddish blond hair. We kept topping each other with snappy one-liners, like a Katharine Hepburn/Spencer Tracy act. So I was disappointed when he insisted on sticking around the disco rather than going someplace where we could have a drink and talk. I found out later that he was working undercover that night, along with his partner, tailing a mob figure who was partying at the club. But he did ask for my number.

We had our first date a week later, and he fascinated me with tales of his exploits on the job. Growing up in the black-and-white TV era, I had longed to be a crimebuster like Eliot Ness on *The Untouchables*, my family's favorite show. Ness was a mythological figure in our house, for during the Great Depression, my then-teenage father had actually worked for Ness as an informant. When the Feds raided the speakeasy where he was bussing tables, the great man himself had shoved a gun in my dad's face, just for show, before moving on to arrest the real Prohibition flouters. Ness was our hero, so I was thrilled to know a real G-man. For someone who had been married for so long to an ordinary, workaday human being—decent enough, if wrong for me—Clay was like a fantasy come true, the wild, romantic cowboy riding to the heroine's emotional rescue. I had never been around such a macho guy, which I mean in the best sense—burly, muscular, and manly. He could pick me up with one hand.

My father had gently quashed my childhood fantasy by telling me that Ness had to do a lot of "rough stuff" with "tough customers" who no woman could handle. That's why women weren't allowed into the FBI. Indeed, J. Edgar Hoover had decreed: "Because of the nature of the duties our Special Agents are called upon to perform, we do not employ women in this position." That edict remained in effect until 1972, when Hoover died, and within hours, legend has it, a few brave women finally scaled the walls of the impenetrable male preserve. After the lukewarm reception I got a few years later, I have to tip my fedora to those intrepid pioneers.

There were several women FBI agents working in Chicago, and through Clay I got to meet one. I was shocked. She was a tiny little thing who could barely have weighed 100 pounds, not the muscle-bound female equivalent of Clay I was expecting. Diminutive as she was, Clay (who was one of the good guys) assured me that she was well trained and plenty capable enough to deal with the "tough customers" and the "rough stuff." I was astounded!

One thing that particularly struck me was the way she was dressed. I knew Clay worked in street clothes, but it never occurred to me to ask what a female agent would wear. This one, because of her assignment, was decked out in a miniskirt and stacked-heel, thigh-high, dark brown suede boots. I coveted those boots—which I could see were making quite an impression on Clay—and even more, the kind of job that would require her to wear them. Though I was only five feet five inches and weighed 110 pounds, I knew that if this little gal could join the FBI, I could too.

I took the exam in January, then four months later got summoned for my "face test," or interview by a panel of agents, before I realized how competitive the admissions process would be. The FBI, then and now, takes only a small fraction of its applicants; in 1999 the figure was 6 percent, while Harvard, by comparison, takes a full tenth. The vast majority of agents in the late 1970s were former accountants and lawyers, the professions that Hoover preferentially recruited, and transferees from law enforcement and the military, some of them highly decorated Vietnam vets. There were a handful of teachers, and I believe that I was the first nurse to be admitted, more likely because of my psychiatric specialty and managerial experience running a ward than because of my health-care training. Had I been a staff nurse in pediatrics, say, I doubt that I would have gotten in. The agent with the oddest "past life" I ever heard about had been a wholesale liquor distributor, a job that probably wouldn't pass muster today (computer expertise is the most sought-after skill, followed by fluency in a foreign language). But she is a first-rate agent—not just one of the best women, but one of the best all-around professionals I have known in the Bureau.

When Clay found out that I had applied, he was a little sulky at first. I think he was afraid I wouldn't see him as such a knight in shining armor anymore. But he and his partner Phil Benson* soon realized how much fun they could have whipping me into shape to be an agent. They had me training like a demon, convinced that I'd be expected to run two miles in ten minutes and do 100 perfect military-style push-ups. When I got to Quantico, I was amazed to learn that thirty-five push-ups was considered excellent, especially for a woman, that not many Olympians can run two miles in ten minutes, and that plenty of my fellow trainees were so unfit that they'd have to hail a cab to catch the bus.

The week before I left I had little jags of crying. It was the first time I had ever been separated from my beloved Seth, who was almost five, for more than a day—and now I would be gone sixteen weeks. But he was at an age when my departure seemed like a great adventure, and he was thrilled that I'd be learning to "catch bad guys."

The FBI Academy, aka Hoover High, is a magnificent facility located on the U.S. Marine Corps base at Quantico, Virginia, about forty miles south of Washington, D.C. It was completed and dedicated in 1972, the year J. Edgar Hoover died. For fifty years, FBI agents had trained in an old converted post office in the shadow of the Capitol, and the world-famous Hogan's Alley, a simulated village street where agents could test their judgment and reflexes in "true-to-life" crisis situations, was a block-long stretch of wooden store façades, with pop-up figures of criminals or fellow agents rigged to spring out of windows and doorways. Today the Academy is a modern campus set on 385 acres of towering pine forest, complete with classrooms, dormitories, a thousand-seat auditorium, state-of-the-art physical education facilities, including the Marine obstacle course, a forensics lab, a library, indoor and outdoor rifle and firearms ranges, a high-speed-chase drivers' training track, and much more. Hogan's Alley is now a realistic facsimile of a small town, where rescue and capture scenarios are staged using live actors. Not only do new FBI agents train at Quantico, as it is commonly known, but its prestigious National Academy division offers a twelve-week program that is like a graduate school for top law enforcement officers from around the world.

My class, Number 80-16 (being the sixteenth class admitted in 1980) had thirty new agent trainees, twenty-three men and seven women. Only one of us was African American, two were Hispanic, and one was Asian. Today the Bureau's priority recruits are minority-group members, as well as women, both to marshal an agent force more truly representative of the population it serves and because it now recognizes how much it needs their unique contributions. But in 1980, women were a novelty at best and, at worst, unwelcome intruders who Affirmative Action was allowing to steal jobs from men. For that, guys, I'm not about to apologize. I worked damn hard to meet the same training standards as any man—while "dancing backward and in high heels," as Ginger Rogers said. And I was still one of only some four hundred women to pass through the Academy, bringing our proportion in the ranks of FBI agents to a measly 4 percent.

Somebody called us "bitches with badges," which is a title I'm proud to claim!

• • •

In those days, the Academy was run like a paramilitary boarding school, where the authoritarian instructors were called "Sir" (there were no "Ma'ams"). Trainees bunked two or three to a room, and for every four there was one shower. If you wanted to soak your aching muscles in a bathtub, you had to rent a motel room on the weekend. There was no drinking and no swearing. For single people, sex on campus was taboo and grounds for dismissal, as if we were all virgins whose virtue the government was obliged to protect—a moral throwback to the era when lovers put on fake wedding rings for trysts in respectable lodgings. But if the amorous parties were married (to other people), we were unofficially warned that the man would squeak through—probably with a wink and a slap on the back—while the woman would pay the price. However, the only expulsion I ever heard of involved a couple who was caught trysting in the swimming pool—and to me, that made perfect sense. Anyone too dumb to find a better hiding place than that isn't someone you'd want to entrust with national security.

The agent-training program was a notoriously rigorous proving ground, with instructors who considered it their job to flush out the weak and winnow down classes to the very best. Many took the adversarial approach to teaching—the old tough, abusive, boot-camp-sergeant style (though our ex-military classmates liked to insist that the FBI Academy was just summer camp with guns). Today the philosophy is different. The standards are just as stringent, but the thinking goes that having chosen you and invested the taxpayers' money in your training, the Academy had better make an agent out of you. But back then the program was a trial by fire, on the theory that if you could survive it, you could make it on the street.

You were required to excel in all three of the program's disciplines: academics, physical training, and firearms. The only acceptable excuse for less than peak performance was injury. A passing grade was 85 percent, and if you scored lower than that on any major test you got one shot at a makeup exam. Should you flunk again, that was the end—you were put on the bus to National Airport with a government-issued, one-way ticket home.

Knowing that all it took was one good screwup to send you packing made for a high level of stress. I've heard of training groups that were backstabbingly competitive, but ours, fortunately, developed an us-against-them cohesion and the determination to pull one another through. I set up study groups and offered tutoring in behavioral science, for example, and the vets and cops coached the rest of us on firearms. We all had nicknames—the usual goofy ones like Mad Dog for the mild-mannered guy and Chainsaw for the man who snored. I was Shark Bait because I was so fair, being an Irish Catholic girl, with legs so white, the guys would tease, that if I went swimming the sharks would spot me a mile away. I had my own secret nickname, Powder Puff, for one of the other women who was pleasant enough but almost stereotypically "girly." I don't know how she made it, but she did and became a pilot in the aviation force the Bureau uses for surveillance. Two of the others in our group weren't so lucky—one washed out on academics the first week, and the other (a cop, no less) on firearms just before the end of training.

For most of us, the academic courses were the easiest—having been to college, we knew how to study—and utterly fascinating: interviewing and interrogation techniques (which can come in handy in your personal life), criminal law, and a range of behavioral science classes that, for shock value alone, far outshone what I learned in psychiatric nursing school. Being a nurse I was less overcome than most by the gruesome slides John Douglas and Ray Hazelwood showed of chopped-up murder victims, but I realized with horror that they could have depicted the handiwork of some of my former patients. I was as fascinated as anyone to hear how Douglas and Hazelwood would hypothesize that a certain killer was a white male between twenty and twenty-five, who lived with his mother and had flunked out of the army—and be proven right. Later I would return to the Academy for in-depth training with these masters, who were inventing criminal profiling.

The class the trainees talked about most was sociology, taught by an expert in gang behavior. An undercover agent—one of us—planted in a biker gang had taken remarkable photos of members vomiting on each others' jackets and posing with bodies stolen from the morgue and shot full of bullet holes, to fake the killing required for their initiation rite. All the bikers were tattooed, and one memorable image showed a penis imprinted with seventeen sets of initials, which could be read when he got an erection. "Yeow!" the class said in unison, squirming. Not exactly your standard university liberal arts program fare.

Physical training (PT) and firearms proved much more challenging. Trainees are tested for physical conditioning their second day at the Academy, at the six-week point, and again before they can graduate. The test involves a two-mile sprint, sit-ups, push-ups, pull-ups, and a shuttle run; and to pass, the trainee must earn enough points in each activity to reach a certain cumulative minimum score. To earn maximum points on the two-mile run, the trainee has to finish in less than fourteen minutes, a fairly fast clip. Scoring the maximum number of points on push-ups requires thirty-five military push-ups done with perfect form—with a ninety-degree angle bend to the elbow, each and every time. No "California" (weird) push-ups were allowed.

Because my boyfriend and his partner had a sick sense of humor and enjoyed seeing me suffer through miserable months of exertions, I passed my second-day evaluation with flying colors. But for women, especially, who had to sweat to achieve the upper-body strength of the puniest man, the tests were arduous. They also brought out the sadism of the more despotic breed of instructor. Many of these petty tyrants were agent wannabes who couldn't cut it on some aspect of the program but who were brought on staff because of their exceptional physical prowess. They lived to bully trainees, and women were the special targets of their resentment.

On my second day at the Academy I watched while a female agent took her final, pregraduation PT test. Her partner cheered her on as she struggled with her push-up quota, while an imperious gym instructor kept count. She had to do thirty-five perfect push-ups to earn the minimum cumulative score to pass, and she was tiring as she reached thirty, thirty-one, and then thirty-two. She barely squeaked out thirty-three, her arms trembling with fatigue, but managed to summon the strength to crank out number thirty-four. Months of hard training—indeed, her very future in the FBI—depended on her doing a perfect push-up one more time.

I was told by another onlooker that she had a master's degree in computer science and was also a certified public accountant, two very impressive accomplishments. The Bureau would benefit tremendously by having someone with her credentials on the white-collar-crime task force—that is, if only she could do just one more push-up!

I couldn't take my eyes off her as she lowered her chest almost to the floor that last time, her face blood red, the sweat dripping off her. I heard her moan in frustration as she fought to push herself up—and made it! But then I heard the instructor say "No go." Her form on the final push-up wasn't flawless, so with a smirk on his face, he flunked her—not just on the test, but because it was her second try, out of the Academy. She had no recourse. Later, a few of us heard the instructor boasting that he had "washed out one more female"—a chilling hint that we might be in for a browbeating.

Since then there have been lawsuits challenging such arbitrary and discriminatory dismissals of trainees, and no single instructor could make such a categorical ruling. More important, the Bureau today is much too attuned to the overall value of its candidates to flunk out a CPA/computer expert over one questionable push-up! But that's not how it was in the bad old days. I resolved right then and there that no self-important jackass of an instructor was going to wash me out of the Academy. Having grown up roughhousing with three brothers, I was never one to back off from a fight, and my experience as a psych nurse had left me pretty hard to intimidate.

But so much depended on sheer luck with instructor placements. There was one fiend with a black belt in karate who routinely had people sent—or carried—to the infirmary with broken wrists and ankles or delirious from heat stroke after hard runs on sweltering, 100-degree Virginia summer afternoons. We called him Ho Chi Minh. Fortunately our group was assigned instead to a coach I nicknamed Captain America because he was a huge man with a Superman physique, who was a tough but decent and, when not pushing us to the limits of human endurance, a genuinely nice guy.

We began each day's session with a run, followed by some kind of workout. One day we did an exercise with medicine balls, which are like six-pound leather globes. We lined up in columns, and then the last person in line would run forward, catch a tossed medicine ball, and fall back into place at the front. When my turn came, I ran up, but instead of catching the ball got smacked right in the head. Getting clobbered with a flying six-pound weight is no joke, and I was knocked down—boom!—and out cold. When I came to, seconds later, with my head ringing, I got a momont's solicitude and an eyeballed checkup by the instructor and then it was, "Okay, back in line!" Even losing consciousness couldn't win you a reprieve from physical training.

Everyone knows that classic abdominal-tightening exercise for which you lie on your back on the floor—ours was hardwood—lift your feet about six inches into the air, and hold it. Believe me, it's a lot more painful to do with a six-pound medicine ball between your ankles. The only way I could get through it was to use the Lamaze breathing techniques I had learned when I was pregnant. I even taught the rest of my group: "When you think you're going to die, focus on a spot on the wall and slowly, slowly breathe in through your nose, then slowly, slowly blow out . . ." It works—it's a wonderful technique. It's just one of those little benefits you get from being a girl . . .

After our workout came defensive tactics class, in which we learned how to disarm an assailant, to prevent an attacker from wresting away our own guns, and to take down someone twice our size with one swift kick. Once we had seized the advantage, we were taught to subdue our captive with a "reverse-wrist-twist-lock" or the infamous "choke-hold," which is now illegal and no longer used. For most of us women, the hardest part of physical training was boxing. Boys are raised to use their fists, but the idea of going hand-to-hand and head-to-head against someone in physical combat is as alien to women as walking on the moon. In the beginning we were paired up with other women in the boxing ring, but once we learned the basics, the instructors felt that it would behoove us to brave the prospect of a real "ass whipping" from a man.

For my partner I chose Frank Evans, the most gracious gentleman in our class, in the hope that good manners would deter him from flat-out clocking me, even if he made it look good enough for the instructors. We squared off in the ring, and when the bell sounded, I laid into him like a madwoman, hammering at him, throwing my upper body into my punches, just as I had been taught, parrying his blows. He endured my slugging as if it were the annoying buzzing of a mosquito—and then with one left hook, put me down for the count.

I slunk off to the shower in humiliation, but Frank's "courtesy" wouldn't allow him to let me nurse my embarrassing defeat in silence. One of our academic courses followed the PT session, and when I entered the classroom, he stood up to greet me. Then, in front of the entire class—just in case anyone missed his triumph—he apologized for knocking me out. "Don't speak to me!" I commanded, indignantly, "I want a divorce!"

Eventually I learned to box pretty well; and one day while looking in the mirror, raising my arms to put my hair in a bun, I noticed a big change. I had Dolly Parton biceps. I had to wonder if all that upper-body strength training was turning me into Charles Atlas. But I needn't have worried. Late in our training one of the instructors took the "ladies" aside for a frank talk. "Everything you're learning here in PT is important," he told us. "One day it might even save your life. But don't get cocky. In a fight, any little shit of a guy is going to have the physical advantage of weight and muscles you'll never have. So always depend on your gun—you don't have to shoot the creep. Just aim it at his balls. That'll yank any guy into line mighty fast."

That was, bar none, the most valuable streetwise piece of advice I received in all those weeks at the FBI Academy.

We were building upper-body strength as much for firearms, the second leg of our program, as for fighting. Guns are hefty, and we spent hours each day out on the firing range, learning to shoot. Nowadays the weapons are a lot more user-friendly—if that term can be applied to guns—nine-millimeter Sig Saur semiautomatic pistols, which hold fourteen rounds and release a hail of fire with very slight pressure, making them very dangerous. We used six-shot Smith & Wesson .38 caliber revolvers, for which you squeeze hard on the trigger each time you want a bullet to eject. So the 3,000-plus rounds of ammunition we shot meant 3,000 individual trigger pulls and taped-up, aching fingers and palms. Sig Saurs come in two sizes, so you can choose one that fits your hand and is comfortable to shoot. But in my day the handgun of choice was the bulky and cumbersome Smith & Wesson .38 revolver, and then there were the even more onerous rifles and shotguns. Just coming to grips with our weapons was one of the challenges of our firearms training.

Like most new trainees, I had never even held a gun. But from the moment we arrived at the Academy we were assured that the FBI program is the best law-enforcement firearms training in the world. "Just pay attention," somebody told me, "and do what they tell you. They can teach a table to shoot!" That became my mantra out on the range.

Firearms, like PT, had its share of tyrannical instructors who thrived on persecuting the weaker candidates and, especially, women. There was one who liked to grab a woman from behind by the nape of the neck, shove his knee between her legs, and bark, "Spread 'em." To him this was "improving her shooting stance," but today it would be called intimidation verging on sexual harassment—and he would be gone.

One of my own firearms instructors, who was very outspoken about his belief that women had no place in the FBI, had a subtler (and more vicious) method of hassling trainees. Right in the middle of my legal studies class, he summoned me to his office. It was very early in my training when I was still overawed by my instructors, so I was terrified. What grave infraction could I have committed that would warrant such immediate attention? The instructor sat me down and told me, very seriously, that he was "concerned" about me—that he doubted that he could ever "certify" me as a "safe shooter." "Why?" I protested. "No one on the range ever said that I was making a mistake . . ." Performance had nothing to with it, he claimed. Even if I did well, he was convinced that I could never kill anyone.

Now completely flustered, I wracked my brains for the correct reply. On one hand, I felt that I had to counter his well-known view that women were too "soft" to be good agents. But just how bloodthirsty was I supposed to sound? On the other hand, who of us can ever know until we face a crisis whether we can kill? At that point I had never been exposed to a situation in which lives, including my own, were endangered and I had a gun. And would this "deficiency" in me that he had "detected"—inability to kill—get me kicked out of the Academy?

He must have loved watching me squirm. Since I was too nervous to call other teachers' attention to my supposed Achilles heel, I kept my mouth shut—so it was almost graduation before I discovered that there was no such thing as "certification" by an instructor or being judged a "safe shooter." All you had to do was hit the target enough times to pass. The whole thing—calling me out of class to make the matter seem urgent, his earnest look, the "concern" he expressed—had been a cruel mindgame, aimed at sowing the seeds of self-doubt and inadequacy in a brand-new, eager, and impressionable trainee. What a power trip!

I wasn't about to let his emotional thuggery defeat me, but it did increase my misery on the firing range, adding an extra new layer of performance anxiety to what was already a mettle-testing course of training. It crossed my mind, naturally, that there was no way for me to prove a taste for murder, short of committing one, and thus earn my "certification," but his declaration shook my confidence—if only because it meant that I had one of my evaluators gunning for me.

Our firearms sessions usually started in the classroom and finished out on the range, where we each shot hundreds and hundreds of rounds at a male silhouette drawn on a target at the end of a fifty-foot lane. The shooting drill was choreographed, like a dance recital. We would begin "proned out," lying on our bellies, practice-firing with both our weak hands and our strong hands. Next we shot two-handed from behind barricades, then holstered our weapons to dash up to the twenty-five-foot line, where we dropped to our knees. Kneeling, we fired off some strong-hand rounds, then jumped to our feet to shoot switching off between hands. The movement would conclude with us kneeling, shooting from strong-hand and weak-hand positions, before breaking to reload.

When the instructor blew his whistle from the tower, Act Two began. Running up to the fifteen-foot line, we would empty our guns into the target before us, reload, and then, switching hands, empty them again. Pausing once more to reload, we would holster our weapons, and then move up to complete the movement at the seven-yard line, plugging the target with only one hand. The entire dance was to be executed within two and a half minutes, and to "qualify," or perform acceptably at firearms, a trainee had to score 80 percent—in other words, shoot 80 percent of the fifty bullets into the "kill zone" of the target, which was the torso of the man, not counting the head, arms, or legs.

Before I entered the Academy I, like so many other laypeople, wondered why police officers don't "shoot to maim" rather than "to kill," unless absolutely necessary. Now I knew the answer—even after twelve weeks of superb firearms training and daily practice, virtually none of us could aim and consistently hit the limb of a stationary target, and never one that would be moving and shooting back. You just don't have that much control of a handgun, even up close. About 90 percent of shootouts take place between cops/agents and suspects who are six feet apart or closer. That's why we shot half of the fifty rounds in our "qualifications" drill at fifteen feet or less—and why I can assure you that proximity doesn't make it that much easier to hit a limb. The extremity most likely to get hit at close range is the gun hand, especially when you're shooting in the dark. The muzzle flash of a weapon will draw your eye, and your aim will automatically follow. Both you and your opponent, unconsciously, will be firing at the other's gun hand, and so one of you is likely to get clipped. Our frequent switchovers during practice were to ensure that we could shoot effectively with our weak hands should the strong hands be disabled.

Still, you can't reliably aim to shoot a gun out of someone's hand. That's a Hollywood myth. And that TV show finale that has the "policeman" (whose real-life counterpart fires his gun at a person a handful of times in his whole career, not fifty times a day) trading shots with an assailant during a chase down an alley, then from a block away infallibly winging the perp in the leg or arm as he scales a fence—thanks to his righteous intent only to maim—is utter hogwash. If only real shoot-outs could go that way!

The truth is, law enforcement agents often have a certain antipathy toward handguns and tend to see their own as a necessary evil (though in the Bureau, at least, few men will admit it and risk being labeled "pussies"). There are some notable exceptions: marksmen, who have elevated shooting to a fine art, and the undeniable bad element, male

and female, who see their weapons as penis extensions. But you're not
going to find many cops and FBI agents—who too often find themselves
facing down some squirrelly or crazy armed amateur—out campaigning
on behalf of the NRA.

After handgun training came the roughest stretch of our firearms
course, shotguns and rifles. One of the kindlier instructors would ease
trainees' dread by warming them up with the old Junior Walker song,
"Shotgun." Accuracy isn't the problem with these—it's the kick. On a
raid men won't usually trust a woman with the shotgun, but I've never
heard a gal argue about it: "Hey, it's my turn, give me that!" It's hard
enough for a big man to absorb the shock of a gun butt slamming with
sledgehammer force into his shoulder, but the impact can nearly knock
an average-size person off his or her feet.

Rifles, pistols, and other handguns—even machine guns—shoot bullets one at a time, which are aerodynamically tooled to discharge easily
from the barrel, creating minimal kick. But a shotgun takes what is called
a rifle or a deer slug, about as big around as a dime, which is like a
marble of pure lead that can blow enough of a hole to drop a moose
dead in its tracks; or else double-ought buckshot, in the form of a shell
containing twelve lead pellets, each about a quarter inch in diameter,
that when fired burst the shell and spray out, fanwise. You don't have
to worry much about aim when packing buckshot, for whatever you
hit from, say, fifteen feet away will be riddled with shrapnel. That's why
it's used, and why in the movies, the normally fearless villain will drop
to his knees in terror when he hears a shotgun racking.

You learn to anticipate and compensate for the kick of a shotgun,
though only the burliest macho types will ever claim to like them.
Everyone in our group who was still standing at the end of training
managed to "qualify" with both shotguns and M-16 rifles by scoring
their 80 percent. But as our last day on the firing range approached, one
of our more sadistic instructors assigned us the challenge of shooting
seventy-five rounds of rifle slugs and double-ought buck from shotguns.
Just the thought of such a punishing exercise stopped my heart. And
why the hell do it? Nothing short of all-out trench warfare in some
postapocalyptic Mad Max realm, with modern rifles unavailable, would
ever approximate this experience in real life.

But a fledgling agent never says "I can't." We all took our places and started blasting away. After a few dozen rounds, even big men were crying out for ice packs to dull the ache of their bruised and battered shoulders. Moans resounded, and with continuing fire, some shooters wept in pain—but kept on plugging. Eyeglasses knocked to shards by the pounding recoil lacerated brows and cheeks. One by one, with our throbbing bodies black and blue and bloodied, we dropped off the firing line. I did enough damage to the brachial nerve, which runs through your shoulder, that I still can't sleep on my right side, even to this day. No one could shoot the full seventy-five rounds.

Every year, agents have to qualify with handguns, rifles, and shotguns, just to be sure that we're practicing on the range and keeping up our skills. Since that injury at the Academy, I've had to shoot with the shotgun on my hip, which makes it harder to control. I still score my 80 percent, of course, but how ironic that a training exercise that was probably meant to toughen us up—that's the most charitable explanation I can think of—instead compromised my ability to use a shotgun for my entire career! Recently a San Francisco firearms instructor, claiming that the Bureau was getting away from hip shooting, insisted that I fire from the more conventional stance. "Sorry," I said. "I can't do it. My right shoulder is a wreck." "So shoot on the left," he suggested. "If you don't mind, I'm going to stick with my way," I replied. "I've already screwed up one shoulder for my country, so I think I'm entitled to keep the other one intact."

Once we were fairly proficient with firearms, our drills became fun, racing through Hogan's Alley—then still a cardboard model town that we ran through—jumping over fake walls, and playing "Shoot/Don't shoot" with targets that looked like bikers, housewives, kids, pets, and cops. Today Hogan's Alley is big enough to drive through, and trainees rescue "hostages," played by actors being held in the nearly life-size post office, and collar the "terrorists" trying to blow up the reasonable fac-simile of a library.

We also had to master the infamous Marine obstacle course, which involves maneuvering over and around a series of barricades, avoiding booby traps, and—worst of all for me, being afraid of heights—climbing what looked like a huge jungle gym, far above the ground, inching over its gaps on narrow beams, climbing lattices, and swinging from precipice to precipice on ropes. We heard lots of stories about injuries on the obstacle course, such as broken collarbones and ankles—and even necks and backs, leading to paralysis—but I suspect that these tales were apocryphal and designed to scare us. I dreaded running the obstacle course, knowing that if I was injured, I would not graduate on time but be "recycled," held back until I was well enough to join another class and pass the PT test. But an encouraging instructor counseled: "Just go through it slowly and methodically, solving one problem at a time. No one is expecting you to set any speed records"—which still strikes me as pretty good advice for anything you'll ever face in life. So we all took it easy, helping each other through it, and we all made it unscathed.

One day we were divided into competing teams for a "capture the flag" exercise that had us running through woods and jumping off diving boards into pools, fully dressed in fatigues and boots and carrying our M-16s. Though I am an expert swimmer, keeping afloat is a lot harder when you're trying to keep a rifle dry. Luckily, it's not a challenge that I ever faced again in my FBI career—there's just not much demand for armed water rescues in downtown Chicago and San Francisco—but you never know. Seth just loved hearing about this exercise. "You jumped in the water, Mommy?" he would ask, over and over. "And your hair got all wet? And your clothes got all wet? And your shoes got all wet?" And he would laugh—it was adorable.

I missed him so much! I could only get back to Chicago to see him twice during training, but I would send him little presents every week and try to talk to him for at least a couple of minutes each day. It's hard for a child to be separated from a parent for so long, but he was a little trouper. I got a kick out of what he used to tell people I was doing at the Academy: "Learning how to kill people, but only the bad ones."

Some of my colleagues were a lot less understanding than Seth. Back in 1980, most married women quit their jobs when they had children. Divorce was still a stigma, and single mothers had much less of a presence in the workforce than they do now. Those who thought women were unfit to be agents were even more outraged that a mother would be admitted to the Academy—and I was the only one in my class. So it was inevitable that I would be needled: "What are you doing here? Don't you belong at home? You've got a kid to take care of." Most of the time I managed to avoid the obvious rebuttals: "One reason I'm here is that I have a kid to take care of. I have to make a living, just like you!"

I would be scolded because of the physical risks of the job: "Haven't you ever thought about what would happen to your child if you were injured or killed in the line of duty?" Of course I had, and I had agonized about it. I would continue to agonize about it, as all parents do every day of their lives, whatever their line of work. The fact is, more parents are killed in car accidents each year than while working as cops or FBI agents—but more to the point, male agents faced the same potential risks that I would. Didn't they have children? Somehow fathers who placed themselves in physical jeopardy were deemed valiant and courageous, while mothers were considered irresponsible.

The reproof that pushed my exasperation to the breaking point, because the bias behind it was so obvious, came from an instructor who began with a seemingly innocuous question. "Is it true that you are a registered nurse?" "Why, yes," I replied, a little flattered by his interest in my background. He shook his head. "We have such a shortage of good nurses. I just can't understand why you quit. How could you leave a field where you are so sorely needed to do this?"

"Well, then," I sighed. "I guess you just wouldn't understand my answer."

In fact, my answer would have sounded like a combination of giddy idealism and derring-do. I wanted to lead a heroic life! I had become a nurse to serve humanity, but after dedicating ten years to tending the infirm in the medics' tent, I now wanted to be out on the front lines, battling evil with the troops. My starting salary would be half what I had made as a head nurse but I didn't care. I'd catch up soon enough. Some of my fellow trainees had walked away from jobs in law firms that paid real money. I was thrilled to be an agent—fascinated by the investigative techniques I had learned and by the workings of our legal system, intrigued by my introduction to criminal psychology, proud of my new muscles and firearms skills—and eager to actualize my powerful sense of mission in the real world.

Amazingly, after twenty years on the job—though now I wouldn't express it with such breathless naïveté—that shining idealism, only a little tarnished by lost fights that should have been won and the inevitable bureaucratic gnawings, is still with me.

Graduation day was almost an anticlimax. During our last week, when we had finished all our qualifying exams, we were finally welcome in the Boardroom, where you could get a beer and a burger or a pizza and for the first time mingle with the pros—cops from all over the country and full-fledged agents back for specialized training. Spinning tall tales to wow the graduating class was the Boardroom's chief order of business, but liaisons made there over a few drinks could last a lifetime. One of the overblown war stories I heard there actually turned out to be true. Dave Martinez, an agent I met, once posed as a desk clerk in a New York City hotel to try to catch a "Top Ten" fugitive who had killed several people, including two cops. Dave's partner, Ron Burkiewicz, was hiding and waiting in the lobby. But when the suspect came to pick up his key, the sting went bad. He pulled a gun and pointed it at Dave, then at two other agents coming up the stairs. In the shoot-out that ensued, Ron shot the felon twice before the man finally succumbed to his wounds. Weathering a shoot-out was so rare in the FBI during the Hoover days, you were rewarded with the duty assignment of your choice. But in Ron's time, and ours, all you got was a pat on the back and then it was, "Well, see you at work tomorrow morning." Such was the world we were entering, but inspired by such stories, we celebrated nightly with boozy cheers and toasts. We would be heroes too!

My family was too far away to attend the ceremony, which involved a handshake from the director (in our case, his designee) and presentation of the highly prized FBI credentials, known as "creds." This coveted identification folder bears the Bureau's gold shield, the photo and signature of the agent, the signature of the director and the seal of the FBI, and a personal agent number assigned in perpetuity—mine is 1609.

When you retire you turn in your creds and the Bureau mounts them for you on a plaque, inscribed with your dates of service. It's a time-honored ritual.

The first place we would show our creds was the Academy gun vault, where we were each formally issued a Smith & Wesson revolver. Women got the bonus gift of a specially designed gun purse, which proved that the FBI was still unaccustomed to female agents. Bad enough that it was ugly—it looked like a tan saddlebag with a gun pocket inside—but it was also treacherous. Mine flopped open the first time I used it, and out popped my weapon, right on the floor at Safeway. "Special Agent, FBI," I hissed at my fellow shoppers, plucking my gun from under the wheels of a supermarket cart. But on graduation day, I wore my handbag proudly.

Back home, I received a more eloquent acknowledgment of my achievement from my father, who had maintained that girls could be nurses or housewives or mothers—I'd been all three!—but not special agents for the FBI. He had watched bemused as I was admitted to Quantico, managed to endure the "rough stuff," and graduated with an assignment to a Chicago squad. Now he redressed his error by presenting me with the gift of a lady-size, blue steel, snub-nosed Smith & Wesson .38. I felt profoundly honored. It was as if he had bestowed the keys to the world on my generation of women.

3

ROOKIE'S WORK

Chicago boasts two federal buildings, right across the street from each other—massive towers dozens of stories high, with vast, cavernous lobbies and row upon row of elevator banks. Though they are stately and imposing, they have a starkness, without the gleaming marble and architectural fillips that might grace a commercial building, that proclaims them to be government owned. Their sole decorative touch is a huge orange flamingolike Calder sculpture out front that seems more formidable than welcoming. It is impossible to enter these buildings without feeling overshadowed and a little cowed.

But at 6:50 A.M. on November 3, 1980, my first day as an FBI agent, I swaggered into 219 South Dearborn with a near fatal dose of self-respect. I had decked myself out in a navy three-piece suit—every agent owned such a suit, nostalgically called his "Hoover Blues," after our late leader—and yes, a trenchcoat and a fedora, shades of Eliot Ness. I had always loved hats, but as a psych nurse, rarely dressed formally enough to wear one; and I was disappointed to discover that they were no longer standard FBI agent gear. But now that I would be wearing a suit to work every day, I could justify investing in a sharp black felt fedora with a grosgrain band, which I secured with a large hatpin to withstand the Chicago winds. I drew a few snickers at first but more often, "Hey, good brim!" "Nice lid!" I soon had a wardrobe of classic fedoras, one to match each of my suits, and for summer, a crisp white straw. My fedora became my signature.

On the ninth floor I presented my creds with a flourish ignored by the guard and was directed to the interior staircase to find my tenth-floor squad. I began my ascent with the proud posture of a queen, but at the top immediately blew my sophisticated cover—in a cliché, made-for-TV moment, I tripped over my unaccustomed high-heeled pumps and went sprawling, flat on my face. My briefcase (mostly empty and carried for show) flew out of my hand and smacked right into a desk where an early-bird agent was sitting reading the paper.

"Look out, boys, she's he-eere," he called out, adding in a fake stage whisper, "These damn new guys! I hope she's not on our squad." As I tried to scramble to my feet, out of wind, with stinging scrapes and holes in the knees of my hose, he asked, "Didn't they teach you how to climb stairs at the Academy?"

I had tumbled onto the turf of the famous Chicago fugitive squad, also known as the macho squad, who commanded the front of the tenth floor. They were a tightly knit cadre of guys who had worked together for years, kicking down doors to capture desperadoes in all the most exciting, high-profile cases of extortion, murder, kidnapping, and bank robbery. They openly smirked at less capable male agents, and no woman had ever darkened the doors of their squad. They were not the kind of colleagues who would look forgivingly on a klutz.

Had I known that, I might have been intimidated. As it was, I summoned up my dignity and asked to be steered toward Squad 5C, ignoring the snorts behind my back as I turned away.

At the head of each field division, as the regional satellite bureaus are called, is a Special Agent in Charge, or SAC. In a city the size of Chicago he or she would serve primarily as chief administrator, with broad discretionary powers, and as liaison to other branches of government and law enforcement, as well as the press. Below him are Assistant Special Agents in Charge (ASACs) who oversee the major programs, such as white-collar crime, foreign counterintelligence, organized crime and drugs, and Violent Crime/Major Offender (VCMO). Next in the pecking order are the squad supervisors, who do the day-to-day management of agent task forces dedicated to specific criminal activities such as fraud, terrorism, and, in the case of the macho squad, fugitive apprehension, as well as expert service squads, specially trained in such skills as surveillance, who are farmed out to help with individual operations. In 1980, there were some 350 agents working in Chicago, only fourteen of whom were women. I was the fifteenth.

Squad 5C, my first assignment, was a white-collar-crime squad of roughly twenty agents focused on wire fraud—any fraud perpetrated via "wire services," such as telephone lines. Most of its senior members were accountants and stockbrokers, and it was a popular launching pad for new female agents. The handful of rookies did a lot of the scut work—combing through records, doing background investigations, and the like—and learned the ropes by being paired with more experienced "training agents." Every investigative protocol—from evidence packaging for shipment to the FBI lab and witness-and suspect-interview procedures to what to do if you were first on the scene of a murder, bank robbery, or bombing—was outlined in our bible, the Manual of Investigative Operations and Guidelines (MIOG). The training agent's role was to help a rookie develop the judgment to flesh out the MIOG guidelines.

The squad supervisor, Kurt Cannon,* set me up with a great bear of a man, Jim Kruger,* as my training agent. It was under Jim's aegis that I set out to do the first major interview of my career, with the president of one of the world's largest banks, from which a substantial sum of money had disappeared. Thrilled that the "case agent," or chief FBI investigator of the crime, had chosen me to help collect statements from the principals, I studied the MIOG, rehearsing its prescribed procedure and reviewing possible approaches with more experienced members of the squad. Still, I was nervous as I set out for my public debut as an agent, dressed in a sober black suit and white silk blouse, with my long red hair pinned up beneath my fedora in a prim French twist. "Hey, Miss America!" my fellow agents catcalled. "Got your gun? Look out for that bigshot! You want backup, Shark Bait?"

I glowered at them, but I was laughing to myself as I approached the doors of the great bank. The president's office on the top floor, forty stories up, was a beautifully paneled walnut suite. After accepting a cup of tea from his secretary, whose suit made mine look like a bargain-basement special, I was ushered into the presence of a distinguished gray-haired man who had Harvard or Air Force Academy written all over him. I shook his hand, then snappily presented my creds. He took them, a Bureau taboo that I was debating how to protest when, peering at them, he asked, "Is this really you?"

At the time, most people didn't realize that the Bureau employed women as agents. After a few months on the job, I was already out of patience with patronizing smirks, comments—ranging from, "Well, well, since when are there gals in the FBI?" to "Who do you think you're kidding?"—and calls to my superiors to confirm that such an improbability as a female special agent did exist.

"Why, yes," I replied, stifling annoyance.

"Are you sure?" The faint humor in his tone pushed me deeper into irritation.

"Yes, sir," I stated, in my most authoritative FBI voice, "of course it is." I reached into my purse. "Here's my business card."

He compared the names and laughed out loud. "Well, Miss DeLong," he said, "if this is really you, would you have dinner with me tonight?"

Indignant, I snatched at the credentials he held out. All I could do when I saw them was splutter, "Those bastards . . ."

It seems that my new colleagues on Squad 5C had "enhanced" the head shot on my creds. Below my proud, smiling face, they had attached the reclining body of a voluptuous nude. It was a perfectly slick, professional-looking job—so well executed that I remain convinced that the graphic artists in Special Projects at FBI headquarters were involved.

The bank president and I laughed ourselves sick at the gag. I had to decline his dinner invitation—both for professional decorum and because the photo was false advertising—but he still gave me free checking for a year.

Back at the office, the agents who had seen me off were all suddenly too absorbed in mysterious tasks to acknowledge me. The case agent and Jim, reacting with surprise that I am sure was feigned, claimed innocence of the caper. There were female agents who saw the credentials prank as so sabotaging and offensive that they urged me to file an official complaint. Not a chance, I thought, even if that made some consider me an "Auntie Tom." There would be bigger battles ahead, I suspected, and I figured I had better pick my shots. Besides, being the butt of a practical joke suggested that I was gaining a measure of acceptance on the squad. And it was funny!

Jim would not only educate me in tradecraft but would also initiate me into the Chicago division's rites and customs, many of which involved food. Though we were required to clock in each morning at 7:00, our official workday began at 8:15, so the squad breakfast—by invitation only—was an important daily ritual. I achieved acceptance at wire fraud breakfasts early on, but there were other squads where rookies (especially women) could suffer months of exclusion, signifying their colleagues' mistrust. The breakfasts were held at a nearby dive, where agents in that pre-health-conscious era would wolf down five-egg omelets deliciously gooey with cheese, towers of toast or pancakes drenched in butter, and logpiles of sausage and bacon. No girlish muffin nibbling was allowed. I once tried to order tea and dry toast and was scoffed at and booed.

Jim loved sweets, and once while we were stuck for hours on stakeout, bored and hungry, he tried to trade me to another surveillance team for a doughnut—he wasn't kidding. He was irredeemably addicted to the chocolate cream pies at Baker's Square. Several times a week, he would reach over and tap his pen or a ruler on my desk, raising an eyebrow suggestively. That meant, "Strap on your gun. We're heading out. It's Pie Time!"

Rookie agents belonged to their entry-assignment squads but they could be tapped by any case agent in the division to assist on an operation. We were encouraged to vary our experience as much as possible—to practice with and in effect audition for different squads in order to select one as a permanent home. So we were all eager wannabes, circling the office and trying to chat up senior agents, telling them, "Look, if something comes up, I'm available . . ." In those days the Chicago office didn't have walls or even partitions. Each squad was a cluster of twenty desks, with two phones for every four, separated from the next by a six-foot aisle. When you heard rumbling or laughter across the room, you'd make it your business to ferret out the cause, just in case it meant something exciting was in the offing that you could assist on, like an arrest.

I felt very lucky when Phil Benson,* Clay's old partner, decided to give me a break. Working undercover in organized crime, Phil had long been resisting "fixups" with eligible women connected to the mob. Now he had a mob banquet to attend, and it was time to produce the steady girlfriend he had been claiming as an excuse—or as the guys charmingly put it, he needed "some federal pussy."

I didn't have a thing to wear. Kurt told me to take the afternoon off to shop for something suitable, which turned out to be a crepe evening suit with sparkly sequin accents and a skirt slit high up my thighs. With stiletto heels and my long hair ratted up like a thundercloud, I felt like the embodiment of dangerous glamour. "Perfect," Phil said when he saw me. "You're supposed to be a dumb broad, and you look like one. Now act like one. Can you handle that?"

Lou was my name for the night—short for my middle name, Louise—and Phil was "John." Had I not known him for so long, the ruse would have been easier. As it was, after "John" headed off with the men, I was stuck at our table with the wives, who wanted to know all about our relationship. Not wanting to fabricate a history that "John" might contradict, I focused on describing my own hopes for the future and even the wedding I envisioned, waxing imaginatively until suddenly one woman asked, "Why did you call him Phil?"

I was aghast. It may have been my imagination that all conversation ceased, but there was nothing fake about the horror that gripped me. I was certain that she was about to signal her husband, and Phil and I would be shot down. Not knowing what I had done, poor Phil wouldn't even see the threat coming and get to his weapon, never mind that we were outnumbered 100 to 2. At the very least I had blown Phil's cover and compromised a multiyear investigation, so would deservedly be fired from the FBI.

It was "ass-pucker time," as the Bureau expression goes.

I started spewing words: "Don't tell him!" not sure at first just who

I meant or where I was heading. "John gets so jealous! Phil's my ex, and John would smack the shit out of me if he knew I ever thought about him . . ."

She didn't doubt it. "Don't worry," she said knowingly. "It's okay." But it must have been ten minutes until my pulse slowed down.

Phil and I escaped unscathed, and when I confessed my mistake, he just laughed. "That happens all the time," he said. "People hardly notice, and they forget about it right away." He approved of the way I'd re-covered. "That's something I can pick up on. I'll mention that I have to slap you around once in a while."

On my first arrest, the danger was much more real. I was chosen to assist by John Slone, a legend in the Chicago division. A tall, powerfully built, soft-spoken black man, he exuded integrity and authority, commanding respect by his presence alone yet rarely saying a word. Celebrated for his record of fugitive captures, he belonged to the macho squad, but unlike most of the others never threw his weight around—he didn't have to. Many highly effective agents have what we call "I-love-me walls," to show off mementos of their cases and plaques and "attaboys" or commendations. All John displayed were pictures of his wife and children. Because he wasn't a self-promoter, he wouldn't win his rightful promotion until it was long overdue, but then he distinguished himself as the head of a squad that cracked some very complex and important civil rights cases.

Slone wanted me on his team because the fugitive we were hunting was a woman. Now that the Bureau had female agents, it had come to recognize that they could both defuse tensions and prevent case-complicating fabricated sexual incidents when women were arrested. For similar reasons, because the subject was black—as was the victim—it behooved Slone to bring along another African-American agent, and he chose Lon Jones,* whom I had known from the Academy. These choices seem obvious to us now, so commonsensical that it is impossible to imagine how law enforcement agencies managed to function effec-tively in the days when they employed only white men. But in 1980, those days were still very recent.

The suspect had been classified a "fugitive" by the police, who had asked for the help of the FBI. We had a tip that she was holed up in an apartment in the Robert Taylor housing projects on the South Side. Chicago's housing projects are notorious, an ill-conceived response to the postwar housing shortage that replaced neighborhoods, which had social structures, with miles upon miles of anonymous high-rises that became petri dishes of violence. The most infamous illustration of life in the projects was the Cabrini Green incident, in which a thirteen-year-old boy raped a four-year-old girl and tried to throw her out the window. She grabbed the ledge, but as horrified residents watched from below, he pried away her fingers and she plummeted ten stories to her death. Enraged, the onlookers stormed the building and killed the boy. Then there was the story of the marksman who had come back from Vietnam, mad at the world, and settled in the projects. One day a woman was walking her little boy to school and, as they paused for a stoplight, suddenly lost hold of his hand. She looked down and found him dead. The sniper—her neighbor—had taken a sniper rifle and just picked him off from the window, like it was target practice.

Disturbing as these stories are, they were not atypical.

No one at the projects welcomed the presence of "the law," including the Chicago Housing Authority guards at the door. They checked our identification so officiously that at one point I had to tease, "What's the matter? You got a lot of gals breaking in here?" He just laughed and waved me on. Our next obstacle was the broken elevators—the city never made it a priority to maintain elevators in the projects—so up the dark, urine-spattered stairs we trudged to the eleventh floor. Word was spreading fast that the FBI was in the building.

At that point I was still having the gun-adjustment problems that bedevil new agents, especially women. Our clothes, even suits, tend to be too fitted to conceal a gun and a holster, and in a crisis you'd better not have to fumble for a gun in your purse. I had come up with what I thought was the brilliant solution of having my tailor sew an expanded, heavily reinforced pocket into my trenchcoat, with supportive facing to keep my gun from lopsidedly weighing me down. I had practiced pulling the gun at home, but when I furtively tried it again on the stairs, the pocket now seemed way too snug to allow me a quick draw. So as we climbed, I kept one hand in my pocket, surreptitiously ripping away at the stitching, but ready to shoot through the coat if there was trouble.

Finally we reached the apartment and caught our breath as John banged on the door. "Open up, it's the police."

There were scurrying sounds and shouting and children wailing, then at last the door opened. With guns drawn and credentials held high, we waded into a crowd of naked toddlers and angry, cursing adults. Though it was January and well below freezing outside, the steam heat and the bright sun streaming through the unshaded windows kept the apartment hotter than 80 degrees. My silk blouse and stockings, already clinging from the climb upstairs, felt like they were melting. There was pandemonium until John's deep, authoritative schoolteacher voice quelled the commotion.

"Where's Mary?" he demanded, warrant in hand. "I know she's here, so don't even try to lie to me."

Indignant denials rang out, and John signaled to us to fan out and search the apartment. We had been briefed to seek not only our suspect but also the murder weapon, a gun. Three of us began searching a back room; and I was down on my hands and knees, checking under a bed, when I noticed that one of the toddlers had broken away from his mother and was tearfully watching me, just about to break into a sob. "Hi, sweetheart," I said, sitting up. "Don't cry, darling . . ." He began to murmur shyly, building to a soft singsong, and I caught a few words. Was he saying Mommy—or Mary? "Where's Mary?" I whispered to him. "Is she hiding?"

He began to smile, and babbling away, seemed to be pointing to a huge pile of clothes in a corner of the room. "Stay here," I said, sitting him down, out of the way.

Quietly I moved across the room and flattened myself against the wall, with my gun aimed at the pile. Then, with one quick swipe, I knocked a load of clothes off the top—and there, buried underneath, was Mary. My colleagues rushed over and wrestled her into handcuffs. One of them had already found the gun under a mattress and secured it in a plastic evidence bag. The whole bust was over in minutes.

Now we had to get out of the building. Encircling Mary, we marched her out of the apartment and down the stairs, the agents in front keeping the way clear, as curses and catcalls trailed us. By the time we reached the ground floor, a belligerent mob had gathered, taunting us with insults and invective. We kept heading for the cars, impassive, still surrounding Mary, with our guns trained on the crowd. Poor Lon, who was bringing up the rear, got the worst of it—not only walking backward but being threatened, spat at, and reviled as a traitor to his race, though both killer and victim had been black.

I can hardly imagine what was going through his mind and how conflicted he must have felt. He left the Bureau a few years later. My own exhilaration at making my first arrest was a little tarnished by guilt at having taken advantage of a child, just a few years younger than my son. I was a mother, I knew how to talk to a toddler who wanted to play "hide and seek," and I had capitalized on it. I wondered if a man would have done that. I had no compunctions about using whatever wiles I had, not to mention my gun, on an adult—but on a three-year-old? Just how hardass was I going to have to be to do my job? It wasn't the kind of question I could talk over with the guys.

Nor could I discuss it with the other woman on my squad, Nancy Fisher, because she was married to one of the tough guys in the division, and she had been an agent only a few months longer than I had. Nancy and I had been getting friendly, and what cemented our relationship was making an arrest together. I was working the complaint desk, a duty that rotated daily among the rookies, when a woman called to ask if we had an Agent So-and-So in the division. He wasn't in the directory and no one seemed to have heard of him, so I told her no. She got very upset.

She had been shopping at Carson's in one of the wealthy North Shore suburbs when a man came up to her and flashed a badge. They started talking about his work for the Bureau and they wound up going out to lunch. Everything was perfectly pleasant until he asked if she would do him a favor. He wanted her to try on a particular dress he had seen on a mannequin in Carson's, not in some secluded place but right there in the store. The request seemed harmless enough, and besides, he was an FBI agent.

"Did you do it?" I asked.

"Yes," she said, "though it did seem kind of strange."

She had gone into the fitting room, put on the dress, and then come out to model it for him. He kept telling her to shift poses—front, back, side, front again, back again—staring at her intently all the while. Then all of a sudden he said, "See you around," and quickly strode away.

"He knows my name and phone number," she added nervously. "He said he was going to call me. And he can easily find my address."

It seemed likely that the man had been using her to play out some sexual fantasy, and that he had left abruptly because he was having an orgasm.

I wish I could have reassured her that he was just some innocuous fetishist and that if she discouraged his calls he would lose interest and seek out another "model." But as John Douglas, in his book *Obsession*, maintains,

> Often enough, so-called nuisance crimes and nonviolent offenses are warnings of much more serious, dangerous offenses to follow . . . Certainly there are a lot more peeping toms out there than serial rapists, so a simple fetish does not always lead to violent crime, but a man arrested for voyeurism today may well evolve into a rapist in the future, when merely watching women through a window and masturbating as he fantasizes about them no longer satisfies him.

Douglas elaborates in *Mindhunter*: "I'm not meaning to suggest that every man attracted to stiletto heels or turned on by the thought of black lace panties is destined for a life of crime. If that were true, most of us would be in prison. But . . . this kind of paraphilia can be degenerative . . ." He cites the case of Jerome Brudos, who "went from mildly strange all the way to deadly." At the age of five, Brudos found a pair of gleaming high heels in the trash and defied his mother to keep them, then graduated to stealing women's garments from clotheslines and even housebreaking in search of underwear and shoes. Douglas calls this a "textbook escalation of activities . . . a continual refinement of the fantasy . . . [We] see in [Brudos]—and so many of the others—an obsession with and 'improvement' of the details from . . . one level of activity to the next." For Brudos, the progression would eventually culminate in serial murder. As a souvenir of his first victim—a nineteen-year-old girl who had mistakenly come to his house on an encyclopedia sales call— he kept a severed foot locked in his freezer, decked out in a high-heeled shoe from his collection.

So, while there was no reason to assume that the caller's "dresser" had more on his mind than lunch and a fashion show, a degree of worry was certainly warranted. And he had committed the crime of impersonating an FBI agent, right down to the badge. This in itself was a danger sign, being a popular strategy among serial sex offenders, many of whom are police buffs. When I described the situation to my supervisor, Kurt Cannon, he said, "Go get him."

I told the woman that when the "agent" called, she should suggest that they get together at Carson's, saying that she wanted to bring a friend, who had never gotten to meet a real FBI agent. The "friend" would be Nancy. I would hang around, pretending to shop, and we would bring along a couple of the guys as backup. Nancy was petite and beautiful, with long blond hair, and I planned to wear my red hair down—no one would "make" us as FBI agents. As we expected, the "agent" took the bait.

We got there early and spotted a man of his description loitering near the fitting room entrance, watching the women. He was tall, handsome, and genteel—the kind of man juries never believe could harass a woman: "Why, a guy like that could get any girl he wanted!" He soon zeroed in on our caller, who introduced Nancy as her friend, as I hovered nearby, riffling through the racks. "Ooooh," Nancy squealed. "Are you really an FBI agent?"

"Why, yes I am," he said proudly.

"How cool!" Nancy was laying it on thick. "Do you have a badge, like a cop?"

He pulled out his badge—it was plastic, not even a good facsimile.

"Gee, that doesn't look like mine," Nancy said, as she "badged" him.

I moved in, announcing, "FBI. You're under arrest!"

I still remember how the blood drained from his face—he turned dead white—as the guys, who'd been loitering like impatient husbands of shoppers, dashed over and cuffed him.

By the time we got back to the office, word was out that we'd made our bust. The charge would be a piddly little misdemeanor, but ideally we had thrown a scare into a guy who was a public nuisance. So we were proud, even if we were doomed to months of merciless teasing.

"Hey, DeLong! Is that the only way you can get a boyfriend—bust him?" went a popular refrain. "You can't get a man with a gun . . ." someone would sing, echoing the old show tune. That wasn't far wrong. I was already discovering that gals with guns could intimidate some would-be suitors.

Then came the morning when I arrived at work to find my desk and chair bound up with crime scene tape. They had been "secured," I was told, pending investigation of my lawless acts, including the most egregious—my daily impersonation of a federal agent.

4

"THE ONE IN THE HAT"

Word was getting around that there was a new female agent in wire fraud who was looking to make arrests: "the one in the hat." That's probably how Al Lennon,* a senior agent on the terrorism squad, happened to pick me out. For two years, he had been working the case of a Croatian terrorist who had murdered three Serbians in Chicago; and now, having finally pinned him down, was ready to make the arrest. When I showed up as directed in the conference room, I was sure that I was in the wrong place. The arrest of a murdering terrorist, I figured, called for at least twenty people, including the Chicago SWAT team and a sniper or two—maybe even a tank.

But the only person there was an agent I'll call Brian,* who had graduated from the Academy about six months ahead of me. Telling me, "Sit tight, little one"—which I didn't take amiss because Brian's ranginess dwarfed most people—he reported that Al and his partner, Pete Harrigan,* were on the way.

"Just the four of us?" I asked, amazed.

"Did you think we were going to call out the National Guard?" he said. "What is this, your first arrest?"

"No, but it's my first terrorist," I told him.

He chuckled patronizingly. "Don't be scared," he said. "If you stay in the car, you won't screw anything up."

"Oh, the voice of experience!" I countered. "Have the big boys been making you sit it out in the car?"

"I guess you didn't notice that I am a big boy, little girl."

"You're bigger than me, but I guess you didn't notice that our guns are the same size."

We exchanged "my-badge-is-bigger-than-your-badge" banter until Al and Pete arrived. From a folder he carried, Al passed each of us several photos of the suspect taken by the surveillance team, plus some shots of his home and car, and a fact sheet listing his age, height, weight, identifying marks such as tattoos and scars, and other personal data. Then he handed us detailed maps of the neighborhood, which made me wonder if we were in for a car chase. I secretly hoped so, never having done one, for it wasn't until 1986 that the Bureau schooled its agents in high-speed driving. (Nonetheless, in its ninety-five-year history the FBI has never been involved in a car chase that resulted in the injury of an agent or an innocent person.)

"Could be," said Al, tolerant of my enthusiasm. He emphasized that our suspect would most likely be armed and dangerous.

Lengthy surveillance had established that the suspect left the house every morning at seven sharp. The plan was to seize him the moment he reached the sidewalk, before he got to his car. Generally, it's safer to arrest someone outdoors, engaged in his daily routine and probably least vigilant, than to knock on his door and give him a chance to dig in with his heavy artillery. And once he gets in his car, he is effectively in possession of a one-ton weapon, never mind whatever might be stashed inside. I'd rather take a bullet than a dead-on hit from a Cadillac or a great big Chevy—my chance of survival would be greater. That's why law enforcement agents are allowed to shoot at suspects in oncoming cars, which may imperil those in their path, but not at cars leaving the scene, which are no longer a direct threat.

We began our stakeout at five, and because it was so early, Al and Pete thought it would be safe to go pick up coffee. They went together, leaving me and Brian, two rookies, to keep watch.

No sooner had they left than the front door opened. "Hey," Brian said, "someone's coming out. What are we going to do?"

"Oh man," I replied. "That's our guy!"

I wasn't even wearing my bulletproof vest at that point, for in those days they were too cumbersome and heavy to wear in the car. Most agents waited until the first hint of action to wrestle them on—which was foolhardy, as I was about to learn.

But the way I saw it, we had no choice. Just sitting outside the house at 5 A.M., we ran a very high risk of being "made"—showing the suspect that we were after him and washing weeks of surveillance down the drain. Even if we weren't spotted, if we let him go, there was an excellent chance that we would lose him altogether. He might well be breaking with routine because he was on the move.

"Let's get him," I told Brian.

My head was swimming with the MIOG procedures and legal guidelines for arresting a dangerous suspect. The worst thing an agent or a cop can do is to apprehend a suspect and, because of some mistake, have to unarrest him. Lawsuits usually ensue, which may be thrown out if the reasons for the arrest are good enough, but still . . .

Although Brian's experience was as skimpy as mine, he said, "Okay."

By now the suspect had nearly reached his car. "Cut him off," I said. "Block him so he can't pull out." Brian swung the car around to box him in; and the moment we stopped, I said, "Let's go!" and jumped out the passenger's side. Before the suspect knew what hit him, I was at his window with my gun drawn, screaming, "FBI! Get your hands on the wheel! FBI! FBI!"

The suspect raised both hands to the wheel, gaping in fear and shock, his mind not grasping what was happening and who I was, yelling outside his window. He never imagined a woman would come after him. Later he told me that all he could imagine was that I was a Serbian assassin, bent on avenging the murders he had committed. "Out of the car!" I said, yanking the door open and grabbing him by the scruff of the neck. "Hands up!"

He knew what to do—the "hands-up" posture has universal currency, probably because of TV—and then, out of the blue, so did I. Flashing on the confidential talk we women got from our PT instructor at the Academy, I pointed my gun at his groin. In my whole career, I've never seen a man do that. It seems to be sort of a gender courtesy never to threaten another man that way. But it works. A long moment passed as I watched a dark stain seep across the place where my gun was aimed.

All the while, I assumed that Brian was right behind me, and I now expected him to move in and cuff the suspect. Where was he? I couldn't take my eyes off my prisoner long enough to check. Finally I heard the screech of brakes and a bump, as Al and Pete's car jumped the curb, coming to the rescue. They leaped out, guns in the air, and quickly pinned the suspect down, slapping handcuffs on his wrists. Only then did I dare cast a glance around for Brian. He was just getting out of our car—a little sheepishly, I thought. He had been there the whole time, radioing for help.

Suddenly I grew weak in the knees, as it dawned on me how much I'd done wrong, barreling ahead without a bulletproof vest, taking it for granted that I had backup. I could have been killed so easily.

Al and Pete were now frog-marching the suspect away, and he came to a stop where I was standing. As he glowered at me, it abruptly struck me as hilarious that, all alone, I had terrified a killer—who had mercilessly, in cold blood, executed three people for political reasons—so badly that he had wet his pants. "Guess I scared you," I said, glancing at the spot.

"You don't scare me," he said, sneering. "You are just a woman. Women are pigs, you are a pig, you pig-woman—"

"That's Miss Federal Pig to you," I said, laughing.

Astonished at what I'd done—but not as much as I was—Al and Pete treated me and Brian to a glutton's breakfast at Mitchell's, a classic Chicago diner that served double-yolked eggs. "So the little girl got the bad guy," they teased, laughing about my rejoinder, "That's Miss Federal Pig to you." That got around the office fast, becoming the first in a string of "DeLongisms" associated with me. (Another one was "Well, I'm not the one wearing handcuffs," which I blurted out when confronted by another cursing suspect.) A lot of the guys razzed me for making the subject wet his pants. "Ooooh, what a badass, scary broad you are."

I felt like one too, for a time. Anyone who has ever ridden a roller coaster knows what a physical thrill you get from danger—and when the risks are real, the surge of exhilaration is that much greater. My first arrest seemed like a baptism, and I recognized that at least part of what had drawn me and so many others to law enforcement was that adrenaline rush. I wanted to feel it again.

Most of the other assists I did were less dramatic, usually involving surveillance, one of the most challenging and important jobs we do. Surveillance may seem like passive observation, but it can escalate in seconds to deadly confrontation if the agents get "made" or must intervene to prevent a serious crime. Just to cite one case, a Chicago surveillance unit tailed a woman, believed to be half of a bank robbery team, driving through a peaceful suburban neighborhood. All they were doing was watching, having no reason to approach. Had she hooked up with her partner/husband outside a bank, they would have moved in, for agents are required to thwart crimes. But something set off her alarms, and realizing that she was being followed by the FBI, she started shooting. The quiet street became a Wild West scene as speeding cars traded gunfire, and then it was all over—she was dead, having provoked a wholly unexpected showdown. Later, in her VCR at home, agents found a videotape of *Bonnie and Clyde*, the classic film about a gangster couple who robbed banks and perished in a hail of bullets. She and her husband would watch it as often as five times a day. Her life, and death, had mirrored it.

There is a specially trained surveillance squad (SOG, short for Special Operations Group) that handles surveillance on major operations. The SOG will be called in, for example, to track suspects of kidnappings or big heists, in the hope that they might lead to the abductee or the money, or probable serial killers, who tend to revisit the scenes of their crimes, their victims' graves, or their secret hiding places for bodies. The squad also does surreptitious entries to plant court-ordered wiretaps and "bugs." On more long-term operations or for more routine activities such as watching known associates of fugitives, tracking garden-variety suspects, and monitoring racketeers, case agents tend to run their own surveillance.

It was on one leg of a long-term sting that I got my first lesson in surveillance from Ron Elder, one of Clay and Phil's colleagues on the organized crime squad. One night, in his undercover role as a mobster, Phil was to meet a Mafia kingpin in a restaurant in Cicero, Al Capone's old stomping grounds. The late, legendary gangster still loomed large there in the racketeering of his spiritual descendants and in the nearly life-size photo that hung in the Cicero police station. Phil needed agents watching from the wings, to document the event for the case we were building and also to protect him, should the meeting go sour. Ron recruited me to come along.

It takes at least two people to work an effective stationary surveillance, one to have "the eye"—that is, to hold his or her gaze locked on the objective—and the other to assist with the surveillance and keep the log, a detailed record of every action taking place in the target zone. This is not just busywork, for the log may become the foundation of an agent's testimony in court and because, sometimes, a seemingly insignificant observation can hold the key to an entire case. A major breakthrough in a foreign counterintelligence case came with the discovery that two Thursdays in a row, a man chucked an empty pack of Salem cigarettes into a garbage can. The garbage can was a dead drop, and the cigarette pack was the signal summoning the spies to a secret rendezvous. So logs are scrupulously kept and analyzed to detect patterns. God is in the details.

No matter how many hours you are stuck on surveillance, you can't read the paper or do your nails to pass the time, for your full concentration must stay focused on your target—in our case, Phil, whom we could see through the restaurant windows as we sat in the car. You can't even look around much, and that singularity of focus is one reason why surveillance can be dangerous. Agents have been shot to death sitting in cars, too intent on their targets to sense the approach of danger.

About the only thing you can do to stave off boredom on a lengthy surveillance is to eat. The longer you'll be sitting, the more sensory stimulation you'll want from your snacks, making potato and tortilla chips, popcorn, candy, and that beloved law enforcement staple, dough-nuts, the foods of choice. When a surveillance drags on for weeks or months, you can easily pack on twenty or thirty pounds. (An agent greeting another who has obviously bulked up will ask, "Oh, so how did the surveillance go?") Fortunately, that night we were covering Phil for only a few hours.

Ron and I passed the time chatting, and it was my turn to have the eye when Phil and his host wound up their meal with coffee and got the check. I watched Phil stand up to leave. Then Ron said something, and unconsciously I turned my head to answer. When I looked back a split second later, Phil was gone. He didn't come out of the building.

"Oh my God," I said. "Where the hell is he?"

Had Phil been shot or stabbed before he reached the door? Was he lying inside, wounded and bleeding and needing backup? Had he been strong-armed out the back, into a waiting car?

Fortunately none of those things had happened, we learned through radio contact a short time later. But anything could have. During my moment of inattention, Phil and the kingpin had slipped outside, turning the corner and vanishing before I spotted them. I was devastated that I'd missed them, but Ron was soothing, assuring me that everyone screwed up when they were new and underscoring what a valuable lesson I'd learned. "It takes practice," he told me. "You just got a crash course on what a difference just a couple crucial seconds can make. That's how fast trouble can come down."

The novel *Hannibal* by Thomas Harris opens with Special Agent Clarice Starling on surveillance in a mirror-windowed van, trying to forestall suffocation in the Virginia heat with a 150-pound block of dry ice. I've been in that situation myself—real agents don't get ice—dripping sweat for hours in triple-digit temperatures, thankful that my partner was female so I could strip down to my panties and bra, keeping my shoes on and my shirt close by in case of action. I can only guess what someone might have thought, peering through the mirrored windows and spying two nearly naked women sitting there, mopping perspiration.

In Chicago we were also challenged by the cold—winter days when the thermometer dropped to 15 or 20 degrees below zero, not counting the windchill factor. On an outdoor stakeout, you couldn't run the heater in your car, for a cloud of exhaust would be sure to draw the suspicions of the neighbors, if not your suspect. So we would work in teams of two or three cars, each of which would periodically turn over its motor for a few minutes to get a short blast of heat. I once surveilled a suspect who went out to his car, only to find it stuck in the snow. He kept gunning the engine, which dug him in deeper and kept his tailpipe spewing steam that was encasing his back wheels in a block of ice. "Sheesh," snorted my partner, after watching him for twenty minutes. "When the hell is he going to wise up?"

"No kidding!" I said. "I'm freezing. Why don't we get this show on the road?"

So we slipped out of our car and, pretending to be passing Good Samaritans, offered to help. We rocked out his car, for which he thanked us profusely and even proffered a folded bill, which we nobly refused. Then he drove off, and we followed. He led us straight to what we later learned was a secret meeting of his terrorist cell.

Now, that's a token of appreciation!

Even indoors, wintertime surveillance in Chicago can take resourcefulness. One day the Bureau got a tip that a group of terrorists was plotting to break in and plant a bomb in a building downtown. I was assigned to do overnight surveillance, along with an agent named John Smart,* from what's called a "perch," meaning a site overlooking the target zone. We were told to report to the perch at midnight and to dress warmly. The building, an ancient warehouse right on the lake, was semivacant, and the heat was turned off on the floor where we would be "perched." It was 20 below outside.

John and I took our places at the window, armed with snacks and huge thermoses of coffee to keep us awake. We had scrounged some old chairs from deserted offices, on which we sat rocking and stomping our feet, taking turns getting up and moving around to get warm. Though I was wearing heavy mittens and doubled-up woolen socks under fleece-lined boots, my hands and feet grew so numb after a couple hours that even clapping and pacing couldn't thaw them. We were both so miserable that I finally told John, "Take the eye. I am going to find something here to warm us up."

I set off in the darkness, guided by the light glazing the windows from the moon and from the street lamps below. Once I got closer to the center of the floor, which ran to thousands of square feet, I used my flashlight to peer around. That yielded nothing, so I crept down-stairs, hoping that I was only imagining the skittering of rats, and there—hallelujah!—was a janitor's bucket, one of those wheeled metal contraptions with a built-in wringer. More poking revealed a huge old sink against one of the walls. Since some of the other floors seemed to be occupied, I figured that the water was still running in the building, and when I tried the antique faucet, a little trickled out. Eventually it built to a thin, rusty stream, never growing hot but definitely on the warm side—warmer, in any case, than our hands and feet. Little by little I filled it up, using a small basin I found on the floor. That must have taken ten minutes, and it probably cost me another ten to wrestle it up the stairs.

When I got back, John was marching in place, slapping his arms against his shoulders, but with his eyes unwaveringly glued to the window. "Where have you been? I was getting worried," he growled. I took the eye so he could see what I was pushing, telling him, "Look at what I've got here! Relief is just a smile away!"

Then I tore off my shoes and socks, rolled up my pants, and nearly barking my shins on the wringer, plunged my feet into the dirty water. Warm at last! All night long, as the water cooled off, I kept refilling the bucket, playing footsie with myself to keep my circulation flowing. Poor John just sat there in misery, refusing to commit his own feet to the rusty brew.

But luckily, he didn't bandy my brainstorm around the office. Our squad had an "Asshole of the Month" award, a dubious honor for which the winner would be wheeled all over the floor in a desk chair, with a sign around his neck, like a dunce cap, to the merriment of all. The award was never bestowed on a real jerk but instead was granted to a good-sport agent who had done something goofy in the line of duty. With my janitor's bucket strategy, I would have been a shoo-in.

We were on overnight surveillance for the rest of the week, but from then on I came prepared with battery-powered electrified ski socks to keep my feet warm. The terrorists never showed. They probably had more sense than to come out in the cold.

•   •   •

Over time, I got a reputation for being good at surveillance. John Gray, who headed the Chicago surveillance squad and taught at Quantico—there was no formal course back when I attended the Academy—maintains that women are much better at it than men. Not only do they tend to be more patient and observant, but also they look less suspicious. A woman in a station wagon with a baby seat looks like a soccer mom picking up a kid from a play date, while a man sitting in a car looks like he's up to no good. Later, when I surveilled suspects for long periods, I made it my practice to switch cars frequently with other agents and to carry along a selection of wigs and hats to alter my looks. Once a relief team came out and nearly missed me, with my red hair hidden under a flowing blond wig, topped by a baseball cap pulled low, shielding my face. "What's the matter with you, DeLong?" one of the agents asked, laughing. "You have a case of the for-reals?" Meaning, "Do you think this is for real, not just some case, and important enough to risk looking foolish to do it?"

"Yeah," I replied, "as a matter of fact I do."

I'm not saying that they took their work less seriously than I did. For the police, it is standard operating procedure to use disguises and switch cars to foil detection, but such strategies—though common sense might dictate their benefits—were less entrenched in the culture of the Bureau at that time. J. Edgar Hoover never believed in "deep cover" work, preferring to cultivate informants inside investigated groups than to plant his own people. Since his death, it has become an important area of specialization, with its own training program at Quantico, but in the early 1980s, "deep cover" and its trickle-down tactics, such as using disguises, were relatively new and discomfiting to many of the old-line veterans. It is only fairly recently that the Bureau routinely began to use agents who could blend in for surveillance in nonwhite neighborhoods—and had the personnel to do it—rather than deploy white, middle-aged men who stuck out like throbbing red thumbs.

As head of the Chicago SOG, John Gray made it his business to diversify the squad and to encourage creativity on surveillance. Coming from a military intelligence background in Vietnam, he was comparatively free of the old Hoover baggage. So we had agents dressing like homeless people in booze-scented, raggedy clothes and lolling on the ground next to Dumpsters to surveil suspects. One agent masqueraded as a Chicago cop and directed traffic while on the lookout for two men purportedly trying to fence a stolen Picasso. As he stood watch, the suspects drove by in a car with a broken windshield and missing taillight, giving the "cop" a legitimate reason to stop them—and lo and behold, there, in the backseat, in plain sight, was the painting. Not quite aware of the value of their haul, the amateur thieves had been storing the masterpiece, uncovered, in the filthy basement of their apartment house, so it was littered with mouse droppings and stank of cat urine.

Funny surveillance stories abound. In one classic, two agent partners watched a suspect for sixty straight days, without a break, waiting for him to make a move. Finally the moment came when he set off in his car, and they followed, heading east, out of the city. By the time they realized that he wasn't stopping anytime soon, they were too far out of town to summon help from their squad. Loath to risk losing the suspect and whatever confederates he might be meeting, they had little choice but to keep driving. There were no cell phones in those days, so whenever their quarry pulled off the freeway for gas or food, they would find pay phones and ring Bureau outposts up ahead in hopes of mustering a relief team. But no luck—the suspect kept shifting course, so there was no way to know where they were going; and when they could guess, it happened the smaller satellite offices they called were too frantic with breaking cases to join a wild-goose chase with a less-than-top-tier suspect. Even in Boston, every available agent was committed, owing to a major drug bust and an organized crime sting that was just cracking open. The chase continued for fifteen hours, all the way up the eastern seaboard to Maine. Thanks to their frantic phone calls, the entire Bureau east of the Rockies knew of the agents' predicament. But nobody thought they were crazy—instead it gave everyone a big, sympathetic laugh! They understood perfectly well how agents could get caught on that hook.

Surveillance gets in your bones. If you have any gift for it at all, it quickly becomes automatic, as I was surprised to learn. One Friday, I had gone down to Kankakee, a little town an hour or so south of Chicago, to pick up Seth, who had been staying with his father. I was driving a car my ex had given me after his mother's death, her twenty-two-

year-old, bright sky-blue Chrysler Newport. It was so ancient that I had
to have seat belts installed, but it rode like a dream and could accelerate
in seconds to 120 miles an hour. Seth and I dubbed it the Whisperjet. I
loved that car, gas hog that it was—I even put WSPRJT on its license
plates—but did my best to keep it hidden from my colleagues. If they
ever saw me in such a huge blue whale of a car, I knew that I'd be
teased without mercy. My own brother was too embarrassed to ride
in it.

Seth was fast asleep in the backseat, and the traffic was heavy when I
approached the outskirts of Chicago. As I pulled up to an intersection
near my house, stopping on the yellow light, I idly looked over at the
cars that were gunning their motors to pass in front of me. To my
amazement, at the wheel of one of them, I saw Gina,* a woman connected to a bombing, whom I'd been surveilling for the past week. What
could she be doing way out here in the suburbs? This could be our big
break!

Without thinking, I whipped to the right and merged in, a car behind
her. Grabbing my "Handy-Talky," or two-way radio, off the seat, I
punched up our channel and could hear the guys talking. They had
gotten stuck and were now behind us, trying to catch up. It takes four
or five agents for a moving surveillance—a couple to travel on parallel
streets, one in front of the quarry and one or two behind—and I could
hear the team member closest to the suspect, who had the eye, calling
out the litany to the other cars:

"Subject heading northeast on South Canalport Avenue. Crossing
South Ruble, right blinker on—hold it! No turn!

"Crossing Des Plaines, right blinker on.

"Turning—heading south on South Jefferson.

"Redboard at West Twentieth [meaning, stopped at the light]. That's
West Twentieth Place, not Street, left blinker on.

"Left turn, heading east on West Twentieth—shoot, we're redboard—"

"Twelve-five," I announced—we used signal numbers instead of
names on the radio—"I've got her." I was stating my location, when
suddenly I heard scuffling from the backseat. Then a small, sleepy voice
asked, "Where are we going, Mommy?"

Seth! He had been sleeping for so long that with my adrenaline rush at spotting Gina, it had utterly slipped my mind that he was there. And he had heard my transmission because his next question was: "Are you trying to catch somebody?"

Not wanting to scare him, I explained calmly that I had caught sight of a lady I had been following, and I had just wondered—aloud, unfortunately—where she was going. But he was too excited to be put off and bombarded me with questions: "A bad lady? What did she do? She's a terrorist? What's a terrorist? She bombs things? Does she have a bomb with her now? How do you know she doesn't? Are you sure? Where is she? Can I see? Mommy? Let's get her!"

We were stopped at a red light about fifteen feet behind her, so I quickly pointed to the back of her head. "That's her. Now you have to lie down flat on the backseat, and don't get up till I tell you."

The light had changed, and the traffic was sweeping me ahead. It would be a while before I could turn off. In the next few minutes, I hoped, the guys would catch up, so she wouldn't get away and I could take Seth home. Then I remembered that when they did, they would catch me driving the Whisperjet.

Sure enough, moments later, my signal number squawked over the Handy-Talky. One of the guys had spotted me despite my unfamiliar car—he recognized my hat. Evidently they had also determined that the suspect was headed someplace innocent enough that only a single car would remain on surveillance once she was inside. The others were going to wait at a nearby Dunkin' Donuts. "Be there," I was told.

Rather than explain over the radio how I'd wound up, though not officially on duty, tracking the suspect whom I'd been surveilling all week—and worse yet, with my son in the car—I decided to drop by the Dunkin' Donuts for a brief hello. Simply to have disappeared into the night would have raised more questions. I couldn't drop off Seth, who was barely six, and leave him home alone, so in the parking lot, I bribed him with a doughnut to stay down. "It'll only be for a little while longer," I told him. "I'm just going to talk to the guys for a few minutes."

They pulled in, already laughing. "Damn, DeLong, what are you doing in that horrible car? What the hell is it? What have you got under that hood? A V-eight? Who's WSPRJT? Your boyfriend? He must be some fat cat to drive a car like that."

Too embarrassed to confess that I had named the car the Whisperjet, I explained that it had belonged to my late former mother-in-law and tried to shift the subject to Gina. "God damn, you are so dedicated coming out here on a Friday night," one guy said. "Didn't you think we could handle Gina? And why didn't you get your Bureau car?"

"Because, uh, well—" I began. And Johnny Eshoo, one of the cops on the case, who had two little boys himself, looked past me and said, "Because there's a little blondie in the backseat. Isn't there?"

I turned around, and there was Seth, overjoyed, waving at the guys. He loved coming to the office with me and playing with them. Meeting them in a parking lot at night, like we were all on some kind of mission together, was beyond thrilling. Now I was really in trouble, because Bureau policy strictly, rightly, forbids having children present during any investigative procedure. (The cable television show *Cover Me*, which features a married FBI couple who often enlist their children's help to spy on people and the like, bears no relation to reality.) At least one agent I know of was fired for bringing a child along on surveillance. What I had done was a less flagrant violation—zeroing in on a suspect and, almost by reflex, switching into the pursuit mode, though I was off duty—but it was still a serious breach of the rules. The guys just sort of winked empathetically, and I knew then that they wouldn't betray me. When we worked together, my life was in their hands, so I could certainly trust them to keep my confidence.

At no time during the pursuit was Seth exposed to any danger. I was never even physically close enough to Gina to put him in harm's way. My ex-husband, however, would have viewed the risks quite differently. He still wasn't entirely comfortable with the notion that his teenage bride and mother of his child had traded her stethoscope for a Smith & Wesson. So on the way home, I was begging: "Seth, you know how you're never, ever supposed to listen to an adult who tells you to keep something secret?"—referring to advice I had given him myself about child molesters—"Well, this is the one and only exception you'll ever have in your life. What we just did tonight is our big secret, one that you won't tell Daddy and you won't tell your friends, all right? This is just for you and me. This is our FBI secret. Just this once—and never again, with anyone—you can be a good little agent by keeping this our secret. Okay?"

"Yeah," he said. "I can keep a secret." And he did. He never told a soul. But now and then, he would bring up the incident when we were alone, still delighting in the memory. "Remember that time we chased a terrorist with the guys—"

"Shhhhh!" I'd say.

During my first year in the FBI, I worked enough surveillance stints to feel like a de facto member of the terrorism squad. I loved the work it did, which had an anything-can-happen rigor, yet without the erratic schedules and spur-of-the-moment travel of the "reactive" squads, such as the fugitive squad, which would defeat anyone trying to raise a child alone. Organized crime appealed to me too, but the only female roles in mob operations were cameos—Mafia men were still too Old World to let women get anywhere near the action. I felt close to several members of the terrorism squad, whom I respected and viewed as my big brothers in the division. So when it came time to choose my permanent assignment, I applied to terrorism, hoping that the contributions I'd made as a rookie would foster my acceptance.

The only catch was that the Chicago Joint Terrorism Task Force, a coalition of FBI and Secret Service agents and specialist cops from the Chicago Police Department's intelligence wing, had never employed a woman.

Part of the reason, to be sure, was our meager number. With only fifteen women in the entire Chicago Bureau—many of whom, because they had families to raise or had special skills, such as languages, tended to gravitate toward the white-collar-crime and foreign counterintelligence squads—there were precious few of us to go around. But terrorism's two-fisted masculine self-image was undeniably a factor, as was the personal view of the task force chief, whom I soon nicknamed the Grinch, a male chauvinist of the patronizing stripe. Devoutly religious and the father of many children, he was particularly unsettled by me, an Irish Catholic girl who was divorced—which was bad enough—and was also the mother of a child. By his lights, I should have been home rocking the cradle or, if I had to work, should have remained in my suitable, honorable, female job as a registered nurse.

But the Grinch had been told that he had to hire a woman, and my friends on the squad went to bat for me. They cited my assists on surveillance and my single-handed arrest of the Croatian terrorist, kindly omitting my errors. An arrest was a shining accomplishment for a fledgling male agent, but for a female it was seen as a fluke. "Yeah, but can you rely on her all twenty-eight days [of the month]?" the saying went—as if at any moment hormones could drive the woman to distraction, rendering her hysterical or flighty or trigger happy, and jeopardize their lives.

One of my strongest advocates was Rick Hahn, a slender man with thick, eye-magnifying glasses, who by appearance seemed the antithesis of the tough-guy terrorist tracker but who was in fact one of the most formidable, canniest case agents in the division. It was a pattern I would see again and again, with John Slone, Rick Hahn, and others—the more accomplished and effective the agent, the more generous he would be at "bootstrapping" rookies and the less likely he would be to sandbag others, especially such easy targets as women. Happily for me, Rick, Al Lennon, and a few others would prevail. To my delight, I was admitted to the Chicago Joint Terrorism Task Force as its first female agent.

But I was determined not to dwell on my "first" or "only" status, and if the Grinch was lukewarm, I didn't care. I vowed to win him over with easygoing humor, loyalty, enthusiastic energy, and, if that's what I had to do, by working twice as hard as anyone else.

5

OVER THE COUNTER

Whatever he may have thought about hiring me for his squad, the Grinch threw me some leads in the beginning. One of them sounded like pay dirt—a tip on a possible terrorist trying to buy arms through a classified ad in *Soldier of Fortune* magazine. Founded around the end of the Vietnam War, *Soldier of Fortune* is an adventure magazine offering firsthand accounts of combat around the world: "Escape from Angola," "American Mercenary in Lebanon," "Seychelles Mercenary Fiasco"—just to pick a few titles from the early 1980s—as well as features on tradecraft and weapons: "Anatomy of a Combat Knife," "Marine Desert War Exercises," "Testing the UZI." Many of its ads featured armaments, some of exotic provenance and otherwise hard to obtain in this country. Something about a response to one of the ads made the seller believe that he was not dealing with the typical hobbyist or military buff and alarmed him enough to call the FBI.

Every line we checked on the respondent hit a dead end—he had no driver's license, telephone, utilities accounts, or credit cards in his name. Clearly he was using an alias, so the Grinch told me to reel him in. I was thrilled to have a case to work up all by myself and to be backed by an illustrious team of pros: Rick Hahn, John Sun,* who would go on to join the Hostage Rescue Team, and Mark Rosser,* a former Secret Service agent who had what I jokingly called "double-D" biceps, which

were probably as big around as my hat. With support like that, I felt
ready to take on an entire army of terrorists.

It is said that if you stand long enough on the corner of Randolph
and State streets in Chicago, under the magnificent old clock, everyone
in the world will pass you by. That's where I arranged a meeting with
our suspect, whom I nicknamed Rambo, after Sylvester Stallone's fic-
tional Green Beret. "Be there at noon," I told him. "Stand under the
clock, and wait for me to approach you. I'm going to drive by in a blue
four-door LTD."

That alone could have told him that I was a federal agent. Our
"Hoover blue" cars were so identifiable that they might as well have
had the Bureau seal embossed on the sides. That, and the fact that I was
going to be driving up State Street, which was closed to all vehicles
except for buses and police cars. But he went along with the plan, apparently seeing the official cover as just part of the scheme. It wouldn't
be the first time one of our quarries chose to overlook the obvious.

Once we connected, I was to tell Rambo to get in the backseat. Then
the guys, who would have been milling in the crowd under the clock-
tower, would slip into the car and hem him in on all sides. The capture
would be effected in minutes. "How will I recognize you?" I asked.

He told me, "I'm five-ten. I'm blond and have a brush cut. I'll be
wearing army fatigues."

"Same here," I said.

At 11:30 we were in position. I made a pass or two by the clocktower
just to get the feel of it, keeping an eye out for someone of Rambo's
description. No one yet. Precisely at noon, I circled by again but there
was still no tall blond man to be seen. Then, on my next sweep, I spotted
a guy. I prayed that he was just some weekend warrior who happened
to be downtown shopping at Carson's right at the time I was supposed
to be meeting Rambo. He looked to be in his mid-forties. He was about
my height, five-five, and he must have weighed 300 pounds. I believe
in coincidence—but not that much.

"Doggone it!" I radioed the guys. "It looks like Rambo couldn't
make it. What we have here is Fat Albert in fatigues."

That didn't scupper our plan, we decided. The man had made noises
about illegal arms purchases, and it was possible that he had some terrorist

connections; appearances do lie. Maybe he was some kind of front man for Rambo. But judging by the way he lunged for the car door when I slowed down, I didn't think so.

"Get in," I told him. "In the back. Hurry!"

Just as we had plotted, the guys melted out of the crowd and in seconds were beside him in the car, frisking him. As soon as the doors closed, I pulled out. "What's going on, where are we going?" he protested.

At that, we all whipped out our credentials. Instead of breaking a sweat or trying to resist, the guy started giggling. "Really?" he said. "You're really the FBI? That is so cool!"

He was nothing but a wannabe, trying to play out some kind of James Bond fantasy. He wasn't even worth rousting. Rick, Mark, John, and I rolled our eyes in exasperation, silently communicating: *Let's teach him a lesson.*

So, as I drove around in circles, they took his fingerprints, warning him sternly never again to try dabbling in the illegal weapons trade. "You're lucky it was your own government who caught you," they told him, "not some crazy group. You might have gotten killed. And now that we know who you are, we're going to be watching you, just to make sure you weren't jerking us around today. We know where you live, and now you know that the FBI is everywhere. Don't screw up again . . ."

For all the time and man/womanpower he wasted, I was sorry that we gave the guy the story of a lifetime, which I am sure that he is telling in much-embellished form to this day: "And when I was hooking up with my arms connection, I was nabbed by the Feds, a bunch of beautiful gals, kind of like Charlie's Angels, who I sweet-talked into letting me go . . ."

We dropped Rambo off right where we'd found him, under the clock-tower. Then we all burst out laughing.

In 1981 the terrorism squad's biggest priority was the pursuit of the FALN, a Puerto Rican nationalist group that was waging the most successful terrorist campaign in American history. They first came to light in 1974 after a Puerto Rican solidarity rally at New York's Madison Square Garden; four bombs were planted that night, and the FALN claimed credit. In December of that year, the false report of a dead body drew the cops to a New York apartment booby-trapped with a bomb. Officer Angel Poggi, who, ironically, was Puerto Rican, would be blinded in one eye. Over the next eight years, the group would prove responsible for at least 120 bombings and incendiary attacks. Their deadliest salvo was the 1975 bombing of New York's Fraunces Tavern, a 1760s landmark building, where George Washington bade farewell to Congress, which had remained a popular Wall Street eatery. The weekday lunch-hour explosion wound up killing four people and injuring sixty-eight.

No arrests were made, but several suspects were identified, including William Morales, thought to have crafted the explosives. One day in 1978, in a safe house in Queens, New York, Morales misjudged the pressure when trying to screw the cap on a pipe bomb and blew off both his hands and the lower half of his face. Certain that he was mortally wounded, he was determined not to die alone. He made his way to the windows of the apartment, streaming blood, and elbowed them shut, then crawled to the kitchen to turn on the gas. When the police arrived, summoned by the blast, he theorized that they would break down the door, throwing off sparks that would detonate the fumes and obliterate themselves, his body, and the apartment, full of incriminating evidence, in one huge blaze of glory.

Again he had misjudged. When the police burst into the apartment, all that happened was that they found William and carted him off to jail. When he had recovered sufficiently, he was transported to Bellevue Hospital to be fitted for prosthetic hands and somehow managed to escape. He would remain underground for three years.

Fast forward to Evanston, Illinois, the Chicago suburb that is home to Northwestern University: One day in the spring of 1980, when a little old lady looked out her window, she saw several young Hispanic men and women, dressed like joggers, going in and out of a van parked on the street. Some of them were smoking, which struck the old lady as incongruous for people in sweat suits, and fearing that they were burglars, she called the police. In fact, they were foot soldiers of the FALN, which had now set up shop in Chicago, and the van—which was loaded with guns—figured in their plot to rob an armored car to fund the cause. The bust failed to capture their ringleader, Oscar Lopez, but six months later, he was apprehended while trying to steal a car. As a result of that single phone call to report suspicious activity on the street, eleven terrorists wound up in prison. Talk about a hunch that paid off!

The benefits of the old lady's suspicions didn't end there. While the group awaited sentencing, one member (possibly because he was facing decades in jail) grew ideologically disenchanted and became an FBI informant. Through him we learned that when a member of the aboveground, political arm of the FALN, the Movimiento Liberación Nacional (MLN), wanted to undertake more hands-on, confrontational activity, he would phase out his visible participation in the group. We knew of three recent dropouts from the MLN and now put them under intensive surveillance. Rick Hahn took charge of the Chicago leg of the operation, which would parallel the investigations in New York; San Juan, Puerto Rico; and Washington, D.C.

Rick assigned me to follow one of the MLN dropouts, Edwin Cortes, code-named "the Rabbit." By all appearances, the Rabbit was an ordinary, respectable, middle-class man with a job, a wife, and two young children. But as Mark Rosser put it, "I don't know what he's up to, but whatever it is, he sure doesn't want to be followed." He was clearly well trained, given the measures he took to "dryclean" himself (shake off surveillance), a master of disguise and a genius at navigating the Chicago subway system. That made him hard to tail—he would slip from one train to another and vanish in the crowds. Eventually we determined that every Tuesday night he would take a circuitous route to some meeting place or safe house, which we could never find. He put us through our paces for a whole year.

I was part of a first-class team that included such old pals as fellow agent Mark Rosser and Chicago police officers Johnny Eshoo, Curt Blanc, and Marty Barrett. Local police play a major role in most federal crime investigations, not only because they lend needed manpower but also because they have more intimate daily involvement with the community, so their ears are closer to the street. Since in those days surveillance techniques weren't taught at Quantico, I learned a lot of what I know from the cops—tricks like watching your subject's movements in window reflections rather than staring directly, which might let the subject sense your presence and also give him or her a chance to get a good look at you. Now and then, however, I managed to ad-lib a useful stratagem of my own.

One Tuesday Rick Hahn spotted the Rabbit in the downtown crowds, recognizing him despite his reversible jacket, snap-brim cap, and sunglasses. Fearing that he might be identified in turn, he set me and a colleague named Jim on the Rabbit's tail. We followed the Rabbit into a subway car, which emptied out, leaving the three of us virtually alone. With nowhere to hide, we had to come up with a way to prevent our quarry from suspecting that he was under surveillance. So I started in on Jim: "I told you to slow down. You know I can't walk that fast. What if I missed the train? You wouldn't even know. You'd be running up ahead and I'd be standing there . . ."

Jim was jolted at first but quickly stepped into the role of the brow-beaten husband. He assumed such an angry face and projected such a stolid, impassive air of sulking that I almost felt like a genuinely annoyed, exasperated wife. "Are you even listening to me?" I went on. "Damn it, pay attention when I talk to you . . ."

"Who can stand listening to your bitching?" was all he would say. "Shut up!"

The Rabbit, who had been peering at us quizzically at first, apparently couldn't stand it either and turned away. No one wants to act like he's eavesdropping on an argument. Jim and I moved into Phase 2 of the fight, the silent treatment, staring out the window and occasionally sneaking glances at the Rabbit. That night we were able to stick with him longer than ever before, finally losing him at the transfer point for the train to the North Side.

Now we at least had a hint of where he was headed. We set up what is called a "picket surveillance," with pairs of agents posted at selected North Side subway stops. Johnny Eshoo and I were waiting at the Morse stop when our strategy paid off and I spied the Rabbit, descending the station stairs. Once before, he had gotten a close look at me, on the train with Jim, so when he suddenly spun around and stared right at me—or so it seemed—I had to think fast. I grabbed Johnny, and throwing my arms around him, pulled him into a make-believe deep, fervent kiss. Over his shoulder I kept one squinting eye trained on the Rabbit, watching him through my eyelashes, until he lost interest in us and moved on. He disappeared down Lunt Street.

"I didn't know you were so hot for me, Candice," Johnny said when we came up for air.

"I'm not. I don't even like you," I told him. "I kissed you because it was my duty."

He feigned hurt, knowing, of course, that I was joking.

It was on nearby Buena Street, a short time later, that we would finally discover the FALN bomb factory and blow the case wide open.

Before that happened, however, I got pulled off the case and loaned out to the north suburban satellite office, which had a frightening string of mysterious deaths on its hands. The first victim was twelve-year-old Mary Kellerman, who woke up with a sore throat and was dead within hours. That same day, Adam Janus, a twenty-seven-year-old postal worker, came home sick from work and soon died, apparently of a massive heart attack. When his family gathered at his home for comfort, Adam's younger brother, Stanley, and his new bride, Theresa, just nineteen years old, were stricken with a sudden ailment that claimed their lives. Worried that the family had been killed by some bizarre, extraordinarily virulent disease, health authorities quarantined the paramedics who had tended them. But in a few days—and after three more deaths—a factor common to all seven victims was discovered: They had taken Tylenol, which somehow had been laced with cyanide, a lethal poison.

The last time Chicago had seen a mass murder of such proportions was in 1966, when Richard Speck broke into a town house on the South Side and, in a blitz of terror, raped, stabbed, and strangled eight student nurses. A ninth roommate, who was tied up but managed to roll under a bed, survived. But that was a very different and all-too-familiar kind of murder—an act of obsessional rage, allowing the killer to revel in his power over his hapless victims. The Tylenol murderer, by contrast, never witnessed a death or even knew when and whom his weapon would strike. It was a bizarre, entirely new kind of crime in our culture, which seemed to be minting new categories, including the murder of celebrities by fanatic fans (John Lennon was shot in 1980), as the twentieth century waned.

There was no detectable link among the victims, beyond the fact that they'd taken Tylenol. The poisonings seemed to have occurred completely at random, so there was every chance that more contaminated bottles lurked on drugstore shelves or in the medicine cabinets of the unlucky. There was no way to know whether the killer had targeted Chicago specifically or whether he had unleashed a nationwide lethal threat. There was no reason to assume that he lived in the area, or even that a "he" was behind the fiendish scheme—while mass murders are committed almost exclusively by men, poison is most often a woman's weapon. The murderer could have been anyone, male or female, young or old, fit or disabled—living anywhere in America, or even the world.

The only immediately obvious suspects were the two firemen who had first figured out the Tylenol connection. Lieutenant Philip Cappitelli was listening to his police-band radio and got suspicious when he heard two emergency calls to the Janus home in one day. Then his mother-in-law came home shaken by the death of Mary Kellerman, her co-worker's daughter. Cappitelli called Richard Keyworth, a firefighter friend in Mary Kellerman's town, and when the two men compared the paramedics' reports, they discovered the link.

Though it seemed unlikely that either man was the killer, both were carefully scrutinized. It is not unknown for murderers to insinuate themselves into the investigations or discoveries of their murders, especially when their crimes seem to be going unnoticed. There was one serial killer, an ambulance driver and the son of a cop, who ingeniously parlayed both his father's job and his own into his modus operandi, to double his thrills. He would spot an attractive young woman, copy down the license number of her car, and then call the police department where his father worked, to say, "Hey, can you run this plate for me?" Since they'd known him his whole life, they were happy to do him the favor, probably assuming that he was trying to identify a woman he wanted to date.

Thus armed with her name and address, he would stalk the woman, waiting for the day when she was alone in a public place, such as a restaurant. Then he would call the manager, claiming to be trying to locate the owner of the white Ford sedan with such-and-such license plate, which he had hit accidentally in the parking lot. When the unsuspecting woman came out to check on the damage, he would clobber her over the head and drag her off in his car, to be raped and killed. After dumping her body in a visible spot along his ambulance route, he would then go into work and wait for the corpse to be discovered. Then he would drive out in the ambulance to collect it, no doubt commiserating with the cops working the crime scene about how dangerous the world was getting to be.

Risky as this scheme was, the killer managed to pull it off three or four times before he was caught. It is now forbidden by federal law for agents to run a name check for personal reasons—enforceable because anyone doing so must log in a name—and most states have established similar restrictions.

The firemen were soon cleared. At the express request of the U.S. attorney general, the FBI joined the Illinois state police on the case, now code-named TYMURS, though the only "nexus" or federal offense the killings could be linked to was the slightly flimsy charge of "product mislabeling," an FDA violation. A task force was set up, comprised of agents from both law enforcement bodies and jointly run. Kurt Cannon, my first FBI supervisor, and Ed Cisowski of the Illinois state police, with whom I would work some important cases in the future, were the co-managers; and Roy Lane of the FBI and Jimmy Flannigan of the state police were the co-case agents.

Just to give a sense of the scope of the investigation, here are but a few of the efforts mounted by the task force: extensive interviews of the victims' families, friends, and neighbors; examinations of the facilities and questioning of employees at the manufacturing plants, trucking companies, and warehouses that handled Tylenol, as well as area stores and medical offices; scrutiny of stock transactions to determine who would benefit from a hit on Johnson & Johnson—and more. Over a hundred federal, state, and local law enforcement agents would be deployed on the case and would follow up on more than five thousand leads.

I was assigned to the hot line fielding anonymous tips from the public—work that is considered too important to be done by civilians yet also recognized as time-consuming, onerous sifting for needles in a mile-high haystack of unproductive and crank calls. There's nothing like a hot line to draw the lonely, crazy, and vengeful out of the woodwork. It is a measure of how low the hot line lay on the investigative totem pole that most of the agents "manning" it were women, even though there still was only a couple of double handfuls of us in the entire Chicago Bureau.

One of the female agents loudly complained about the "gender discrimination" that kept us glued to the phones while the men hit the street every day, chasing down tips. She wasn't wrong, but her tactics were. I knew that bellyaching would never work. I was determined to pick up a lead decent enough to get me out of there—and fast.

The first lead I got that sounded solid came from behind bars. The worried caller reported that a convict whose crimes reflected "medical interests" had boasted, "If you thought what I did before was bad, wait till you see what I do next." Nonetheless, he was paroled. A short time later, the Tylenol murders began.

In fact, I remembered that particular convict's original offenses very well. I had been a young bride studying at the University of Illinois at Champaign-Urbana during the time they were going on. The perpetrator would pick out a coed, break into her apartment with a bandanna covering his face, tie her up, rob her, and then forcibly give her an enema. It was a substitute for sex, rape by proxy.

Yet whenever it made the headlines—"Enema Bandit Strikes Again"—everybody laughed, as if it were a harmless prank. He was even viewed as sort of a gentlemanly eccentric because when a would-be victim pleaded, "I have the flu. Please don't do this to me," he spared her, consoling himself with her roommate. It was five years before he was caught and, fortunately, sentenced by a judge who recognized his shenanigans for what they were: sexual assaults. But he resented every minute of his jail term, maintaining that he didn't deserve it because he had never actually raped anybody. By the time he was released he was, according to my caller, very angry and "very, very dangerous."

Hearing those words from someone in prison, where everyone is menacing, certainly got my attention. We pulled him in for questioning, but he turned out not to be our guy. I wasn't completely surprised—it seemed unlikely to me even then that a predator who got his kicks from the up-close-and-personal contact of administering enemas would derive much gratification from such a hands-off crime as long-distance poisoning of total strangers. Now, it would shock me if he had been the Tylenol murderer. With my training and years of experience in profiling—backed by the research of John Douglas, Robert Ressler, Roy Hazelwood, and others from the Bureau's Behavioral Science Unit—I know that sexually oriented "nuisance crimes" tend to escalate and are as often as not the prelude to more, not less extreme, and violent personal assaults.

We had to check out any lead that seemed at all viable, however. We had four big piles—hot leads, interesting leads, handle-later leads, and finally psychics. The first time I picked up a call from a psychic, I thought, *Hmm . . . you never know.* The police used psychics, with some success, and I didn't think that extrasensory perception could necessarily be ruled out. But when I told Tom Schumpp, the state police commander who was overseeing the hot line, he shrugged it off. "Start a stack," he said. I soon saw why. The "psychic" pile quickly grew to tower over all the rest. That's how many people believed that they had occult "seeing" powers.

Finally, mercifully, a tip came in that got me off the hot line and out into the field. Legitimate callers, as opposed to grudge-bearers and nuts, tend to identify themselves and give you their addresses and phone numbers without resistance. That's how this call started out, so I sat up and took notes. The female caller said that she had taken her husband to the emergency room of a local hospital, and while he was being treated, overheard a couple in the waiting room whispering about putting Tylenol in bottles. The conversation had made little sense to her until she read the news accounts of the murders and decided that she had better call the FBI.

She sounded elderly, earnest, and responsible. When I brought the details to Tom, he didn't jump up and down with delight. Ever the cynic, he simply said that he would have it checked out. "Let me check it out," I begged. "I've been on the phones for weeks now and I know my way around emergency rooms. I was a nurse."

"Well, Scoop," he said, "if you really think that this will crack the case, why don't you take that guy"—he gestured toward a state police agent named John Beck—"and see if you can run it down?"

The caller and her husband lived in Cicero, Illinois. She reiterated the details she had given me on the phone—another sign of veracity, when a story doesn't change—the dates and time they had been in the emergency room and the name she thought she heard when the attendant summoned the couple. I knew that any hospital would keep a log of emergency patients but also that it would closely guard the information, given the confidentiality laws. We would have to ferret it out somehow.

At the hospital, which was on the North Side of Chicago, I went straight to the head nurse. "You know, I used to be a head nurse at University," I told her. "Now I'm an agent." She oohed and aahed, and I started to believe that we had a chance. We gave her the name of our caller, and she bent the rule a little to confirm that she was indeed listed in the log.

"Who else was there at the same time?" I asked. "Was there a dark-haired couple in their thirties or forties? The name sounded something like 'Sotheby.' "

"You know I can't tell you that," she replied.

"I do know," I said, "and I understand how important confidentiality is. Part of your job is to protect people's privacy. But on the other hand people are dropping dead all over the place. Seven people in just five days. If this lead pans out, we could save a lot of lives . . ."

At this point, the Tylenol murders were the biggest news story in America, all over the newspapers and on TV. Everyone was terrified. Even my own son was scared, tormented by the death of the youngest victim: "But her mommy gave her the pills!"

How do you explain to a seven-year-old that it's still okay to trust his own mommy? I had been trying to soothe him, saying that it was the fault of "one bad guy, who we're about to catch." But I worried that he—along with a lot of other children—was starting to see the world as a fearsome, unsafe place.

The nurse was thinking, turning over the rightness and the wrongness of the situation in her mind.

"We could just wait here while you go for some coffee," I told her. She got my drift. "Excuse me," she said. "I'll be right back."

The logbook lay open on the desk and we quickly copied down the names of everyone who had been in the emergency room that day. Among them was a name that sounded like the one we were looking for, Somberly.* "My God," said John. It looked like our informant was on to something.

Now came the hard part, tracking everyone down for questioning. One of the first people we called on thought he remembered the couple: "Yeah, dark hair. They were in the waiting room, and when I sat down near them, they moved."

It now seemed certain that we had a tiger by the tail. With Tom's blessing, we started working the lead ten, twelve hours a day. We weren't turning up any Somberlys—none were listed in the Greater Chicago directories or Department of Motor Vehicles records—but everyone we talked to remembered seeing a couple or to recalled hearing the name. We had started running checks on alternate spellings and interviewing the people that turned up. Then too, we had to face the possibility that they had registered at the hospital under an alias.

We were eating, sleeping, and breathing the Tylenol murders. Every morning John would pick me up at six, and we'd get home at midnight. I was living on Diet Cokes and sandwiches eaten in the car. Once we stopped off at a gas station to use the bathroom and to fill up—we were burning through a tankful of gas every day—and parked next to a car full of people speaking Spanish. One of the men got out and popped the trunk, and almost automatically, I glanced inside. It was strewn with empty boxes and bottles of Tylenol. I got goosebumps! What were the chances that two investigators on the Tylenol case would just pull into a gas station and park right next to the murderer?

Moving up to stand in front of their car, I grimaced wildly, silently signaling John, who was just coming out of the station, to hurry over. "They have Tylenol in the trunk," I murmured. "Lots of it."

The man had just slammed the trunk shut—meaning that we'd have to get a search warrant if he didn't cooperate—so we braced him, pointing at the trunk and demanding that he open it. "No," he said in Spanish, "I won't. Who are you?"

Using the Spanish I'd picked up as a nurse, I finally made him understand what was going on. Amazingly, he knew nothing of the Tylenol murders, though the Spanish media was covering it as intensively as the English-speaking press.

But it turned out that he not only had a receipt for the Tylenol, which he had just purchased, he had a reasonable explanation. His mother had arthritis so she took a lot of Tylenol but couldn't twist open the small bottles (even in the pre-childproof era). So he would buy her a supply and dump the bottles into a plastic container, which he had on the front seat, in the same bag with the roast chicken and the casserole dish of rice and beans he was bringing her for dinner. I thought I would faint at the smell of the food—it had been so long since I had eaten a hot, home-cooked meal. The other people in the car confirmed his story—they were all on the way to visit their *abuela*.

"Good Lord," I told John, "we've been working this case too long. We're being haunted by Tylenol. I'm seeing Tylenol killers everywhere."

We finally did find the Somberlys. When we got to the house, a tiny black woman answered the door. Yes, she had gone to the emergency room because she had a "spell"—her blood pressure was high. She was now feeling much better, thank you. A neighbor couple had brought her in. The wife turned out to be home. She was middle-aged, as was her husband, she said, showing us his picture, which stood on the mantel beside a framed thank-you from her church. They too were African American.

These people didn't fit the crime, and neither had the Hispanic family we had questioned in the gas station. With very few exceptions, such as Colin Ferguson, who opened fire on the passengers of a New York suburban commuter train, mass murders are committed by white people. And they were also so open and forthcoming that it was hard to believe that they had anything to hide. They didn't fit the crime because they weren't the criminals. A blind person could see that.

It was time to talk to our informant again. We had been checking in with her on details others told us, but we clearly needed another face-to-face meeting—without her husband in the room. She had never mentioned that the Somberlys were black—a rather important omission.

We leaned on her hard, and little by little her story started to shift, but she remained utterly credible. She was so sweet and well spoken and absolutely sure of what she had observed that I think that she could have passed a polygraph. She had convinced herself that her story was true. Finally I had heard enough. I told her that she had one last chance to confess before I placed her under arrest for lying to an FBI agent in an official investigation: "Give me the truth. You never heard a couple talking about Tylenol in the ER, now, did you?"

"Well . . . ," she began. She allowed as how someone had said something about Tylenol, maybe saying not to take it, that aspirin would be safer—maybe she had misinterpreted what was being said . . . Maybe it was a doctor who had been talking about the Tylenol—or a nurse . . .

"Why did you tell us all that about the couple?" I demanded. "Why didn't you think the story through after all those times we called you?"

She didn't really know, the part about the couple had just come to her, and now that she was thinking about it again, she could see that she had gotten confused . . . It wasn't the couple . . . And when all those other people we were talking to had also heard the name, she just assumed that we had dug up something . . .

Then she said something that utterly shocked me: "Does this mean I don't get the reward?"

At this point the reward money being offered by McNeil, the division of Johnson & Johnson that made Tylenol, for information leading to the arrest of the killer had reached $100,000, a vast sum of money in the early 1980s. But could the woman possibly believe she had a chance of collecting it for a phony lead? I would grow to hate investigations where there was a large reward on offer, for the money seemed to exert a gravitational pull on the crazies, who would overwhelm us with bogus tips.

John and I got up and walked out of her house in disgust. We had invested two back-to-back, around-the-clock weeks running down the lead she had given us, and we were tired and angry. Fake tips aren't at all unusual, but they tend to blow up quickly. It's rare to get one that has enough true elements to hoodwink two investigators for that long. It never fails to amaze me that people actually believe they they'll be able to pull off such stunts. And why do they do it? For the attention? To bring drama and color into their pallid lives? Why would they want to tie up the resources of the very law enforcement agencies they depend on for their own protection?

I keep a mental file cabinet that I've labeled "If the Taxpayers Only Knew . . ." In it is a big folder for cases like this and Rambo and the other boondoggles I've gotten stuck with over the years. If the taxpayers only knew how much time and how many millions of their hard-earned dollars law enforcement agencies must waste each year on phony leads, they would demand that their imaginative fellow citizens be billed—or that we bring back the pillories!

While John and I were out chasing our bogus lead, a handwritten note came in to Johnson & Johnson: "For a million dollars I'll stop the killing."

Accompanying the demand were particulars on a bank account into which the money was to be deposited. We doubted that the killer was dumb enough to use his own account, but we assumed that he had the means to transfer the money out, seconds after the deposit was made. That meant that we were dealing with a fairly sophisticated murderer— that is, if the note was real. We began to wonder when a second letter, which FBI experts determined to be a handwriting match, showed up at the White House, threatening to bomb it with remote-controlled airplanes if Johnson & Johnson did not accede to the extortion demand.

We traced the bank account to an Illinois business called Lakeside Travel, the owner of which, Frederick Miller McCahey, was quickly eliminated as a suspect. It seemed likely, however, that he had an enemy who hoped to implicate him in the scheme. But who? It would take a gargantuan grudge to make someone want to frame you for killing seven people and extorting a million dollars. And who had access to his account numbers? Quite a few people, it turned out. It was his payroll account, so the employees he compensated every week would have the number right on their checks.

When investigators questioned the travel agency employees, one woman told them that the husband of a co-worker, LeAnn Richardson, was enraged at McCahey and had been trying to rally the rest of them against him. McCahey had suffered some financial setbacks, bounced a set of payroll checks, and filed for bankruptcy. He had made it up to some of the employees but still owed LeAnn $50, prompting her husband to file a complaint with the Department of Labor. He got no relief, and the couple had moved to New York.

To ferret them out, investigators in New York combed the rooming houses and hotels and also set up surveillances and circulated "wanted" posters at newsstands and public libraries. The reason for the newsstand and library surveillances was that the extortionist had directed Johnson & Johnson to approach him through ads in the *Chicago Tribune*. Indeed, it was at the New York Public Library that Richardson was discovered and arrested. His fingerprints matched the ones that had been picked up from the envelope of the extortion note.

At that point, the case took some bizarre twists and turns. Richardson's photograph had been released to the press, and we got two calls— one from a Kansas City postal inspector, who informed us that there was an arrest warrant out for him for mail/credit card fraud, and the other from a homicide detective. In those days, fingerprint records were not yet computerized, and it could take a while to get them matched to a specific name. But both our callers knew his name, and it wasn't Richardson—it was James W. Lewis.

From what the homicide detective told us, it seemed that Lewis had changed his name after he was arrested for murder in Kansas City. He had worked for an old man, whom he had been accused of killing and then hauling the body up to the attic, with a rope and pulley, to conceal it. The weather was cool, and the body had mummified by the time it was discovered, with its arms hacked off, presumably so it would fit through the attic's trapdoor. A length of rope matching the one used to hoist the body was found in Lewis's car. But because of a series of technical problems—including the fact that the state of the body prevented the coroner from determining the cause of death—Lewis was never charged but remained the chief suspect.

Meanwhile, armed with search warrants, the Bureau had put the couple's homes in New York and Illinois, their cars, their places of employment—every nook and cranny of their lives—under a microscope, in the hopes that we could tie Richardson to the murders, as well as the extortion. But we could find not a solitary shred of evidence proving that either of them had ever purchased Tylenol or had access to cyanide. That wasn't surprising. Back in 1982, before computerized bar codes were widely used, there would have been no records of who bought such a common, over-the-counter drug as Tylenol, and there were more than two hundred companies in Greater Chicago alone that sold cyanide. The FBI lab was able to trace it by its chemical composition to one manufacturer, only to find that the firm kept no records of which lots of chemicals its customers, who were scattered across the country, received. But even if there had been traces of cyanide clinging to the Richardsons' furniture or clothing, they could well have been obliterated by time and the move from Illinois. It was profoundly frustrating.

Lewis denied committing the Tylenol murders. At his arraignment, he would plead not guilty to the extortion charges but at trial admit writing the letter—not for the money, Michael Monico, his lawyer, claimed, but to expose the financial wrongdoings of Frederick McCahey, whom he considered the "enemy" for having bounced LeAnn's paycheck. The prosecution would attack this claim as "ridiculous," and Monico himself admitted that his client was "bizarre" when it was revealed that Lewis had committed "horrible acts" against his adoptive parents that had led his mother to sleep with a gun in her bed. Monico would close by telling the jury, "You may convict him of being stupid, foolish, and reckless, but you cannot convict him of this crime."

The jury didn't buy it, and Lewis would ultimately be convicted of extortion, plus six unrelated counts of mail/credit card fraud.

While awaiting sentencing on the extortion charges, Lewis evidently got restless in jail, for he contacted Roy Lane and offered to help him solve the Tylenol murders. Lane jumped at the chance and brought along Jeremy Margolis, the assistant U.S. attorney who had been "first chair" on the case and was a great favorite of FBI agents—flamboyant, outrageously funny, media savvy, highly effective, and the only federal prosecutor I have ever known to carry a gun. The two were coached ahead of time by Roy Hazelwood, who told them that in the course of "fantasizing," Lewis might well leak some valuable information.

At first Lewis claimed to know nothing about cyanide but would later blurt out that it was used for "jewelry cleaning" and was a "cash" business, mentioning the name of a chemical supply store in Kansas City where it could be bought. He then outlined in careful detail, even illustrating his points with sketches, how the killer might have "hypothetically" doctored the capsules. He "probably" would have drilled holes in a board that were slightly smaller in diameter than the capsules. He then would have separated the capsules, dumping out the medication, and inserted the halves into the holes. Pouring some cyanide onto the board, he would use a triangular "cake knife"—Lewis was specific on this point—to scrape the poison into the capsules, which he would then reassemble and put back in the bottle. A cake knife like the one he described had in fact been found in the search of his home.

"What might have motivated the killer?" Roy asked.

Echoing his own defense, Lewis posited that the cause was a dispute that was not getting resolved, a wish to get "multijurisdictions" of law enforcement to look at what the "true crime" was—the source of the conflict between the killer and the "other party."

Lewis's detailed speculation on the methodology of the Tylenol killer was taken into account by the judge, and he was sentenced to twenty years in prison. At the time, U.S. Attorney Dan Webb advised the court that in the opinion of the "government," Lewis was responsible not just for the extortion but for the murders as well. Nonetheless, he would serve only some fifteen years of his sentence and be paroled in 1998.

To date, no one has been charged with the Tylenol murders, but the effects of the killer's acts are still with us—the seals on every bottle, jar, and plastic container of ingestibles or cosmetics that we buy. Almost as important, the killer added a new entry to our lexicon of crime. The moment the news of the murders broke, the copycats came out—adding cyanide to Anacin, tainting Excedrin with mercuric chloride, and even more creatively, spiking eyedrops with acid, contaminating mouthwashes and nasal sprays, and planting pins in soda cans, just for starters.

Within a month of the Tylenol killings, there were a hundred verifiable malicious product tamperings nationwide, with the heaviest concentration around Chicago, and the number has continued to burgeon ever since. A crime that was virtually unknown twenty-five years ago is commonplace today. Every year, people die.

6

THE WONDERFUL
WORLD POLICE

Once the investigation began to focus on James Lewis, action on the TYMURS case slowed down, and I returned to the terrorism squad. I was eager to get back on the FALN case, but I had some trepidation about working for the Grinch. I realized that my loanout hadn't been just a matter of seniority, because new and less experienced members of the squad were easiest to spare, but because some kind of animus had developed between us. It was no secret that having been compelled to hire a woman, against his will, he had taken me only as the least of the possible evils and because I had the support of some key members of the squad. Apparently, that was still sticking in his craw.

At a staff meeting when I wasn't present, he referred to me as "lame." Though my performance reviews were uniformly glowing—he couldn't put in writing what bothered him about me, even if he consciously knew— he never stopped carping, though always to others, not to me. The stream of criticism was so constant that one of the case agents who was overseeing me directly felt obliged to come to my defense. "She puts in sixty, seventy hours a week. She works nights and weekends. Sometimes, even though it's our case, she's the only FBI agent out there on surveillance with the cops. The guys pack it in for the day, but she stays . . ."

But even that didn't satisfy him—try as I might, there seemed to be nothing I could do to overcome the Grinch's antipathy. I was working such a rigorous schedule because I still had to prove myself, not only to the Grinch but also to my fellow agents. I rarely had trouble with the veterans, who had come up in the Hoover era but seemed adaptable when it came to working with women, but did with men closer to my own age. One of them, forced to acknowledge that I had done a good job, actually said to my training agent: "Admit it, you're sticking her, aren't you?"—as if competence were a bug communicated by sexual contact and only by "catching it" from a man could a woman do well.

The younger guys' attitude didn't spring from misogyny, exactly. It was more as if recognizing that a mere woman could do their job dealt a devastating blow to their self-image. Once I realized that pride was often the problem, I tried to handle every contretemps with humor, and often it worked. Just to cite a commonplace example, there was one guy of whom I asked a procedural question, and then later asked for clarification. "Didn't I just tell you that?" he snapped. "I don't know what I said that was so hard to understand."

He would never have spoken that way to a man who was his equal. But I didn't say that. Instead, I made sort of a pouty, hangdog face with a pouched-out lip. "Would it be really hard for you to tell me just one more time?" I asked. "If it is, I'm so sorry . . ."

He had to laugh and we became fast friends. There were other agents who I just couldn't win over. A few refused to speak to me for two full years. One morning, as I headed out for breakfast with a bunch of squad-mates, I overheard a particular young fogey declare, "Well, if she's coming along, I'm not."

The colleagues I was with had the grace to look embarrassed and, urging me to ignore the snub, insisted on treating me to breakfast. So that wound up being his loss—or so I told myself.

But every woman in the division knew that she was under pressure and that if a coup, such as an arrest, would allow a man to coast for a while, a woman would soon be asked, "So, what have you done for us lately?" It was as if our achievements just didn't compute, but should we screw up or slack off, a gong would sound, sirens would blare, and it would be broadcast all over the office. Being the only woman on my squad, I was especially visible—and so often became grist for the office rumor mill.

"Hey, DeLong," I was asked one day, "did you really kick a gun out of some guy's hand?"

As if I were Bruce Lee! The rumor wasn't a compliment. It implied that I was a daredevil and a show-off, and it was utterly unfounded—I hadn't even been involved in an arrest for months. The chief way I exhibited bravado was through verbal self-defense. How being outspoken got translated into acting like a reckless stuntwoman, I can't imagine. But the rumor persisted, and I got the undeserved reputation for being something of a cowgirl on the job.

My consolation was the camaraderie I shared with the task force members, agents and cops, with whom I worked on the FALN case. We formed an exclusive club called the Wonderful World Police, which was headquartered at Mike's Bar, a popular hangout for cops. From the roof of Mike's, initiates were told, the Freedom Beacon glowed, but it was visible only to those who were "True of Heart, Pure of Mind, and Willing to Do the Right Thing." Rick Hahn was elected president of the club, and Assistant U.S. Attorney Jeremy Margolis was appointed our Supreme Commander. The club held informal meetings nearly every week, at which members could unwind, laugh, swap lies, and salute one another with the hoist of a beer or shot glass, declaiming our motto "Let the Beacon of Freedom Shine Brightly!"

One of my contributions to the merriment of the group was the story of a plan I cooked up to help Rick Hahn, our leader on the investigation, find out where a suspect lived. We knew the address but not which door in the four-flat (so-called because there were two apartments upstairs and two downstairs, which shared a front porch and opened on a center stairwell) was the right one. So I told Rick, "I know! Why don't I put on my old public health nurse's uniform?"—it was an unflatteringly dowdy light blue striped pants suit—"and then I'll just ring a bell in the building, claiming to be a visiting nurse, and ask?"

"Good idea," he said. "It's worth a try."

So I went home to change, and when I returned to the squad room, wearing my uniform, Rick pointed out, "There's no place for your gun."

If there was trouble, it would be too awkward to scratch for a gun in my black leather nurse's bag. So Rick told me that he would lend me his ankle holster, which I strapped on over the panty hose I was wearing under my uniform, as I got out of the car. The holster closed with Velcro. I was terrified that it would fall off as I walked the couple of blocks from the car to the four-flat, so I pulled it as tight as possible before inserting my little five-shot Smith & Wesson backup gun.

It felt snug at first, but the farther I got from the car, the more it seemed to be cutting off my circulation. I had pins and needles in my foot, which was getting sore. But I told myself, "This is how they're supposed to feel—tight. Men probably don't notice them as much, with their heavy socks." If I lost my gun, I would have worse problems than an aching foot. Besides, I couldn't figure out how I could fix it out there on the sidewalk, with nowhere to sit and without showing the world that I was packing a weapon.

But by the time I reached the house, I was in severe pain and limping. I was sure my foot was blue. So, propping my foot on the lowest step of the communal porch, I tore open the Velcro—relief!—and quickly slapped it back down. But as I climbed the stairs, the holster was smacking against my ankle—too loose. There was no way I could keep fiddling with it and not draw attention to myself, so I went ahead and rang the doorbells, hoping that no one would glance down and wonder about the bulge at my pant cuff. I got the information we needed and then shuffled back to the car.

"Whew," I said to Rick, tearing the thing off. Beneath it my panty hose were shredded, utterly ruined.

"These panty hose were brand new," I cried in protest. "They died in the fight for truth and justice!"

"Voucher it," Rick said. "A good agent can always get a new pair of stockings out of the U.S. government."

The guys all laughed at my story, especially the punch line about the voucher. "Man, it's tough being a woman in the FBI," one of the cops said.

He didn't know the half of it.

Meanwhile, the FALN case was heating up. Surveillance teams had staked out the North Side subway station where, a few months before,

Johnny and I had spotted the Rabbit exiting the train. They had tracked him to an apartment that we felt certain was a safe house but couldn't prove until we got a court order permitting us to install microphones, as well as a secret video camera. Never before in history had a law enforcement agency tried closed-circuit TV surveillance of suspects at home. The technique was controversial—there was case law supporting eavesdropping but none as yet on visual monitoring of suspects—but then so were the FALN's tactics, which had already exacted a heavy toll of injuries and deaths.

Rick Hahn had come up with the idea of planting the camera out of frustration, because audiotaping of the FALN had yielded so little. They were always careful to talk in code (referring to bombs as *plantanos* or plantains, the starchy Caribbean bananas, for example). With the information Rick supplied, Jeremy Margolis began the arduous process of drafting an affidavit—which would have to move through channels at the FBI and the Department of Justice before it ever found its way to the local judge who could approve the search warrant—explaining why the video was needed.

In the meantime, on New Year's Eve, bombs went off at four government targets in New York City: the federal courthouse in Brooklyn, the Manhattan U.S. attorney's office and the government offices at 26 Federal Place, and NYPD headquarters at One Police Plaza. At this last site, a patrolman had encountered the bomb when he kicked a Kentucky Fried Chicken box that he saw lying on the floor. It blew off his foot, and the FALN not only called the press to claim credit but were also overheard in Chicago, on wiretap, referring to the "fiesta" in New York. The video surveillance was then approved.

It took a few weeks for the hidden camera to bear fruit. Eavesdropping surveillance ran sixteen hours a day, but the video could be turned on only when the audio suggested suspicious activity. Finally the day came when Roger Gomez, the Illinois state police agent who was surveilling the safe house from a nearby perch, called Rick, stammering with excitement: The Rabbit and two confederates were sitting at their kitchen table cleaning guns. There was talk of sending in the Chicago SWAT team to arrest them, right then and there, for illegal possession of weapons, but Rick Hahn and others insisted that holding off and watching would allow the Bureau to cast a wider net for the terrorists. They procured a search warrant, waited until the terrorists left the safe house (trailing surveillance teams), then broke in.

But where were the guns? All the searchers found at first were the table and chairs in the kitchen and a floorlamp, with a high-power bulb and no shade, standing by the one living room wall that abutted another apartment. When the terrorists met there, they would scrutinize every inch of the wall under the harsh glare of the bulb, looking for tiny holes that might mark the presence of hidden microphones. (They were so careful that at one point, Alejandrina Torres, the stepmother of Carlos Torres, the head of the Chicago cell, would run a propane torch over every surface of a safe house that might bear fingerprints, to burn off any evidence.) But the FBI tech agents had been too meticulous to leave tracks.

Then one of the searchers noticed that the nails in the floorboards by the sink were new and shiny. They pulled up the floor, and underneath were thousands of rounds of ammunition, twenty-four pounds of unstable dynamite, enough to blow a ten-story building sky-high, forty blasting caps, and more raw material and paraphernalia for making bombs. Clearly a big operation was in the offing.

Again, the Bureau was faced with the decision of whether to seize the explosives and take the Rabbit and the others into custody or to maintain our vigil, in hopes that we could lop off more heads of the FALN hydra. But it was one thing to monitor a houseful of guns and quite another to leave live explosives lying around. The safe house was an apartment in a forty-one-unit building. What if there was an accident like the one that had befallen William Morales, with potentially a much deadlier outcome? So Rick Hahn hatched a daring and ingenious plan. We would leave the explosives in place but "neutralize" them, replacing them with phony lookalikes, and continue our surveillance.

It would take time to assemble everything needed to make the switch, so that night, Rick Hahn stood guard in the apartment. There was a surveillance team ringing the perimeter of the property, but there was no telling whether a terrorist might return and slip through the net— the Rabbit, especially, had proven exceedingly canny about eluding surveillance. So he spent the night hyperalert in a chair in the front hall, clutching his gun tightly, ready to spring into instant action. Tick-tock, tick-tock—he was practically counting the minutes until dawn. Finally Bureau explosives experts arrived and crept into the house to remove the "live" materiel and substitute the innocuous fakes. When Rick emerged from the building, he recoiled from the cool air, staggering and slurring his words as if he were drunk—with the windows shut in the apartment, he had grown besotted from a night of breathing nitroglycerin fumes.

Through the surveillance we learned that William Morales was hiding out in Mexico but was in close touch with the Chicago FALN. At the behest of the FBI, the Mexican Federales placed him under surveillance but botched the job, leading to a shoot-out that claimed lives on both sides. Morales survived and was jailed in Mexico, as the United States negotiated unsuccessfully for his extradition. He would be convicted in the Mexican courts on the charge of being an accessory to murder for the shoot-out and would serve only four years of a seven-year sentence before the government accepted Cuba's offer to repatriate him and take him off their hands.

Under the floorboards, we had also discovered a schematic drawing of what looked like a penitentiary, though we couldn't tell which one. Since convicted FALN operatives were being held all over the country, we sent the sketch to every federal prison. Authorities at Leavenworth, where Oscar Lopez was serving a lengthy sentence, recognized the layout as their own. For months, Lopez had been feigning illness, and we surmised that the group would try to free him while he was being taken to a Wichita, Kansas, hospital for tests. Sure enough, with an FBI team looking on, the Chicago FALN crew showed up fully disguised in the prison parking lot, where they waited in vain—alerted to the plan, prison officials removed Lopez from the prison population, as if he were going for tests, but instead transferred him to a holding pen.

Not only did our surveillance team capture them on tape, as evidence of a prison-break plot, but when we followed them back to Chicago, they led us straight to another safe house that we hadn't known existed. It was there that we found plans for one of the group's biggest operations yet—blowing up a National Guard Armory. The date was chosen to

underscore their Puerto Rican independence mission, the Fourth of
July. The armory was located in the middle of Chicago's West Side
barrio, so had they succeeded, most victims of the blast would have been
Hispanic. Although I often encounter such moral contradictions in my
work, I never cease to marvel at them.

The Fourth of July was only six days away, so it was time to move
in. We arrested the Rabbit and Alejandrina Torres at their places of
employment, where they would be least likely to be armed, and captured
two other confederates on the expressway. A fifth group member managed to escape. After the arrest, a photo of me at one of the safe houses,
with a streak of fingerprint soot painted on my nose by a fellow agent,
was pinned on the squad corkboard, with a label below it reading: GOOD
GUYS—4, BAD GUYS—0.

The FALN prosecution would be held up while the constitutionality
of our closed-circuit TV surveillance was argued, all the way up to the
U.S. Supreme Court. Finally the justices ruled in the Bureau's favor,
affirming that the privacy guaranteed by the Bill of Rights did not extend
to making bombs at home. In 1985 the Rabbit and the others finally
stood trial for their terrorist acts, before a jury that thrilled to the FBI's
account of neutralizing the ammo and the explosives. They were convicted of seditious conspiracy, among other charges, and sentenced to
thirty-seven years in prison. They would still be in jail had President
Clinton not granted them clemency in 1999.

For pioneering closed-circuit TV surveillance, the Chicago terrorism
squad became celebrated in the U.S. law enforcement community, with
Rick Hahn singled out for special commendation. In 1984 he received
the Attorney General's Award, the highest honor given in federal law
enforcement. That night he picked up the tab for all of us at Mike's Bar,
and one of the many toasts we made was an ironic nod to *1984,* the
George Orwell novel featuring "Big Brother," an all-seeing government
monitor. We had been accused of "Big Brother" tactics in the FALN
case, so it was only fitting that those efforts would be rewarded in 1984.
All told, Rick would wind up dedicating fourteen years of his life to the
FALN, and later, recognized as one of the Bureau's top bomb scene
investigators, he would be called in as the crime scene commander on
the World Trade Center and Oklahoma City explosions.

There would be less felicitous fallout from the FALN case for the Grinch. After the safe house had been wired up, agents were assigned to monitor the microphones, which would detect activity, on a rotating basis. After a few weeks with little action, the Grinch lost patience with the surveillance and arbitrarily reassigned an agent who was supposed to be listening—in effect undermining the groundbreaking work of his own squad on its hottest case. Finding the microphones unmonitored, Rick checked the duty roster, tracked the assigned person down, and demanded to know why. The Grinch had canceled his shift, the agent explained. "He said that there was nothing going on."

"Get back on it right now," Rick ordered.

As they walked back into the audio room, the scene that set the whole operation in motion—the Rabbit cleaning the guns at the kitchen table—was just starting to unfold. "Look what we would have missed!" said the case agent. Before long, the higher-ups replaced the Grinch with a new supervisor who had more enthusiasm for the case.

The Grinch would prove equally uncomfortable with the next woman who worked for him, Dora,* who was known to be a very competent, easygoing team player. Sympathetic as I felt toward her, I was also relieved that the problem wasn't mine alone. For some reason that I never learned, however, he continued to bear me ill will and—though no longer my supervisor, and never to my face—to complain about me right up until his retirement a few years later. By then I had enough allies that I could laugh it off.

I guess the old saying about lovers can apply to female employees, for certain men: You never forget your first.

With the FALN case winding down, I worried about where the Grinch would place me next. Maybe he'd try to loan me out again—or maybe I'd be put on coffeepot duty. None of us knew that he was about to be reassigned himself. So I put in for a transfer to a new squad, foreign counterintelligence (FCI), where I could make a fresh start with a new supervisor, Don Thompson, who was reputed to be more supportive of women.

At the time, two of the organized crime squads were embroiled in a

three-year undercover operation code-named GOTCHA,* which was
in its final stages. Then came the Thursday when we were all summoned
to a three o'clock meeting in the conference room, which was buzzing
with excitement. GOTCHA was going out with a bang the very next
night in a simultaneous citywide blitzkrieg raid on twelve mob-owned
strip joints thought to be mare's nests of money laundering, prostitution,
racketeering, and drug dealing, with suspected links to corrupt officials
in the Cook County Sheriff's Office. The sweep would knock out one
of the legs of the mob's financial infrastructure. It would be my first raid
and my first intimation of what my father had witnessed when Eliot
Ness and the G-men descended on the speakeasy during Prohibition—
my primal, indelible image of the FBI.

We were told to report at 4 P.M. that day dressed in our best professional business attire. If the press showed up while the raid was in progress, the Chicago SAC, Ed Hegarty, wanted us to look good on camera.
But even though I knew everyone would be dressed up, it was a heady
sight that greeted me when I reached the top of the internal staircase
leading to the tenth floor: two hundred strapping male agents milling
around, arrayed in dark, elegant Hoover blue pinstripe suits with snowy
white shirts, silken ties, and gleaming black shoes. It was like a Brooks
Brothers convention up in heaven or an army of gentlemen thronging
the ballroom at a debutantes' cotillion, waiting for the band to strike up.
I had never seen so many of my colleagues decked out in their finery,
all in one place, looking so masculine and suave—and I felt proud to be
among them.

I had chosen a conservative black and white suit that was more formal
than my usual officewear. It gave me a boost of confidence that I sorely
needed when I learned who I'd be teamed with for the raid: the SAC
himself, Ed Hegarty. He had wanted a female agent at his side when we
broke through the door—whether to disarm our targets with the unexpected sight of a suited-up woman in a brothel or to make some
statement about women's role in the "new FBI," I wasn't sure. But what
I did know was the agents within earshot were all laughing. Catching
the attention of the SAC was considered the kiss of death. When summoned to his office, you faced punishment for a serious transgression or
else commendation—but his praise would subject you to a new level of

scrutiny sure to spotlight any future slipups. We avoided him as assid-
uously as Catholic schoolkids trying to dodge the Mother Superior.

"Have fun tonight, DeLong," one of my colleagues whispered. "I
hope you enjoy your last night in the Bureau. Hey, can I have your
window seat?"

I failed to see the humor.

That night, our team of six rendezvoused at 7:30 in front of Michael's
Magic Touch at Ogden and First Avenue in the blue-collar suburb of
Lyons. I had passed its flashing neon sign countless times but never took
much notice of the dingy, two-story stucco building. The first floor was
an ordinary dive, with Formica tables to the left and a long bar to the
right, its top sticky, fronted by battered stools. The small stage was strewn
with aging black amps and electrical cables; it was way too early for the
show. The room stank of stale smoke and booze. Patrons scuttled away
as we presented our search warrant, and it struck me how much seedier
this joint seemed than the glamorous speakeasies I imagined Ness raid-
ing—but then, maybe it wasn't.

We surged up a flight of stairs, with Hegarty leading the charge, and
broke through the deadbolted door at the top: "FBI!" he bellowed. I
was almost vibrating with zeal as we pushed our way in with our guns
drawn—and with curiosity. I had never been in a whorehouse before.

Inside was a warren of rooms. We all pounded on the doors that lay
off the dim hall, our shouts rising in a chant: "Open up! FBI!" Mine
was opened by a scantily clad young woman with a twenty-year-old
face but the hardened expression and weary air of middle age. Clearly
she knew the drill, for she exasperatedly started dressing, without being
told. Behind her on a mattress on the floor, half covered by a sheet, lay
a man who was hyperventilating.

"Hold it," I said. "Both of you, keep your hands where I can see
them."

I addressed the girl: "What's your name?"

"It's Candy," she replied.

It would be, I thought. Then I asked the man, "Where's your ID?"

"Don't shoot," he gasped. "I'm a doctor, I'm not a criminal . . ."

I moved in closer. "I'm not a cop. I'm an FBI agent. No one's going
to arrest you, as long as you cooperate."

"My chest . . . ," he said. "I'm having a heart attack."

He didn't look especially pale, and I could see that he wasn't sweating. But he wasn't trying to pull a fast one either. He was gripped with fright.

"I'm a nurse," I told him, feeling for his pulse. "It looks to me like you're having an anxiety attack. Take a couple of deep breaths and try to calm yourself down."

He started gulping air, huffing and puffing as I flipped through his wallet, looking for ID. In it were pictures of two girls, as babies on his knee, then in school uniforms, and finally as glossy-haired teenagers, lounging beside what looked like their backyard swimming pool.

"Your kids?" I asked.

He nodded, not meeting my eyes. He was probably ashamed.

"Nice," I said. "Okay, you're free to go. Why don't you get dressed and get out of here?"

"I can't move," he protested, "I'm having a heart attack!"

I was sure he wasn't. "You're a doctor—think about it. What are your symptoms? It's more like a case of nerves."

He made no effort to rise. All I could think of was his daughters' humiliation when their father's taste for the low life came to light. If he was bent on betraying his wife by hiring prostitutes, he had the means to do so with the utmost discretion, with a high-class call girl in a luxury hotel. He was at Michael's Magic Touch—risking exposure and disease—because that's what he liked. It would be bad enough for his family if he was called upon to testify, but it would be devastating for them to catch him that night on the eleven o'clock news.

"Listen to me," I said. "If you're having chest pains now, you're going to drop dead when the press shows up. So get moving! Channel Five is on its way!"

That got him going. He dressed quickly, and I escorted him out to the parking lot. His car was a "chick magnet," a hot little foreign sports coupe that screamed "midlife crisis."

I then rejoined my colleagues, who were searching the place, and found my pal Ron Elder rummaging around the bar. Halfway shoved behind the cash register was a little wooden file box, filled with index cards, which I passed to him. Thumbing through them together, we found a man's name on each card, along with a credit card number—exactly what we were looking for!—and a column of girls' names: Babs, Bunny, Deirdre, Candy (several of these), each marked with a number. Were these the clients and the notations the number of times each had been with a particular girl? The johns would have had to use their real names if they were putting the charges on their credit cards.

I looked up the doctor, and sure enough, there was an index card for him. At the bottom, in the apparent "Comments" section, was jotted "Big dick." "Good God," I said. It hadn't even occurred to me to look, and the very idea embarrassed me. I must have been as red as a lobster when Ron looked over and asked, "What's the matter?"

He came to peer over my shoulder as I shuffled through the cards. We paused at one labeled Larry Green,* which had a lot of writing at the bottom. I recognized his name, for he was a prominent judge. Larry's requirements were spelled out in detail because they were rather, well, special. It seemed that he would bring along a jar of spiders, and as he lay naked on the mattress, stroking himself, his girl was expected to pull the legs off the spiders and let them flutter down onto his body.

Now I was hyperventilating, and Ron was laughing out loud. Having been a psychiatric nurse, I thought I was unshockable—but I had never heard of a predilection quite like this.

Thereafter, Larry's proclivity became a joke between us. Ron would sneak up behind me and scrabble on my back with his fingers, as if they were spider's legs, saying, "Ooooh, DeLong . . . It's Lar-rrrry?" as I shrieked.

As a result of the raid seventy-five people were convicted—racketeers of every breed, mob denizens, and corrupt officials from the Cook County Sheriff's Office. A brothel patron who testified in court would amuse the jury with the revelation that on one visit, he was charged $96 for a glass of water.

GOTCHA would be spun off into various TV movies, including one starring Brian Dennehy as Jack Reed, a Cook County Sheriff's detective. It would yield hundreds of news stories and remain in the headlines for years, astonishing even cynical Chicagoans with wild tales of dirty mayors and police chiefs, prosecutors frolicking at a brothel Christmas party, police officers paid in sexual favors for protecting a strip joint from raids, a county superintendent using school funds for sex club expenses, and more.

As for me, my night on the town with SAC Hegarty didn't affect me at all, to the disappointment of colleagues who had been hoping to keep teasing me about that unholy liaison. But there was one consequence of my brothel raid: No one in my personal or professional life was ever again allowed to call me "Candy."

7

UTOPIA

In 1983 I bought my first house. It was in LaGrange, Illinois, a small suburb southwest of Chicago, famous for its Victorian homes and the graceful Dutch elms arching in fifty-foot canopies over its streets. My house was one of the smaller ones—more of a cute bungalow than a turn-of-the-century mansion—and one of the shabbier ones, a handyman special begging for a facelift. But it was the best house I could cobble together the down payment to afford, and LaGrange seemed like a wonderful place for Seth to grow up. It was close enough to the city to let us enjoy its cultural amenities, yet still the quintessential, picture-book Midwestern small town. Norman Rockwell could have painted it.

Much as I loved the town's charm, it did make me feel self-conscious about not exactly being a Norman Rockwell mother. For one thing I was divorced, still something of a stigma in the early 1980s, and unlike most of the other women with school-age children, I had a full-time job. I worried that Seth would feel deprived and conspicuously different in a neighborhood where most fathers lived at home—which was tough enough—and where mothers, rather than babysitters, were always waiting to greet children after school. So I made it a frequent ritual to race out on my lunch hour and treat him at our favorite local restaurant, Kahoots. I also planned to participate in as many of his school activities as I could.

When we moved to LaGrange, Seth was just starting third grade. Not long into the first term, his homeroom teacher, Mrs. Caneer, called to see if I would be a "hot dog mother."

"A what?" I asked.

It seemed that the first Tuesday of every month, the class had a special hot dog lunch, with mothers doing the serving. "Sure," I said. "Sign me up."

I felt certain that with a little juggling, I could keep one day a month clear to establish a reassuring presence in Seth's school. I also thought sharing hot dog duty might help me befriend some of my new neighbors. But the first time that I showed up in my suit and high heels, the other mothers, huddled together talking in their sweat suits, hardly spared me a glance. When one peeled off from the herd to retrieve a Diet Coke from her bag, I pursued her. "Hi!" I said, in my brightest, friendliest voice. "Hi," she dutifully responded, then fled back to the safety of the huddle. I was like an ill wind blowing into the wives' inner sanctum from the threatening realm of divorce, single motherhood, and men's work.

Clearly, I was going to have to sell myself at home in LaGrange, just as I was doing at work with recalcitrant male agents. But right then I had only an hour before I was due back at the office. I got busy with the hot dogs.

Seth beamed when he saw me, which wiped out every trace of my hurt at being snubbed. But I must have been more stung than I thought because, as I reached across the table to pass out hot dogs, I wasn't paying much attention to the children's whispers. Then one little boy piped up, loudly, "Seth's mommy has a gun!"

Though it was my lunch hour, I was still on duty and so required to carry my weapon. In those days I wore it in a shoulder holster, hidden under my suit jacket. I hadn't realized how visible it was from below when I stretched out my arm.

Mrs. Caneer rushed over in alarm. "It's okay," I told her, holding out my empty hands. "I'm an FBI agent."

She must have flashed on Seth's records because she said, "Oh, right. That's so interesting! Why don't you tell the class all about your work?"

"She catches bad guys," Seth announced proudly, and all the little eight-year-olds oohed and aahed, barraging me with questions. "Did you ever shoot anyone?" has to be the question most frequently asked, by children and adults alike, of any law-enforcement agent. As I described my work, some little boys mimed shooting each other with their fingers, complete with sound effects: "Pow, pow, kapow." There's no getting around the attraction of little boys to guns—the best thing a parent can do is promote a healthy sense of fear and grave responsibility about weapons. The rest of the children giggled and shrieked excitedly.

That much attention proved too much for Seth, who buried his face in his arms on the desk, but I could tell that when his shyness subsided, he would be pleased. Even the other hot dog mothers, who stopped buzzing around the tables to listen, seemed to look at me with a new, if wary acceptance. Somehow it was better that I had an exotic job.

Thereafter the school invited me, with the Bureau's blessing, to give regular speeches on working in law enforcement, as well as on special topics such as "stranger danger." Seth's stock shot way up. He was no longer the new kid but a class celebrity, thanks to his mother's gun. Inevitable as it was, that dismayed me, but I was grateful that, however inadvertently, I had been able to ease his adjustment to our new home.

We had been living in LaGrange for only a few months when terror struck our idyllic little suburban community. A woman commuter was sexually assaulted as she got off the Burlington train from Chicago, becoming the seventh victim that year. Because rape is so often a crime of opportunity, pleasant suburban neighborhoods, with plenty of green, open spaces and peace and privacy, can unfortunately be an all-too-ideal setting—and these are the neighborhoods where many rapists feel most at home. According to the U.S. Department of Justice's Bureau of Statistics, 56 percent of those who commit "forcible rape" are white men, and when the category is broadened to encompass "sexual assault," that number rises to nearly eight in ten. As Roy Hazelwood maintains in *The Evil That Men Do*: "Every single sexual deviation is overwhelmingly dominated by white males . . . and most sexually related ritualistic crimes are committed by white males."

Because the assaults had occurred at different stops along the commuter line, it had taken authorities a while to compare notes across jurisdictions and determine that, most likely, these were not isolated incidents but the work of a single perpetrator. It was now all too apparent that a serial rapist was on the loose.

As soon as I heard about the case, I called Gene Stapleton, the Chicago division's profiling coordinator. He in turn called Roy Lane, Sr., the LaGrange chief of police, to offer the Bureau's assistance. At the time, profiling was a little-known tool for tracking offenders. Pioneered by psychiatrist James Brussel in the 1950s, it was introduced to the Bureau in the early 1970s by Howard Teten and Patrick Mullany, who invited policemen in their Quantico course to submit bizarre, unsolved crimes for study. By the time I attended the Academy in 1980, it was just coming to be codified as a formal discipline by Robert Ressler, John Douglas, Roy Hazelwood, and a few others. Many law enforcement professionals, even within the Bureau, considered it little better than hocus-pocus. But Roy Lane was more sophisticated than the average suburban police chief, being a graduate of the FBI's National Academy and the father of Roy Lane, Jr., the agent who had been the FBI's chief navigator in the Tylenol murder case. Lane jumped at the chance to apply the new technique to the effort to catch the predator now known as the Burlington rapist.

I got the blessing of Don Thompson, my boss on the foreign-counterintelligence squad, to work the case—maybe a serial rapist seemed as dangerous a menace to the community as a spy. So I went with Gene to a meeting of the task force set up by the police from all the municipalities where the rapist had attacked women. The victims ranged in age from thirteen to forty-five—evidently, he was not targeting any special type of woman—and their descriptions of the attacker varied just as widely. They placed his age at anywhere from twenty to thirty-five, and estimates of his height ran the gamut from five seven to six four.

Was more than one rapist at work?

Not necessarily. Disparate descriptions are more the rule than the exception, for under the high stress of an assault, few victims—or even witnesses—can zero in on the assailant's looks. Fortunately, the artists' sketches worked up from the victims' accounts bore enough commonalities to link them to a single perpetrator. We also had an unexpected factor working in our favor: During the time the rapist was at large, the Chicago Bears, who had been breaking the hearts of football fans for years, were having a miracle season under a hero coach whose distinctive, chiseled features were showing up daily under front-page headlines and on the nightly TV news. So even non-sports-conscious women were describing the assailant in terms that every cop could visualize: "He looks like a young Mike Ditka."

But how the assailant looked was just one variable in the equation; we had to start by figuring out where to look. Listening as each detective presented his case, it struck me how widely the depth of their information varied. "Let me go back and reinterview all the victims," I volunteered. "Maybe with a single questioner juggling all the stories, we can plug some holes."

Today that wouldn't be allowed. Profilers witness or guide interviews from backstage but don't do direct questioning in nonfederal cases, lest they compromise their consultant status and wind up on the witness stand. And it's less necessary—as crimefighting grows more systematic and sophisticated, strategic cooperation is more the norm and multi-jurisdictional investigations kick up fewer turf battles. But back then no Bureau directive forbade my stepping in, and to my surprise, I got little resistance from the detectives—possibly because I was the only woman present. People tend to assume that a woman will be more effective than a man at interviewing a female sexual assault victim, which, in fact, is not true. Some of the most cogent and insightful interviews, among the hundreds I have seen, have been done by men. It's as much a matter of personality as gender and, just as important, of training. My background as a psychiatric nurse was invaluable, and so were the techniques I was taught at Quantico.

In those days many cops didn't realize how deeply their questioning should probe into the verbal, physical, and sexual behavior of the offender—whether he was solicitous or abusive, what he said, how much force he used, the physical acts he demanded, where and when he ejaculated, if he did. Some were too embarrassed to ask for the details or too sensitive about upsetting the victim. You'd see police reports that were highly detailed as to the location, the circumstances, and so on, right up to the point of the attack, which would be summarized in a single line: "And then he raped her." Buried within that line were precisely the details most critical to the construction of a profile.

Profiling is part science, part art. The science part employs statistics the Bureau has compiled from thousands of violent crimes, as well as interviews with offenders themselves. This data tells us, for example, that when a toddler dies at home of blunt force trauma to the head, at least 90 percent of the time the cause is not a fall down the stairs or a shove by an older child but a blow from an angry adult. Obviously, exceptional cases occur, but that figure is hard to ignore; and it gives police a solid reason—as opposed to mere conventional wisdom—to concentrate their energy and investigative resources on the adults who were most likely present in the home at the time of the death.

Analysis of such a vast number of crimes has taught us that the conventional wisdom—such as the belief that fighting back is the best way to foil a rape—is often wrong. Even juries tend to buy into that particular false assumption, confusing submission with willing participation. Of the rape/sexual assault victims polled by the Department of Justice, 71 percent reported that they had taken "self-protective" action, defined as anything from appeasing to attacking their assailant; half of them believed their efforts had helped the situation, while 20 percent claimed that they had made matters worse. (Of course, we can never poll those who did not survive an assault.) There is no one "best" way.

Profilers analyze the "what, when, where, and how" of an attack, scrutinizing even the most minute details to see if they suggest a pattern or offer a useful clue as to the offender's personality. By comparing the attack to similar crimes committed in the same way, they can pull out the most common characteristics of those known offenders to create a personality and lifestyle sketch of the UNSUB or "unknown subject" of the investigation at hand. Profiles are most effective at targeting offenders who act out of psychopathological compulsion, rather than, say, the kid who holds up a liquor store with a Saturday-night special, panics, and shoots the clerk—the pool of potential thieves with access to illegal handguns is simply too vast. But the profile is not an attempt at psychiatric diagnosis, and the "whys" it addresses relate to preventing future crimes, such as: Why was a certain victim targeted? Why was another released unscathed? Why did the violence of the attacks escalate over time?

The "who" of the formula—tracking down and arresting the actual perpetrator—we leave to the police. A good profile will not only point the cops in the right direction but can also help predict where the offender is liable to surface (at a victim's funeral, for example, for certain types of killers), the kinds of public appeals that may flush him out (by encouraging him to communicate with the police or the press, for example), or the lines of questioning that may elicit a confession at the police station or revealing, self-incriminatory testimony at trial. That's the art part.

Even with Chief Roy Lane committed to trying this newfangled profiling strategy, we faced a certain amount of skepticism from the detectives. I was paired with one of the scoffers, Gary Konzak, who dismissed it out of hand as "crystal ball stuff." Luckily, we discovered the bonds of living a few blocks apart and having children at the same school. And even luckier, my reinterviewing scheme soon paid off, with a solid hit that resolved the height discrepancies. One of the victims was very tall. "Agent DeLong," she told me, "I am six one. When he grabbed me, I could feel his chin jamming into the top of my head. He had to be taller than me."

A sensation that vivid was very likely a reliable memory, and it established that our man was at least six four or six five, significantly taller than average. Gary now had to agree that we were on the right track.

Most of the victims portrayed the rapist as almost regretful—having committed the rape, he would apologize, berate himself for the abuse, and sometimes begin to cry. Before raping one woman, he laid his raincoat on the grass, so she wouldn't get wet. One of the most telling descriptions came from the second woman to be assailed, whom the rapist pinned in her car. While kissing and fondling her, he kept asking, "You like my kissing you, don't you? You like my stroking? Do you like the way I'm touching you?"

Calmly and gently, she replied that she didn't like it, but only because she didn't know him. That seemed to confuse him, she reported. After fifteen minutes of groping, he kissed her good-bye and let her go, saying that he was sparing her as a "Valentine's Day present."

Roy Hazelwood classifies rapists in six categories, depending on whether they are driven by the need for power, the need to act out their anger at women, or by other factors—only a slim percentage of rapes arise out of actual sexual desire. The Burlington rapist's apologies and efforts to cast his victims in the role of the willing lover eluding him in real life—cushioning one with his raincoat, expressing the hope that another enjoyed his caresses and giving her a "Valentine's Day present"—place him in the "power-reassurance" category. Through such "pseudo-unselfish" behavior, in Hazelwood's words, the rapist can assert his power over a woman but also feel that he is an adequate, sexually desirable man. It is also notable that the Burlington rapist displayed such chivalry during his early sexual assaults. As their experience and confidence builds, rapists tend to grow hell-bent on completing the act, no matter how their victims respond.

Still, research has shown that many rapists take emotional cues from their victims. Through her calm self-possession, Woman Number 2 managed to escape with just backseat pawing by the fledgling rapist. The other victims weren't so lucky, but at least they weren't otherwise injured if they didn't resist (beyond initial efforts to escape). Screaming and fighting may scare off a nervous assailant in a setting where he risks discovery, but it may also provoke him into unintended violence. One victim fought back hard, even trying to bite her attacker on the penis. If you bit a mad dog, what would it do? She was beaten and nearly strangled to death.

The most seriously injured victim was so angry that she could hardly talk to me. After choking out that she was never going to testify, she just clammed up, burning with fury. Of course I could sympathize with her pain and sense of violation, but finally I had to say, "Look, talk to me or not, we're going to catch this guy, but being mad does nothing to help us get him off the streets." Her barely contained, unarticulated wrath was getting even me agitated. I had to wonder whether she had been such a blast furnace of rage even before her assault and whether that fire, turned on her attacker, had not repelled him but instead whipped up the violence in him.

When the task force reconvened two weeks later, I was able to offer the detectives a lot of information they hadn't uncovered in their own interviews with the victims. To my relief, they welcomed it—it had been nerve-wracking to stick my neck out in a roomful of older men. We now presented my findings, along with the detectives' original battery of reports, to the Bureau's Behavioral Science Unit. With Gene's guidance, I helped work up the profile with Roy Hazelwood himself.

The subject was classified as a "power-reassurance rapist," probably in his mid- to late twenties, a loner with few friends who had never experienced a normal, consenting, intimate relationship with a woman. Probably a high school graduate at best, he would have served in the military but been dishonorably discharged and now hold an unskilled or semiskilled job, with little public contact, if he was employed at all. He would have a police record of some kind, probably for property crimes. He would most likely live within a mile of the LaGrange train station, where most of the attacks had occurred, either in a rented apartment or with his mother in her home, given his low income. The profile even suggested the kind of car he would drive, an old "beater," and the clothes he would wear, a dingy T-shirt and worn jeans.

Some detectives were gung-ho about the profile, but others shrugged it off, disdainful of the "fortune-tellers" at the FBI. Even today, armchair critics will complain that many profiles point to the same kind of assailant—the marginally employed loner with a poor military record and a petty-crime history, living at home with Mom. But it just so happens that such men do commit a significant number of sex-related assaults. Forty-two percent of those incarcerated for rape (99.6 percent of whom are male) report that they have never been married.

Our quarry, meanwhile, was picking up steam. His next victim was a petite young woman, about five feet tall, weighing no more than 100 pounds, who must have looked like an easy mark. But he had misjudged her—she luckily had some martial arts training. As he grabbed her from behind in a bear hug, she ducked out of his grasp, whirled around, and kicked him hard in the solar plexus. She then fled, leaving him gasping for breath.

A short time later, a middle-aged waitress closing up a small restaurant near the LaGrange train station heard a noise at the back door. When she went to investigate, a man startled her in the storeroom. Screaming, she turned to run, but he snatched at the back of her uniform, clubbing her to the ground with a telephone. "I'm going to kill you!" he snarled.

Then, tearing at her clothing, he raped her. She lay still, too frightened for her life to try to fight back. Finally he pulled himself off her and beat a retreat, leaving her dazed with terror and, later, too flooded with shame even to tell her family about the assault.

Fear, shame, and guilt, almost universal among rape victims, all too often conspire to keep perpetrators on the street. In the preface to *Practical Aspects of Rape Investigation*, which he co-authored with Ann Wolbert Burgess, Roy Hazelwood reports that "less than half of all rapes believed to occur are reported to law enforcement," and of those "only slightly more than half . . . [result] in the arrest of a suspect." (Factoring in sexual assaults, the Department of Justice ups the estimate of unreported sex crimes to 68 percent, more than two-thirds.) That means— astonishingly—that the 89,000-odd forcible rapes (excluding sexual assaults) recorded for 1999 by the FBI's Uniform Crime Reporting Program should properly be closer to 200,000, or approximately 1 rape for every 600 or so American women (1 in 270, by Department of Justice figures encompassing sexual assaults). And of those 89,000 rapes in 1999, only around 29,000 resulted in arrests, suggesting that only around 14 percent of the rapes actually committed every year—just a sliver off the top of the iceberg—may ever be prosecuted.

If 89,000 men were raped next year—never mind 200,000—can you imagine the public outrage? Rape would instantly become a capital crime!

Fortunately, the waitress, like the other eight women, found the strength and courage to come forward. We met, at her insistence, at a place where no one knew her, Marc's Big Boy on the corner of 55th Street and LaGrange Road. We chose a table up front, a few feet from the door, and I sat facing the kitchen, giving her the window view. How easily the case might have been solved had our positions been reversed that day!

As she told me her story, I could see that she was painfully unnerved by the rape—tense and edgy, drinking cup after cup of coffee, peering warily at every male who walked by. There was a visible bump on her head.

"He hit you," I said. I had read the initial police report, but I wanted to encourage her to talk.

"Yes," she replied. "I was terrified. He was so angry, and I thought he was going to kill me . . ."

It was the first time that the UNSUB had battered a victim who hadn't resisted—probably a reaction to the little kickboxer who got away, I thought. At six feet four inches he must have been shocked and humiliated that such a tiny woman could thwart him, and he wasn't about to take no for an answer again. It is a very different kind of rapist who derives pleasure from inflicting pain.

"Why did he pick me?" the waitress kept agonizing. "What did I do to provoke him?"

"Nothing," I assured her. "You did nothing wrong. You were just the unlucky woman he happened to come across. This wasn't your fault, so you can't blame yourself."

But she would, I knew, even then. Between my careers as a nurse and an agent, I would see hundreds of rape victims, and for virtually every one, among the harshest psychic burdens of the experience was that tormenting self-recrimination.

Despite her emotional upheaval, which was entirely understandable, I found the waitress to be an exceptionally reliable witness. Unlike some of the others, she was certain of her attacker's height, confirming that he was very tall; and because he had confronted her in a lighted room rather than seizing her from behind in the dark, she had been able to look him in the face. Moreover—considerations no cop or agent can ever overlook—she sounded levelheaded and steady, and if we managed to prosecute her attacker, her gray hair and maturity would make her eminently believable on the witness stand.

So Gary Konzak and I were elated when she called a short time later to report that she had spotted her assailant around town. She had even copied down his license plate number. Gary quickly tracked the man down, convinced that this was the break we were hoping for, and—sure enough—he matched the artists' sketches of the Burlington rapist.

But a few days later, when Gary called, I could hear the defeat in his voice. The police had verified that the man was out of town the night of the attack. The problem was bigger than a simple misidentification, for by a good defense attorney's lights, our star witness had just "cried wolf"—thereby impugning her credibility, perhaps irrevocably. When we caught the guy, it would be that much harder to prove her case.

Meanwhile, we had adopted a more proactive strategy. We knew that it was improbable that our rapist had sprung out of nowhere and, in a yearlong rampage, claimed only nine victims—less than one a month. Many people in law enforcement maintain, informally, that rapists tend to operate on a twenty-eight-day rhythm comparable to the menstrual cycle; and research has shown that serial rapists can be astonishingly prolific. The forty-one offenders in Hazelwood's study, chosen because each had raped at least ten times, were cumulatively responsible for 837 sexual assaults and more than 400 attempted rapes. So chances were great that our perpetrator had at least approached—whether or not he succeeded with the assaults—two or three times the number of women who had called the police. One or more of them might well have invaluable information—perhaps the key to the entire case. Someone may have gotten a glimpse of his car or, possibly, learned his name. Strange as it may seem, power-reassurance rapists quite often tell their victims at least a first name, and sometimes it's the real one.

Even an intense publicity blitz on the rapist had failed to draw anyone out. To flush out the victims who were too skittish to come forward, I suggested that we set up a hot line manned by counselors from a local mental health center. We held a press conference, well covered by the TV and radio stations, as well as the newspapers, to announce that we weren't looking for more victims—all we wanted was information on the attacker. Callers could remain anonymous. The first two days alone pulled in a hundred callers, most of whom we easily dismissed as the usual cranky neighbors, vengeful ex-wives, and other grudge-bearers. We got a few good leads but none solid enough to pan out.

Two weeks passed, and then our waitress popped up again with another sighting of the rapist. This time she was positive, she told Gary.

"I saw him. I looked straight at him. I know it's him. I will never forget that face."

Gary gently tried to put her off, explaining that if we kept bringing in men for questioning on her say-so, it would damage her reliability—and possibly her case—beyond repair.

"I understand," she insisted, "but you have to believe me. There is no doubt at all in my mind that he's the one. And I even know where he works."

She was so convincing that Gary had to ask, "Where?"

"At Marc's Big Boy on LaGrange Road. He's the cook."

I could tell that Gary still had his doubts, but I said, "Hey, what's the harm in looking? Besides, I love their omelets. Let's go there for breakfast together and check it out."

We went the next morning, and again I took a seat facing the kitchen. By then I had been staring at the artists' sketches for months, so the UNSUB's sharp-featured, masculine face, with his close-cropped hair and mustache, were acid-etched on my mind. We made breakfast chatter like a normal couple, but over my open menu, I kept my eyes fixed on the kitchen, some fifteen feet away. When a tall man bobbed up in the doorway for an instant, I had to steady myself on the table so I didn't jerk with surprise. He looked like a young Mike Ditka.

The server arrived to take our order, and when she moved out of earshot, I told Gary, "The waitress is right. It's got to be him."

He snickered. "Come on, DeLong," he said. "I'd like to believe it too, but nothing is that easy in police work. She was wrong before."

"Not this time," I told him.

"You liked her, so now you want her to be right. Don't lose your objectivity. That last guy looked like Mike Ditka too, don't forget."

I felt like he was patting me on the head so I whipped him a big fake smirk. Then I stood up. "Okay, I'll go take a better look."

"Candice—" he warned, but before he could stop me, I was gone. He was probably worried that I'd gape at the cook and tip him off to our suspicions or maybe even confront him, when we didn't have the evidence in place to pick him up, or otherwise totally bungle the investigation. He had no reason to think that I knew much about surveillance. But he couldn't intervene without creating a scene.

I poked my head in the kitchen. "Excuse me," I said. "Are you the cook?"

He didn't answer. Moving fully into the kitchen so I could study him, I pressed on. "My husband and I just ordered Denver omelets, but I'd like to change mine to cheese. I couldn't catch the waitress, so I thought I'd better tell you myself."

Everything about the cook—his height, his angular face, the way he looked me over with his piercing blue eyes, his surliness, his sarcastic reply—"Sure, lady"—matched the descriptions I'd collected from the victims.

Back at the table, Gary's panicky look relaxed into relief when I returned without incident. "You know—" he began, but I cut off him off, declaring: "Bingo. He's our guy."

I was so dead certain that Gary didn't even try to contradict me.

Once the police started digging, it turned out that the cook fit the profile on nearly every count. He was a white male, twenty-seven years old, who had dropped out of high school and enlisted in the military, from which he was discharged dishonorably for stealing. As a teenager he had been arrested a number of times for property crimes. Unemployed at the time of the early attacks, he was hired at Marc's Big Boy as a short-order cook—a semiskilled job requiring little public contact. Until he got the job he had been living with his mother but had just moved out into his own rented apartment, a mile away from the train station. He had recently sold his car, which was an eleven-year-old Datsun—an old "beater." When he was picked up for questioning, he was even dressed exactly as the profile had predicted, in a T-shirt and old jeans.

Roy Hazelwood turned a lot of skeptics into converts with that profile.

The concrete evidence tying the cook to the rapes now started falling into place. A discreet check of the restaurant's records showed that while he worked some sixty hours a week, the cook was off at the time the recent assaults took place. Several of the victims were able to pick his photo out of a grouping. A few were scared that they might later have to identify him in a live lineup at the police station, worried that he would somehow catch a glimpse of them and seek reprisal. Would they be running a big risk? No—people in lineups cannot see their observers through the glass; and if through some peculiar turn of events, a suspect had the chance to spot a victim, say, on the street in the vicinity of the precinct house, it is unlikely that he would recognize her. Commonly, rapists cannot even vaguely describe the women whose lives they have destroyed.

Finally the police felt confident that they had enough "probable cause" for an arrest warrant.

"Do you want to come along on the bust?" Gary asked.

Did I? "You bet," I said. I had been living and breathing the Burlington rapist case for months.

The police arrested the cook at his home, and he came along without a fight. As they led him out in handcuffs, I stood watching, hoping that he was feeling just some of the terror I had heard in his victims' voices. Before ducking the cook's head into the patrol car, Gary gestured in my direction. "See that woman?" he said to him. "She helped capture you."

The cook fixed me with such a snakelike glare that it froze the warm glow of satisfaction I was feeling at his capture. But I held his gaze until they hustled him away.

He was indeed "our guy." He was convicted and sentenced to two thirty-year terms in prison, to be served concurrently. With time off for good behavior, he'll be up for parole around 2010. It is unfortunate that the angry victim, the one who had nearly been strangled to death, refused to testify, for the violence of that assault could have considerably increased his sentence. Far be it from me to propose the best course of healing for any victim, but I had to wonder why she chose to keep all that rage bottled up inside her rather than use it to bring her assailant to the just punishment of the state. Could retribution have brought her closure and, perhaps, comfort?

The little downtime I had from the Burlington rapist investigation I spent fixing up my house in LaGrange—tending the neglected yard, peeling up the mangy carpeting and linoleum inside, stripping off the old, cheap paneling, and brightening the walls beneath with spanking fresh coats of paint. I chose a warm golden yellow for the kitchen, a rich cream for the living room, a lively orange for Seth's room, and for my own, a serene blue. For the bathroom, I even braved the rigors of pattern matching and wallpaper paste. To preserve the spirit of the era when the house was built, I hung lace curtains at the windows. I loved being a homeowner, and I was proud of the cozy little nest the bungalow was becoming.

Of course, all these home improvements cost money, and I was almost down to counting the change in my pockets on the last day or two before each paycheck arrived. Every spare penny I had was going into the house.

The fad toy in those days was the "superball," a high-density rubber ball that would bounce to tremendous heights if you so much as dropped it on the floor. Seth had some imitation version of it, a little Day-Glo orange ball that he couldn't resist dribbling around, trying to get it to hit the ceiling. "Not in the house!" I would say, sure that the bounding ball was going to knock things over, but I didn't really have the heart to nag. Seth's irrepressible, little-boy energy was infectious. So I made a rule that he could bounce it in the hall, away from lamps and other breakable objects.

One rainy day, he was bouncing the ball in the hallway, and it somehow careened into the bathroom. "Mom . . . ," Seth called, in a worried voice. I rushed in to find him standing over the tub. "What's the matter?" I asked.

"My ball went down the hole."

I climbed into the tub and peered into the drain. All I saw was darkness. I got a flashlight and shone it down the hole. "Are you sure, Seth? It doesn't look like anything's down there."

Unfortunately, he was positive. I turned on the water to see if the drain was blocked. Sure enough, the tub began to fill. I tried to dislodge the block with furious pumping of the plunger—no luck. Now what?

Never having owned a home before, I had never hired a plumber in my life. How much would it cost? Having plunked down nearly every cent of my discretionary income on fixup supplies, I was on an airtight budget until payday—still a ways off. And who could even guess how far down the ball was lodged and how much of the plumbing would have to be dismantled to reach it? I had visions of workmen tearing up my floors with crowbars to get at the pipes.

But how could we function without a bathtub? I called an agent friend, Tom Norris, to discuss the catastrophe. "Didn't you have a trap on the drain?" he asked.

"What do you mean?" I had to say, with some embarrassment. As he explained, I felt foolish. As competent as I was growing in the tough-guy world of bombs and guns, I was still a stereotypically hardware-challenged female, far more conscious of the need for curtains, wallpaper, and flowers in the yard than for a fifty-cent metal strainer that could save me a fortune and untold misery. It had never even crossed my mind to check for traps in the drains.

"I'll come over," Tom said kindly.

He spent the rest of the afternoon down in my basement, wrenching apart the plumbing and poking through the pipes with an opened coat hanger. Finally, out popped the ball.

For the second time that day, I was struck with a powerful sense of incongruity. Here we were—a man, woman, and child—in a picture-book town, so charming that it could have been the movie set for *It's a Wonderful Life,* spending an apple-pie American Saturday, with Daddy working on the house and Mommy upstairs making a snack to cheer him on. Only we were colleagues, not Mommy and Daddy. The man working on the house, a former Navy Seal and Congressional Medal of Honor winner in Vietnam, was a team leader of the FBI's famous Hostage Rescue Squad; and the woman in the kitchen dedicated her weekdays not to canning, baking, and darning but to hunting the vicious rapist terrorizing her perfect little Eden. Seth was the only element that fit naturally into the picture—if Norman Rockwell were painting it, that is.

He'd have to add some extra brushstrokes to depict our lives.

But Seth and I were making a place for ourselves in LaGrange. Mothers of his friends who lived nearby would watch him for me after school, and in exchange, I instituted Friday movie nights. I'd take six or seven children out to the movies every Friday, and afterward we'd all go out for dessert at Kahoots to discuss the film. I could have written a children's film review column showcasing the astute opinions of my little band of critics.

But what brought me even greater pleasure was my nightly communal run. Every evening after dinner I would jog to keep in shape, always with my Walkman clipped at my waist, so the music would keep my pace up. Seth would ride alongside me on his bike to keep me company. One night, a couple of neighborhood kids on bicycles started following us. I waved to acknowledge them and then just kept going, jogging to the beat from my headphones down the quiet residential streets, and was surprised, glancing back a few miles from home, to find them still on our tail. They didn't peel off until we veered onto our own front sidewalk.

A few nights later, when I came out in my sweat suit, they were waiting, riding in little circles on the driveway. "How come you go running, Mrs. DeLong?" one boy asked.

"Well, I do it to stay strong and so I don't get fat," I said. I did a few stretches and set off, with Seth beside me and the boys trailing in our wake like a couple of seagulls after a yacht. Soon we were joined by a third child and a fourth. On nights when I stayed home because I was just too tired or the weather looked threatening, one of them would ring the bell. "Aren't you coming out, Mrs. DeLong? You're gonna get fat . . ." My little squad of personal trainers didn't brook many excuses.

Eventually we formed a regular band that would assemble most nights for the seven months of the year that we weren't imprisoned by the Chicago winter. Often we would be ten or eleven strong, headed by a few hot-rodders with high handlebars and banana seats, blazing a trail for the pack, with the more sociable cyclists clustered on the side borders, and a couple of lone wolf cubs, pedaling to their own rhythms, bringing up the rear. In the center, ringed by the children, I would run lulled by a new kind of music—the meditative thrumming of bicycle wheels and the rushing of leaves, as the wind billowed through the treetop canopies high above us—and it filled me with peace.

8

THE MASTER CLASS

The experience of working with Roy Hazelwood on the Burlington
rapist case left me fascinated with profiling. So when the Behavioral
Science Unit at the Academy offered its first new training class for profiling coordinators in four years, I immediately applied. My chances of
being accepted were slim, for I had been in the Bureau four years, short
of the minimum prerequisite of five, and three other agents in the division were competing for the slots. But my background as a psychiatric
nurse must have prevailed, for to my delight, I was chosen, along with
Dan Kentala, who had been a Chicago homicide detective and gotten
a master's degree in psychology before he joined the Bureau.

At the time the Behavioral Science Unit (BSU) at the FBI Academy
was housed in the stark basement bunker of the Quantico library, made
famous by the movie *The Silence of the Lambs,* with windowless cinder-
block walls, bare and dingy linoleum floors, and fluorescent tube lights
overhead. Its fifteen-odd staffers worked at cold gray-metal government-
issue desks jammed two or three to a room. The austere setting reflected
the Bureau's erstwhile estimation of the value of the social sciences in
crimefighting, but by the early 1980s that antiquated view was shifting,
thanks to the growing renown of such masters as espionage expert Dick
Ault. A former Marine who had become an authority on foreign counterintelligence, Ault specialized in personality and lifestyle assessments

aimed at recruiting or "tipping" spies—discovering the personal vul-
nerabilities, such as precarious finances or resentment of superiors or
poor treatment by their own governments, that might incline foreign
officials to commit treason and shift their loyalties to the United States.
Most of his work was classified "top secret."

Much more visible was the work of the profilers, who were reaching
out to police departments across the United States to offer their services
for solving such pattern crimes as serial rapes and murders. Even as recently as the 1980s sexual criminality was a fairly new realm of study.
The Bureau, like most branches of law enforcement, had little instruction on the subject until the late 1950s, when a Philadelphia agent,
Walter McLaughlin, developed his own classes based on his personal
experience in the field and the meager academic resources available. In
The Evil That Men Do McLaughlin is credited with developing "what
was probably the world's first sexual-crime classification system for law
enforcement," which the Academy incorporated into its teaching materials. But despite McLaughlin's efforts, the Bureau continued to walk
the line between "prudery and prurience," as Ken Lanning is cited as
recalling:

> I remember an inservice [class] at Quantico when we were told
> we were actually going to be shown some real pornography. In
> order to see it, however, we had to leave the classroom and go to
> another room, where it was displayed for us on a table. We had to
> put our hands behind our backs and walk around the table, just
> sort of looking at it.

When not having students literally tiptoe around the subject, the Bureau offered courses that were, in the words of Roger Depue, BSU unit
chief in the 1980s, "a porno show for cops." Lanning was counseled by
a colleague when he became an FBI field instructor:

> "Ken, you're about to embark on probably the greatest topic the
> FBI can teach. You can't go wrong . . . Just let me give you three
> little bits of advice.

"One, lots of dirty jokes. You have to have a dirty joke to go with every sexual perversion you talk about.

"Two, get lots of pornography. Dirty pictures. Magazines. Movies. Pass 'em out. The cops love 'em.

"And, three, never allow any women in the class . . . Because if you have women, you can't do the first two things."

Roy Hazelwood's experience was similar. According to *The Evil That Men Do,* when he arrived at Quantico in 1978, "low-grade fraternity humor" flourished everywhere. In his own broom-closet office, he found a box of sex toys, a "flasher" doll with a penis that shot out of its clothes when the head was pressed, and, pinned to the walls, women's black lace lingerie and a whip bearing the legend "Without Pain There Is No Pleasure."

Together Lanning and Hazelwood conducted a study of law enforcement views on sexual victimization, reporting their distressing findings in a paper titled "The Maligned Investigator of Criminal Sexuality," which urged increased professionalism, preservation of confidentiality, and respectful treatment of victims. They overhauled the Bureau's "Sex Crimes" class, changing its name to "Interpersonal Violence," which by 1979 was a forty-four-hour course accredited by the University of Virginia—a far cry from the old "porno show."

That's not to suggest for an instant that my profiling school studies were dryly academic. My teachers—the foremost authorities in the world on their particular aspects of sexual criminality—were some of the most colorful characters at Quantico and, having honed their skills, for the most part, on the police education "road show" circuit, among the most brilliantly effective public speakers I have ever encountered. Part of their appeal, to be sure, was the inherent fascination of their material—the most curious wrinkles in the human psyche. But they also took care to approach that material with enough humanity and to leaven it with enough appropriate humor to make it possible for us to tolerate the daily ration of horror.

John Douglas, who at the time was doing a lot of the hands-on profiling and research, had a wise, fatherly air in the classroom and a mild manner that belied the tough, confrontational interviewing he was doing in prisons for his landmark multiple-murderers study with Ann Burgess and Robert Ressler. Burgess gave a guest lecture on their study; and Ann Rule, an ex-cop who became a best-selling true-crime author, came in to describe her extensive serial killer research. Our most controversial guest speaker was Chris Costner Sizemore, the subject of the famous book and film *The Three Faces of Eve,* in which her psychiatrist claimed to have cured her of multiple personality disorder. While maintaining that she did indeed have multiple personalities—a claim that law enforcement officials always regard as a boondoggle, an excuse to evade culpability for crimes—she debunked *Three Faces* as a complete fabrication, which she redressed in her own book, *I'm Eve.*

Among our regular instructors, Ken Lanning was a world-renowned authority on the sexual victimization of children. It was Lanning who taught me the techniques I used to win the trust of Joshua, the child we rescued from an abductor, to elicit the truth of what had happened to him, and to help him recognize that it was not his fault. Lanning's lectures were down-to-earth and nonsensationalistic but they held his audiences spellbound. He was revered, and he was also a good sport. Each class at the Academy had a pregraduation banquet, to which spouses who had come for the ceremony were invited, but not children. There was always a scramble for babysitters, but counselors would assure their classes: "We've got some good news and some bad news about banquet night. We managed to line up a babysitter for all of you—but it's Ken Lanning."

Not that he was a child molester—he wasn't, of course—but he did know all there was to know about the subject.

Robert Ressler was the greatest raconteur on the staff, known for his biting wit and keen memory for detail, as well as for coining the term "serial killer." He had a famous collection of crime scene photos, some dating back to the early days of the Bureau, which he drew on for his lectures. Among the historical cases we studied with him was the Chicago Lipstick Murders, so named because the killer had scrawled on the wall in one victim's home, using her own lipstick: "For heaven's sake, catch me before I kill more. I cannot control myself." The grisliest of the Lipstick killings, haunting Ressler during his Chicago boyhood and inspiring him to go into law enforcement, was the murder of Suzanne Degnan, a six-year-old whose head would later turn up in a sewer drain.

Then, one summer day, an off-duty policeman on his way home from the beach saw two cops chasing a burglary suspect and beaned him with a flowerpot. The runaway turned out to be William Heirens, a seventeen-year-old University of Chicago student. He was a fetish burglar, who by his own account had broken into hundreds of homes to fondle and steal women's underwear, hiding it at his grandmother's house for later delectation. In time the break-in itself became such a sexual thrill for him that he would bypass an unlocked door to enter through a window, which would arouse him to orgasm.

When Heirens's fingerprints were found at one of the Lipstick murder sites, he confessed, but insisted that the killings were accidental. The court didn't buy that excuse—panic at being discovered might account for one but not three murders, never mind the brutal dismemberment of a child—and sentenced him to a prison term that some fifty-five years later he is still serving, making him the longest resident guest of the Illinois penal system.

One of Ressler's prized photos, captioned "Heirens Signs Confession," showed the killer, pen in hand, being yanked upright by the hair, with his eyes rolling back in his head—treatment that would constitute a civil rights violation, at the very least, today. But it was probably quite gratifying to the more revenge-minded public of the 1940s.

Jim Reese was another gifted, natural teacher as well as an excellent profiler, a tall, handsome man who would teach us important lessons about the limitations of professionalism. With all the repellent acts you may be exposed to in law enforcement, there is a tendency—even a necessity—to become inured to the unspeakable. There is a certain macho toughness that comes with the territory, a belief that if you act as if nothing can touch you, nothing will. But the price of denial, for too many, is very high—addictions, withdrawal from intimate connections, or even violent acting out with loved ones, leading to divorce and isolation, and sometimes, in the saddest cases, suicide.

Reese's lesson was to recognize, not to deny, that we all have breaking points. His own came with Arthur Frederick Goode III, a serial killer who strangled young boys to death with belts and was one of the first murderers put to death once the state of Florida reinstated the death penalty. The execution was controversial because with Goode's low IQ, some questioned whether he had the mental competence to understand his crimes. But Goode had certainly displayed mental competence, even downright cleverness, when he found a way to smuggle a letter out of prison, eluding the censors, to the parents of one of his victims, describing how he had savored violating and strangling their child. The man was a vicious, sadistic monster, the embodiment of evil.

When Reese was interviewing Goode in prison, the killer asked in a suggestive way whether he had a child. That did it for Reese, who was in fact a father. Bureau legend held that Reese had to be restrained from beating the hell out of Goode—which wasn't true, but the story persisted because it was an appealing gloss on Reese's "good guy" reputation. What Reese did say was that he left the cell with a knot in his stomach that would be there for years and then smashed his fist into a prison wall. Then he realized that there was more to coping with stress than "striking out at something." He would go on to become one of the pioneers in stress-management training for law-enforcement officers.

At one point, before I went to profiling school, I would have a similar, if less dramatic epiphany. I felt almost haunted by the crime scene photos I was handling—mostly women, many around my age, savagely butchered in their own homes. Much as it embarrassed me—I was no frail, fainthearted little girl after my near decade as a psych nurse—I found myself sticking my gun in my pocket just to take out the garbage. But when I confided in Gene Stapleton, the chief profiler in Chicago, with whom I had worked the Burlington rapist case, he was wonderful. "Candice," he said, "if that didn't happen to you once in a while, you wouldn't be human. We all get that way."

He took me in hand and, kindly and patiently, sat with me in his office for an entire day, talking me through hour upon hour of horrifying slides with alternating wisecracks and matter-of-fact assessments, showing me how to zero in with the analytical mind before the emotions got a chance to kick in. "But the real key," he told me, "is plain old exposure. If you look at enough of these, they come to have less of a visceral effect." It was like being treated for a phobia—being forced to look at spiders or ride elevators or cross bridges repeatedly, until desensitization sets in, and the stimulus loses its paralyzing power. And the technique worked—within a day or two I was over that speed bump and back in action.

Roy Hazelwood's joking reply, whenever he was asked how he coped with the never-ending stream of abominations, was "Masturbation." Flippant as that may have sounded—and it always provoked gales of knowing laughter when he said it in a room full of law-enforcement professionals—it was a perfectly apt expression of the deep need we all had for some cathartic, cleansing release from the clench of darkness. With his casual air and slight Texas drawl, Hazelwood seemed more like a down-home guy than a man of prodigious intellect who developed many of the measures and distinctions that are now axiomatic in law enforcement and have advanced our understanding of sexual criminality.

It was Hazelwood and John Douglas who defined the two categories of murderers we so commonly cite, the organized and disorganized types. Among "lust murderers," the kind of killers we as profilers would see most often, the organized type is psychopathic, egocentric, amoral, commonly charming though incapable of empathic connection, and often highly intelligent and sophisticated. Organized offenders are usually more mature, experienced criminals and careful planners, who bring their own weapons and restraints. Some devise elaborate schemes either to hunt down their victims (who may be of a particular type) or to fulfill their fantasies. Ted Bundy, a handsome former law student, who was so smooth that he could snatch a child victim from under the nose of a school crossing guard, exemplifies the organized killer, as does Edmund Kemper, who could play out a physical pun like burying a victim's head in the yard, positioned so that she would be "looking up" to his mother.

Such mass murderers as the Tylenol killer, who went to great pains to plot out his scheme and to doctor the capsules with cyanide, also are of the organized type.

Disorganized offenders strike out spontaneously, in a fever, and usually leave a chaotic crime scene and trail of evidence. They are often stereotypical male loners, socially isolated, unemployed, ill-kempt, and of average or lower intelligence. Sometimes they are psychotic, like the subway shover who hears voices in his head, telling him to push some-one into the path of an oncoming train, or they may simply be young, inexperienced, and acting out of panic.

There are also offenders who fall into the mixed category, combining elements of both. The offender may be young, just discovering what he likes, and developing a modus operandi, on the way to becoming an organized type; or conversely, he may be organized but deteriorating psychologically, getting careless in his methods. Still others may act op-portunistically or in a frenzy of rage, like the disorganized type, but retain the presence of mind to conceal evidence, by hiding a body, for example, to elude capture.

An example of the "mixed type" was the Sacramento Vampire Mur-derer, Richard Trenton Chase, a paranoid schizophrenic who suffered from delusions for years before he went on a four-day rampage, killing five people in two separate incidents. He eviscerated his first victim, a woman, with her own steak knives, then drank her blood using paper cups he found in her trash. Also in the trash can was a Kentucky Fried Chicken box, in which he packed up some of her body parts to take home. A few days later he murdered a family—a woman, her middle-aged father, and her eighteen-month- and seven-year-old sons. He dis-emboweled the woman, plucked out her eyes, and harvested a few of her body parts; then he drained the toddler's blood into the tub, where he bathed in it. He would later tell investigators—who caught him with body parts in his blender and a catsup bottle full of blood in his refrig-erator—that his own blood was being "dried up" by spaceships and by the scum in the soapdish in his shower, so he needed a fresh supply from his victims to stay alive.

These savage, psychotic killings had all the hallmarks of the disorgan-ized killer, but there was a twist—before mutilating his victims, Chase had shot them with a .45 he had brought along. And despite his delu-sional thinking, he had the presence of mind to hide the trophies he had brought home from the crime scenes, concealing the toddler's body so well that it wouldn't be found for months.

In this case the killer's capture was the direct result of an FBI profile developed by Robert Ressler and Russ Vorpagel. Investigators went door to door, asking whether anyone knew of a man with the characteristics that they had posited for the offender—and sure enough, neighbors led them to Chase.

Hazelwood also refined academician Nicholas Groth's four classifications of rapists (two power-seeking types and two angry types) for law enforcement. He divided rapists into six categories, making distinctions that have passed into the law-enforcement lexicon, based on the recognition that rape has more to do with the need for power and domination or with hatred of women than with sex. The two types that are primarily motivated by power needs are the power-reassurance type, of which the Burlington rapist was a classic example, seeking reassurance of his desirability and fantasizing that his victims were "girlfriends," of a sort; and the power-assertive type, less common, who seeks to confirm his manliness by prevailing over another person. The power-assertive rapist may use force, even if his victim doesn't resist, just to proclaim his dominance. Date rapists often fall into this category.

I once had a case involving a power-assertive rapist who broke into the house of an elderly couple, who were too frail to offer much resistance. Nonetheless, he slapped them around, raping the woman and calling her derogatory names, then threatened to come back and kill them if they called the police. They reported the rape because they both needed medical treatment, and the story made the papers. Three weeks later, the rapist returned, beating them even more forcefully and throwing the husband into a wall before raping the wife. At one point, he put his hands around her neck, saying angrily, "I told you not to call the police, you bitch!"

I had been taught in profiling school that although many rapists threaten reprisals, they don't tend to come back, preferring to move on to the next victim. So when I called Roy Hazelwood to tell him about the case, he was astounded: "That's one for the books," he told me. It was that rare.

The two types motivated by anger are more likely to inflict serious injuries on their victims. The anger-retaliatory type, as the name suggests, is out for revenge, seeking to punish women for some real or imagined slight. As Hazelwood writes: "The problem is that the episode could be anything from a woman being elected to Congress to a female police officer issuing him a ticket to a fight with his wife." He is likely to strike impulsively, in a disorganized manner, and to prove unable to complete the sexual act because of his anger.

One night when I was working in an emergency room, a fellow nurse was assailed in the parking lot by a furious stranger who beat her so badly that she never completely recovered. Luckily, people came upon them and intervened, saving her life. The assailant was enraged by some woman (or all women) and took it out on an innocent victim who happened to stumble into his path.

Perhaps the most frightening of all is the anger-excitation rapist, a sadist who derives sexual pleasure from his victim's pain. These rapists are highly organized, often with elaborate fantasies to play out—the Bundys, the Kempers, and the Jeffrey Dahmers—and careful plans to execute them, right down to the weapons and restraints they employ. This category is most dangerous, but fortunately, such offenders are relatively easy to avoid by taking reasonable safety precautions. One thing I tell my safety education classes is that women and children should always look askance at any man who asks them for help carrying packages and the like. There's got to be a reason he's not asking another man.

I also urge them to be wary of placing themselves in potentially risky situations, even with men they know. Ken Bianchi, one of two cousins who perpetrated the infamous Hillside Strangler murders, lured a victim—a former neighbor who had spurned his advances—out of the safety of her apartment by claiming that he accidentally had hit her car. Ironically, she had just gotten off the phone with her mother, having assured her that she had securely locked the doors because the Hillside Strangler was on the loose.

Hazelwood's final two categories have a less clear place on the power-anger axis. The opportunistic rapist usually stumbles on his victim in the course of committing some other criminal act—burglary, for example—and decides on the spur of the moment to take advantage of the situation. Participants in a gang rape, the sixth type, may have some of the power or anger motivations of the other types, but the chief force that drives them is the need to prove themselves to one another. There is at least one unwilling participant in every such group, and victims would do well to try to distinguish the leaders from the followers, who will be more likely to give up their confederates to the police.

Obviously, human beings defy cut-and-dried classification, but Hazelwood's categories offer tremendously useful guidelines for identifying the kind of person likely to have committed a given crime and thus narrowing the search—or sometimes, expanding the search. Back then, if a woman was murdered, whatever the circumstances, the police would immediately pick up her husband or boyfriend and dedicate their efforts to building the case against him.

It was a sensible place to start. According to Department of Justice estimates for the period from 1976 to 1994, around 29 percent of the murders of adult women were committed by a close relative or an "intimate"—spouse, ex, or boyfriend—before moving on to the next, more difficult tier, acquaintances, who proved responsible in roughly 47 percent of the cases. But for murders involving rape or sexual assault—which represent 1 to 2 percent of the total—the probable culpability of intimates and family members plummets to less than 10 percent. Acquaintances are found guilty in roughly the same proportion, but the likelihood of a stranger being the killer increases dramatically—to 39 percent. Pinpointing the murderer in a woman's far-flung network of acquaintances is hard enough, and looking for a stranger is like trying to find a needle in a haystack. That's when such profiling can be invaluable.

Hazelwood's classes, like most of the others, had a lecture format, illustrated by slides, many of which were horrific. Twenty years later, I still sometimes dream about one heartbreaking "before and after" sequence—not the bloodiest, by any means—that sickened and outraged us all. The "before" shot was of a blond child who strongly resembled Seth, standing in his little-boy jeans and sneakers, shirtless and pensive, near a fishing hole. In the "after" shot, he was draped across a thicket of bushes, looking like he was sleeping, but with a visible stab wound in his chest. The man who killed him was a child probation officer.

Whenever I think of that image, I also flash on the wall of one of the offices in the basement bunker, inhabited by all these tough, seasoned sex crimes experts, that was covered with bumper stickers all about children: DO YOU KNOW WHERE YOUR CHILDREN ARE?, TEACH YOUR

CHILDREN WELL, and one that kept running through my head like a mantra, IF YOU LOVE YOUR CHILDREN, NEVER LET THEM OUT OF YOUR SIGHT.

But like all our instructors, Hazelwood, though always professional and respectful of victims, made sure to offer us a little comic relief. He came up with a real groaner, as I remember, when someone in the class brought in the shot of a strange crime scene, a car filled with feathers. The student explained that a passing cop had stopped to investigate the car because he heard sounds of struggling inside and saw feathers clinging to the steamed-up windows. When he opened the door he found a lifeless victim lying on the floor—a dead duck, which the half-naked perpetrator had obviously been engaged with sexually. At this point we were all dutifully jotting notes, shaking our heads at the absurd range of human sexual deviations. "Well, folks," Hazelwood said, pausing for effect before delivering his punch line, "that's what we call 'gettin' down.' "

Dopey as the joke was, we all screamed with laughter.

After our classroom instruction, which began at eight in the morning and ran for the duration of a regular workday, most student profilers would go for a run, grab dinner in the Academy cafeteria, and then repair to the Boardroom for the evening. There we could mingle with other agents attending different "in-service" training programs, swagger a little in front of the wide-eyed trainees in their final week before graduation, and most important, make connections with the 250 cops enrolled in the National Academy, who were the wellspring of cases for us to profile. At the very least, we hoped to wangle invitations to speak to their departments about the great new crimebusting tool we had to offer.

I was so thrilled by what I was learning that I became an impassioned crusader for the cause. Showing up in a MY π PIZZA T-shirt, instantly recognizable to anyone from the Greater Chicago area, I had no trouble attracting a little knot of curious cops. It also didn't hurt that I was one of only a handful of women amid hundreds of men. "Oh, you're in that voodoo class," at least one of them would say dismissively. "Don't tell me you believe that fortune-teller shit."

So I would launch into my spiel about the amazing accuracy of the profile in the Burlington rapist case, as well as some of the other major triumphs of the BSU. The unit had first come to prominence after the Atlanta child murders that took place from 1979 to 1981. By the time that Roy Hazelwood was called in to help, ten children had been found shot, stabbed, or strangled to death. Eventually the death toll attributed to the killer would approach thirty. All the victims were black, mostly boys from eight to fifteen years old.

The Georgia FBI was getting tips implicating the Ku Klux Klan in the murders (and indeed, the overwhelming majority of serial killers are white males). But when Hazelwood examined the crime scenes and the body-dumping sites, the curiosity he drew in the all-black neighborhoods showed him that no white man could have moved freely there without detection. The killer had to be black.

John Douglas now joined the investigation, followed by Robert Ressler, amid cries of "Cover-up!" from the black community, who were convinced that the authorities were suppressing the truth to preserve racial peace. But once some red herrings were eliminated and several of the murders determined to be copycat or unrelated slayings, attention focused on Wayne Williams, a black freelance photographer/musician. Eventually some seven hundred pieces of hair and fiber evidence would connect him to twelve of the victims—and he fit the Hazelwood-Douglas profile on every major count, right down to the dog he owned, a German shepherd.

Williams wound up standing trial for only two of the murders, anomalous victims in their twenties (one reason why the case periodically waxes controversial). At the time, hair and fiber evidence wasn't as widely accepted as it is today, but an equally tough challenge for the prosecution was Williams's demeanor. He wore thick glasses and seemed so easygoing and soft-spoken that it would be hard to convince the jury that he was capable of murder. As John Douglas recalls in *Mindhunter*, Al Binder, the defense attorney, tried to turn Williams's appearance to his advantage: "Look at him . . . Look how soft his hands are. Do you think he would have the strength to kill someone, to strangle someone with those hands?"

In fact, it takes as little as four pounds of pressure, about as much as it takes to snap off a light switch, to cut off the flow of blood to an adult's brain, never mind a child's.

Now Douglas strategized with Assistant District Attorney Jack Mallard to figure out a way to penetrate Williams's cool façade. They decided that when the questioning hit a certain pitch of intensity, Mallard would encroach on Williams's personal space by laying a hand on his arm. That did it—Williams snapped and broke into a manic, angry rant, showing himself to be not such an improbable killer, after all. On February 27, 1982, the predominantly black jury found him guilty, and he was sentenced to two consecutive life terms in prison. And now, at least some cops and prosecutors began to look at profiling with a new measure of respect.

As I gushed about such cases in the Boardroom, I told myself that doubting and dismissive as they seemed, at least the cops were listening to me. Someday, some way, my cheerleading was bound to pay off. And, I had to admit, I was getting a little immediate, personal payoff too. For any mother, single or married, working at home or out on a job, a couple weeks away from childcare responsibilities feels like something of a vacation. Of course, I missed Seth, who was staying with his father, and talked to him daily, but it had been a long time—what with Seth, my job, and fixing up the house—since I had felt as much like a single woman as a single mother. I sometimes yearned for a partner and once in a while would have a dalliance when a dear former lover/friend from my nursing days, the wild Irishman Tom Crowley, blew into town from Minneapolis. But now that Seth was old enough to understand what my seriously dating someone might imply, there was no way I wanted to risk seeing him hurt by some unreliable type who might disappoint us both.

Now, here I was, outnumbered a hundred to one by men—big, bold, strapping, courageous men, including some guys from early Hostage

Rescue Teams, who were going through training around that time. It was making me dizzy.

I was surrounded by men all day long, of course, but the guys I worked with were like brothers to me. I also worried about the fallout from an office romance, though I knew of women who had braved the gossip and wound up married to Bureau colleagues—we called them "double agents." Now and then a "civilian" had asked me out, with disappointing results. One was the male equivalent of the "badge bimbos" who chase men in law enforcement. He couldn't stop bragging to everyone we met, including waiters, "This is Candice. She's a federal agent"—as if nabbing me somehow proved his virility. All that public show certainly soured me on ever seeing him demonstrate his manliness in private.

The flip side of badge-bimbohood was "badge-bolting." Badge-bolters would be thrilled about your job when they first met you—"You're an FBI agent? How cool! What's the most exciting case you ever worked?"—only to get cold feet once it hit them that catching bad guys sounded a lot more macho than selling ad space. If they had the nerve to ask me out at all, more often than not they'd stand me up, perhaps scared to risk feeling even for an evening that they might not be wearing the pants in a relationship—not that I wanted to put on anybody's trousers. The guys at work loved to tease me about the bolters, saying things like, "Of course he was scared, poor guy! He knew that the second he got his rocks off, you'd whip out your gun and say"—shifting here into a bitchy falsetto—"Hold it right there, pal! You're not done yet!"

Between bad dates, concern for Seth, and just being dog-tired at the end of every working/parenting/housekeeping day, I had halfway given up on the notion that I might ever find another mate. But just being there in the Boardroom with all that male attention made me realize that I was missing a lot. Maybe a long-distance relationship was the answer—something that wouldn't impinge on Seth's life at all unless it got serious enough to warrant talk of permanence. Not that I had any hot prospects, but maybe it was time to try to scare a few up again.

9

THE UNSUB

Today every division in the FBI is mandated to have a National Center for the Analysis of Violent Crime (NCAVC) coordinator, aka a profiling coordinator. The profiling coordinator serves as a liaison to the police, educating them about what the Bureau has to offer; works profiles and consults, when invited; functions as the bridge between local law enforcement and the resources at Quantico, including the Violent Criminal Apprehension Program (VICAP), which is the world's largest database tracking violent criminal offenses. A large office such as Chicago might have several working profiling coordinators. But back then, the New York Bureau was one of the few to make profiling a full-time position. The brass in Chicago, as in many other divisions, still considered it something of a waste of manpower to dedicate an agent full-time to crimes, such as rape and murder, that fell under state jurisdiction unless they occurred on federal land. Agents like Gene Stapleton who had been trained in profiling worked it in around their regular duties, and the same was expected of me and Dan Kentala when we returned from Quantico. The best I could negotiate for myself was a transfer to the applicant squad, doing full-field background investigations (for Justice Antonin Scalia, prior to his Supreme Court appointment, among others), so I wouldn't be encumbered by complex, ongoing investigations and could devote half my time to profiling and police training work.

Dan and I formed a team and soon became known, predictably enough, considering the grisly crimes we handled, as the Gruesome Twosome. Our first case was a brutal rape/homicide that took place in Elmhurst, Illinois, in spring 1984. The victim was a fifty-year-old woman who lived alone in a comfortable, single-family suburban home. After the assault, she managed to flee to her neighbor's house, where she collapsed of wounds so severe that the coroner was amazed that she could stand, never mind run away. On the way to the hospital, Detective Ray Bradford, who would be assigned to investigate her case, held her hand in the ambulance, as she kept repeating, "He raped me. He tried to kill me," over and over. She was in shock and so unable to give him any information about the offender. She died within minutes of arriving in the emergency room.

Usually such homicides are solved in a few days. Only when a case has dragged on for weeks without a break do police tend to seek the help of profilers, who then work from crime scene photos, autopsy records, a victimology (a description of the victim's lifestyle and habits), and police reports. But the detective sergeant working this case, John Milner, was an innovator and decided to involve the Bureau right from the beginning. The crime scene was still intact enough that it made sense for Dan and me to inspect it and to do some nosing around.

We knew from the various reports that when the victim fled, leaving the front door open, the television and all the lights in the house were on. So she had probably been watching TV in the living room while her assailant was peeping into the windows, casing the house for valuables. He then slit the screen in an open back window and crept from there into her bedroom, where he snatched her jewelry box from the dresser.

With the sound of the TV covering his movements, he let himself out through the back sliding-glass doors to paw through the jewelry box, pocketing a few pieces and leaving the rest, obviously costume, strewn on the ground. He must have been angry at the meager pickings, for he now apparently reentered the house to confront the victim in the living room. There he raped her, most likely on the sofa, which was blotched with semen; and going to the kitchen, cleaned himself off with a dishrag, which was later found, semen smeared, on the floor.

At that point, Dan and I surmised, the victim had tried to bolt. A wash of blood around the front door suggested that he had caught her on the porch, stabbing and slashing to try to halt her escape. The preponderance of the many gashes and gouges appeared on her face and neck, as if he had been slashing at her in a panic, trying to still her screams. Would she have survived, I wondered, if she had lain there silent, praying for him to leave?

Across the street, just beyond her neighbor's yard, lay a cornfield. Dan and I headed over to give it a closer look, figuring that the killer had made his getaway by scrambling through it in the darkness. We were pacing off the distance between the yard and the field when we were interrupted by a woman and a young boy, maybe five years old, who was carrying a package wrapped in newspaper.

"Are you the cops looking into the murder?" the woman asked.

We explained that we were FBI agents, called in to aid the police.

"Well," she said, "my son has something to show you."

"Oh, what have you got there, little man?" I asked indulgently, expecting to see some homemade art project on crossing the street safely or not talking to strangers.

But he said, "Is this what you are looking for, Miss Policelady?"

He proudly peeled back the crinkled newspaper, and all I could do was sputter, "Where the hell did you get that?"

"It was under my swing set," he told me.

There on the newspaper, streaked with dried blood and tissue, was the biggest Rambo knife I have ever seen.

Suddenly the scene felt eerie, like the moment in an Alfred Hitchcock movie when a cloud blots out the sun and the music grows ominous and the ghastly underside of the ordinary is revealed. Seeing the murder weapon materialize out of nowhere, in the hands of an innocent five-year-old—who presented it perfectly matter-of-factly, gore streaked as it was, without turning a hair—was so surreal and horrifying that it made my skin crawl.

What was that mother thinking? How could she have even let him touch that knife? Didn't it give him nightmares?

I gingerly took the knife away from him, still swathed in newspapers, to turn over to the police. I could barely bring myself to utter "Thank you" to his mother. Dan got the particulars of who they were and where they'd found the knife, and we were still shaking our heads about it when we went back to the office to work up our profile.

The UNSUB's race and sex were an easy call: "White male," we began. That was a safe assumption, absent evidence (such as a hair) suggesting otherwise. Any non-Caucasian would have stood out in the virtually all-white neighborhood. Besides, like rape, sexual assault murder is most often a same-race crime: white on white (55 percent, according to Department of Justice statistics), black on black (24 percent), and so on; just 15 percent of black offenders target white victims, and 2 percent of white offenders prey on blacks. Furthermore, the assailant fled on foot—the discovery of the knife under the swing set, inaccessible to a car, established that. There were no reports of an unfamiliar car in the vicinity, and no alley or side street near the victim's home where he could have parked undetected. That meant that he probably lived within a few miles at most of the victim's home.

What was his probable age? The number of stab wounds on the victim's face and neck suggested that he was rattled by her screaming, and the fact that he had killed her on the porch in flight, instead of in the house, indicated that the murder was unplanned. And why kill her at all, instead of knock her down and run away? Anger, perhaps—but if murder was his aim, he was rather inept, since his many stab wounds didn't even fell his victim. All these facts suggested that he was young, not a seasoned, sophisticated criminal. It was also possible that he was short of stature and too slight to subdue his victim, who was petite herself, about five feet five inches and weighing 118 pounds.

But we felt fairly sure that this was no "kiddie crime." A teenager wouldn't have brought his own weapon, most likely, and would have had neither the sense to case the house before the break-in nor the nerve to reenter and confront his victim when he struck out with the jewelry box. The perpetrator had some experience, probably youthful B&Es that were now progressing to rape and murder, which he was still too callow to execute well. For these reasons we placed his age at approximately twenty-five.

What were his personal circumstances? He was after the kind of jewelry that would be kept in an ordinary home, in a box on the dresser, which meant that he needed cash. Our man didn't seem to have a car, either. The fact that he resorted to brute force to control his victim, rather than threats or other intermediate steps, suggested social awkwardness, an inability to handle himself. If he was employed at all, it was likely that he held some kind of menial, ill-paying job, with little public contact. And he probably dressed the part—beat-up jeans, T-shirts, dirty sneakers.

Given his probable income level, we surmised that he was living with someone else on whom he was financially dependent. Since rape had not been his main goal, but more an after-the-fact assertion of power, an expression of anger toward women, that person was probably a domineering female. She would be a relative, perhaps his mother rather than his wife, since married men generally can't move around so freely in the evening. But the semen at the scene, indicating that he had successfully completed the act, showed that he was not a sexually ineffectual loner. He had significant experience of consensual sex and very likely had a girlfriend. A fight with her or with his mother may well have been the "stressor" that precipitated his attack. We viewed him as an "opportunistic rapist," for there had been a rash of burglaries in the area, with women's purses being snatched right off their kitchen counters or tables, for which he was probably also responsible. While our man clearly had rape on his mind, it didn't seem to be his primary aim.

We had completed our profile and were about to submit it to the BSU for review—every profile done in the field must be checked and approved by Quantico before it is turned over to the police—when the Elmhurst cops apprehended a very good suspect. He fit our profile perfectly on many counts. He was the right age and lived with his mother, who "ruled the roost," according to the police, and had a girlfriend with whom he was sexually active. He had a modest level of criminal experience—a few other burglaries, for which he had eluded arrest, but no record of rape or assault. He lived three miles from the crime scene and had canvassed the neighborhood on his bicycle before settling on the victim's home, then hid the bike, planning to retrieve it to make his escape. One thing about him shocked us, however: The suspect was black.

Dan and I were ready to eat humble pie, chastened that our first official profile had been so off-base, until Detective Sergeant Milner (later chief of the Elmhurst police) explained that the suspect was very light-skinned—as fair as I was. Riding his bike around the neighborhood, he could have easily passed for white and attracted little notice.

But from that moment on, the case seemed hexed. The suspect was convicted and sentenced to death but managed to squeak through a legal loophole on appeal. A forensic anthropologist, who had been called in as an expert witness, had testified that the wear on the suspect's shoes matched the pattern on a footprint at the crime—a correspondence as definitive as a fingerprint, she maintained, for no two people wear down their shoes in the same way. It was just one piece of evidence among many, but it was enough to hang an appeal on—and to get the verdict overturned. The appellate court ruled, essentially, that forensic anthropology was an inexact science and so it had been improper to expose the jury to the expert's speculations.

The prosecution retried the case—this time, by the defendant's choice, it was a "bench trial" held in front of a judge, without a jury—having every confidence of winning another conviction. But midway through the proceedings, the judge had a heart attack and the case was held over until he recovered. When he came back, in Bradford's words, "It was as if he forgot everything that had been presented" and out of the blue ruled, "There is no evidence" and dismissed the case. It was one of those astonishing, seemingly capricious rulings that confound and frustrate police and prosecutors; and it was irrevocable. A murderer who had been deemed worthy of the death penalty walked free.

Just a few months later he hijacked a car at gunpoint. Speeding away, he struck another car, killing the young driver, before losing control, crashing, and killing himself. He did get his death sentence, after all—if a little late and, sadly, at the cost of yet another life.

Infuriating as the Elmhurst verdict was, the cases that upset me more are the ones when lives can be saved if the victims' fellow citizens bother to intervene. Nobody has to go busting through a door like Charles Bronson. All it takes to be a hero is to pick up the phone.

That fall I had two such disturbing cases back to back, just weeks apart, in nice suburban neighborhoods. The first victim was cutting across a parking lot one night, on her way home from choir practice, when she was attacked by a rapist—it is worth noting that some 7 percent of rapes take place in parking structures or lots. After the rape, he killed her by slitting her throat. Two days later, when the news broke, a woman called the police anonymously to report, "I live nearby. That night I heard a lot of screaming coming from the far end of the parking lot."

I'll bet she heard "a lot of screaming." The victim put up a ferocious fight. The autopsy revealed skin jammed under her fingernails from her desperate, clawing effort to stop her assailant and "defensive" wounds on her forearms and hands, from trying to fend off his knife. How long do you suppose it took to subdue a furiously struggling victim, effect a rape, and slit her throat? Far more than the minute it would have cost the woman to phone the police and probably a while longer than it would have taken them to respond, especially in a small town. The woman's failure to act may well have cost the victim her life.

The murderer in this case was quickly apprehended. At the victim's funeral, a male classmate showed up with a scratched and bruised face—a red flag for the police, who were also in attendance. Cops often stake out funerals and wakes because murderers tend to turn up there, unable to resist witnessing the aftermath of their handiwork. This one even placed a note in the victim's coffin, saying, "I'm sorry the way things worked out." He confessed to the murder, explaining that he had only wanted sex from the victim but had "accidentally" killed her. How you accidentally show up with a knife, accidentally slash up someone who is fighting you off, and then accidentally cut her throat were all questions that baffled the jury. They found him guilty of murder.

The second case involved a twenty-five-year-old woman who was beaten and stabbed to death, in the neck, in her apartment. This time I accompanied the detective on his canvass of the neighborhood, knocking on doors and interviewing people who lived or worked near the crime scene. (Just as a procedural point, we are trained not to ask, "Did you see anything unusual?" because "unusual" is a matter of opinion. To many people, a deliveryman in work clothes, say, ringing the victim's doorbell, might not seem strange enough to mention. Instead interviewers will simply ask, "What did you see around such and such time?" for often seemingly inconsequential observations hold important clues.) We were working our way through the apartment complex, talking to the victim's neighbors, when we encountered a man who told us that around the time of the crime he had heard a woman screaming "for about twenty minutes."

Twenty minutes! It was probably to stifle those screams that the poor woman had been stabbed in the neck. Certainly a rescue effort could have been mounted in twenty minutes.

Although I already knew the answer, I asked our informant whether he had called 911.

"Well, no," he said, as if it made all the sense in the world. "I thought it was just a lovers' quarrel and so it was none of my business."

It took all my restraint not to shake him and say, "Listen, you jackass. Being killed by a lover gets you just as dead as any other corpse. Stabbing is still savage—a way no one ought to die—and, last I heard, killing a lover still counts as murder on this planet. And under what moral system could stopping a murder possibly be 'none of your business'?"

In any case, this killer was more likely a relative stranger rather than a lover or even an acquaintance, for despite fine policework, he was never found.

Because of the idiocy I encountered in these two cases—and so many others—the first thing I stress in my lectures on women and children's safety is, "If you are ever assaulted, never count on help!" Even direct onlookers may misjudge the situation or be too paralyzed to act—never mind those self-excusers lurking behind closed doors, unapologetically denying the evidence of their own ears while in possession of the most effortlessly wielded, superpowerful crimefighting weapon in existence: the phone.

Cops talk to each other, and apparently word was getting out that the Gruesome Twosome was worth consulting on certain crimes. I myself was getting something of a reputation as an interviewer, thanks in part to a lucky break. I was sitting in with the cops on an interview with a rape suspect who was proving too opaque to suss out. He was stonewalling his questioners, and I couldn't get a feel for what he was hiding or whether he even seemed capable of rape. Then a technique called "elicitation," which we were taught at Quantico, popped into my mind. So I just sprung it on him, as if it were a foregone conclusion: "Well, then, after you raped her what did you do?"

He came back, without missing a beat, "I went into the bathroom and took a piss."

"So that's where we'll find your fingerprints? On the bathroom wall—right?" I asked.

Realizing that he had just confessed, all he could say was, "Damn."

The detectives looked at me as if I had pulled a rabbit out of a hat. I shrugged—"elicitation" was nothing but the psych-major name for one of the oldest tricks in the book, and we all knew it. I had almost been embarrassed to give it a try. But it worked—to my surprise, the guy walked right into it. There was a DeLongism I invoked when criminals made such bungles, which happens more often than you might think: "Aren't You Glad They're Stupid?"

During our first year on the job, every consultation Dan and I got felt like a fresh vote of confidence. So it was professionally gratifying to get a call from the Western Springs chief of police, George Graves, who was tracking a serial rapist, much as it horrified me personally to learn that another serial rapist was at work in my own backyard. Western Springs was the town next to LaGrange, situated on the border of Cook and DuPage counties. I often detoured through it on my nightly jog, just to enjoy the architecture of its lovely homes. So it rankled all the more when I learned that the predator was targeting joggers. That hit me where I lived—figuratively, as well as literally—and I vowed that I would personally be the one to end this rapist's career.

The first of twenty reported attacks occurred at nine o'clock one night when a tall man wearing a hooded sweatshirt stepped out of the shadows to ask a passing female jogger the time. Startled, she pulled up short, and he grabbed her. She was able to wriggle out of his grasp and flee to a neighbor's house, where she called the police. She had looked him squarely in the face and was able to provide something of a description, but with the hood pulled tightly around his eyes, nose, and mouth, he had obscured his appearance enough to make him difficult to identify.

Over the next few months the offender approached five more joggers, all in their teens. Overall, about 22 percent of rape victims and 33 percent of sexual assault victims are thirteen- to seventeen-year-old girls. But this offender also, surprisingly, assailed a few boys, a kind of gender flip-flopping that is extremely peculiar. Pedophiles, who target children, often do not discriminate between the genders because prepubescent male and female bodies are fairly similar, but the vast majority of rapists of adults focus exclusively on one sex.

In all the attacks, he used the same modus operandi. He would approach his quarry, ask for the time, and pull a gun. He would then march his victim away from the houses to more secluded areas, where he would carry out the sexual assault. His boldness was astonishing, for he would pull his victims right off the sidewalk in mid-evening, in front of homes where the inhabitants were wide awake, and sometimes force himself on his victims in between houses that were barely ten feet apart. I wondered if he was on drugs, which were stoking his boldness, or whether for him the risk was part of the thrill.

He must have relied on the gun, possibly a toy, to keep his victims quiet, for he used little physical force or menacing, commanding, language. Because his behavior was so nonthreatening, I began to suspect that he was something of coward, an impression that seemed confirmed by the experience of his thirteenth victim, whom, probably unknowingly, he approached twice. He asked her the time, showing his gun, and she said, "Oh my God, it's you again!"

When he seemed nonplussed, she started scolding him. "What's *wrong* with you? Why are you doing these things? Why are you hurting people? I don't even believe that gun is real."

"Okay, lady, never mind," he replied sheepishly, then turned and ran away. The fact that he could not even muster an argument told us that he was probably of fairly low intelligence, with poor verbal skills and low self-confidence, and had no intention of using the gun, which might well have been fake. Still—much as I wanted to climb to the local water tower and scream to all the teenagers in Western Springs, "Hear ye, hear ye. This man is a chicken-shit wimp. You don't have to succumb to him! Resist!"—I must emphatically discourage anyone from ever chastising an assailant. In too many cases, provocation has resulted in a serious injury to the victim, as in the Burlington rapist case, or even gotten her killed. This one just happened to be very lucky.

The assailant's nonconfrontational behavior was an important factor in the profile I worked up with the BSU. He struck me as a "power-reassurance" rapist. His low verbal skills and lack of social confidence suggested that he was a high school dropout, which alone would make him stand out in a community where most high school students not only finished but went on to college. It would also make him fairly unemployable, and if he worked at all, it would be sporadically and in a low-level job. He knew the area well enough to commit nearly a score of assaults without being caught, though he sought his victims in populous areas, and within a small enough geographical range to suggest that he didn't own a car. Given the price of real estate in Western Springs and the surrounding suburbs, it was likely that he lived with a parent on whom he was financially dependent. I doubted that he was really a jogger because we knew from victim interviews that he was significantly overweight—beefy, with a sizable paunch—white, and between twenty and thirty years old.

We also suspected that he might be under treatment for a mental illness. As in the Burlington rapist case, I personally reinterviewed the victims of the man who was now known as the Hooded Jogger Rapist. Interviewing teenage sex crime victims can be dicey because, being minors, they usually have parents present and so often lie about their familiarity with sex. Very likely because I was a woman and a mother myself, I was often granted the privacy with victims that the cops had been denied. In this case, when the parents of a very young teenage girl let me talk to her alone, she confided a detail about the assault that she had not shared with the police.

Among other acts, her assailant had forced her to perform oral sex on him, and she said, "By the way, his semen tasted funny."

I was a little shocked that she would have much to compare it to—when I was her age, admittedly in a more innocent time, most girls didn't even know what semen was—but the information could be an important lead. So I suppressed my surprise and simply asked her, "What do you mean by 'funny'?"

"Well, it had a metallic taste to it," she said. "It wasn't milky or sort of bitter, like it usually is—you know . . ."

I was having trouble keeping a neutral expression on my face, but in fact I did know, as a nurse, that there are certain medications that can cause sweat, saliva, and other body fluids, including semen, to have a very salty/metallic taste. One of them was lithium, a drug used to treat manic-depressive illness. That opened up a whole new line of inquiry for us with local mental health clinics, where, of course, confidentiality laws would make it tough for us to get an actual name but where it couldn't hurt to sow some seeds. There was always a chance that someone might come forward with an anonymous tip that could steer us, if not directly to the perpetrator, at least somewhere in the right direction.

The fact was that someone, somewhere in Western Springs or in the neighboring towns, had to know this guy. With the assault toll approaching twenty, we felt compelled to be proactive and so embarked on a house-to-house canvass of the entire area—no small feat because the town of LaGrange alone had some 2,000 homes—in the hope that someone would recognize a few key elements from the profile and offer us a name. It was a technique that had worked in many other cases, notably the Sacramento Vampire Murders of a few years before. When the police had gone knocking on doors, asking if anyone knew a pale, emaciated, mentally ill loner in his mid-twenties, they were soon told, "Oh, that sounds just like Richard across the street." Bingo! He was the killer.

I felt in my heart that the profile held the key to this case, and indeed, even after talking to so many victims, we had precious little else to go on. The hood was an effective disguise for a man with relatively undistinguished facial features. I prayed that the profile would work; and meanwhile, being a jogger myself, night after night, I quietly patrolled the parts of town that had secluded crannies where a rapist might take cover, with my handcuffs in my pocket and my gun in an elastic bellyband at my waist—ready, even hoping to be stopped and asked the time. I wanted to be the one to bring him in.

One night a car pulled alongside me and honked. In it was Dave Lucas of the LaGrange Police, waving a copy of my profile.

"Hey, Candice," he called through the open window. "You don't have to catch your boyfriend all by yourself. Don't worry, we'll get him!"

I laughed. "Hey, Dave, I believe it—you're the best. But before you run him over, at least read him his rights."

As it turned out, Dave didn't run him over, but he did run into him. One Saturday afternoon while he was on patrol, he spotted a man who fit the descriptions of the rapist, as well as the profile. He was an overweight white male, who turned out to be twenty-seven years old, and during Dave's brief preliminary questioning, seemed to have very poor verbal skills. He agreed to let Dave bring him to the station for further questioning, photographs, and fingerprints.

It was clear to Dave that the suspect knew exactly why he was there and seemed neither surprised nor indignant when asked about his movements on the nights of the twenty attacks. But he steadfastly denied being in the vicinity of the crime scenes, and lacking the concrete evidence to hold him, Dave had to let him go while proceeding to run record checks and trying to confirm his alibis. The victims were shown his photograph but none could make a positive identification, agreeing only that "it definitely could be him"—which isn't good enough.

But Dave never got another chance to interrogate him. After his release, the suspect went home, doused himself with gasoline, and set himself ablaze.

Fire is a terrible way to die, one of the most agonizingly painful means imaginable of committing suicide. Choosing such a self-punishment seemed tantamount to a confession; and indeed, after that death, there were no more assaults by the Hooded Jogger Rapist. I've seen that kind of rough justice more than a few times in my career, when a perpetrator inflicts a far harsher sentence on himself than any that might be handed down by a judge and jury. Sometimes I get a twinge of compassion for the suspect in such cases—but only for the briefest instant, until I think about the legacy of shattered lives he leaves behind.

With every profile I did, I grew more convinced of the value of the tool in crimefighting. We made mistakes, of course. In one case, very early in my career, a nurse was murdered coming home from a party, and the police were confident that the boyfriend was responsible, though they had no proof. She had been raped, almost never the resort of someone sexually familiar with the victim, but I did not know this back in 1984 and allowed myself to be swayed by their estimation. Of course, they were wrong—the perpetrator was a stranger—and I never took that particular misstep again. We had been told at Quantico, "Once you have a suspect in mind, you're no longer doing a profile, you're doing a personality assessment"—meaning that objectivity is essential to developing a useful profile. (Profilers have been known to cheat, tailoring their findings to known suspects so they can look clairvoyant when the conviction comes down, but that's a fool's game and hard to pull off more than once or twice.) So I would tell the police, "If you've already got a strong suspect, I don't want to know. Let's do the workup first, and then we'll see about your suspect."

Whether on profiling cases or in my police-training lectures, I immensely enjoyed working with the cops. In those days, I would very often be the first female FBI agent they had ever seen. Early on, I discovered that cops love nurses—maybe it was because they spent more time, in the course of their work, in emergency rooms than FBI agents, or maybe they felt that nursing required the same idealism that had attracted most of them to law enforcement. Whatever the reason, when I came to spread the good news about profiling to a roomful of skeptical male cops—including the inevitable few who were thinking, *What the hell does this young girl think she can tell us?* for I never looked my age— I would mention my nursing background and faces would brighten. From then on I was well received.

Even in the Bureau, nursing stood me in good stead, especially during my rookie days. One night, we were out on a raid, and some of the guys were looking in a garage when the door came crashing down on somebody's head. He was knocked momentarily unconscious, and so I was hustled over to check him for signs of a concussion. I did a quick hand-squeeze, flashlight-in-the-eyes neurological exam, and it wowed them all.

Traditionally, there was fierce rivalry between the cops and the FBI, but the joint task forces being established in the early 1980s to combat such shared burdens as terrorism were beginning to allay it. Outreach programs like the one I was conducting, to promote the resources of the BSU, were also helping to heal the rift. But there was still plenty of residual resentment in the ranks, as I would discover one day when—despite my role as a Bureau goodwill emissary and strong contacts in the homicide squads of Greater Chicago—I wound up in jail.

I had gotten an urgent call from the Chicago police to come and interview the victim of an attempted rape, a woman who had been tied up and tortured. I was heading up Lake Shore Drive, doing maybe five miles over the limit, when suddenly behind me there were flashing red lights and a blaring siren. "Pull over!" came the voice over the bullhorn.

"Hi there," I greeted the cop who had stopped me, handing over my driver's license and credentials. "I'm with the FBI and I'm on the job."

He didn't acknowledge me as a sister in crimefighting. Instead he said officiously, "Your license is expired."

It was the day after my birthday, and it had slipped my mind that this was the year I had to renew. "Oh, right. Sorry," I replied. "But look, I'm on my way up to Area Five, homicide and sex crimes. I'm working a case with Detective John Smith."

"I don't care," he said.

"But it's a Chicago Police Department case," I informed him, certain that would set me free.

I wondered why he was even giving me an argument, for he must have known full well that as a government agent on duty, I didn't even need a license. Federal law supersedes state regulations. In case he really had some doubt about it, I asked him, more nicely than he deserved, to call his boss.

Instead, he put his hand on his gun. "Miss," he said, "the only call I've got to make right now is a judgment call—whether to put you in my squad car or let you follow me back to the station, since legally, you can't drive."

I could have radioed for help, but it galled me to need rescue, like a damsel in distress, from the clutches of a big, bad cop. I wasn't even a rookie but an agent of standing and experience, and it was embarrassing—which was exactly the point. Few cops would have dared put a male agent through such a humiliating charade. Still, I saw little choice but to follow him to the station and let him make a fool of himself trying to book me, if he bothered to take it that far. He didn't even try to confiscate my gun, which was really foolish, for he was sorely tempting me to use it.

At the station, the kindly, big, burly, red-haired desk sergeant urged my captor to let me go. "This is ridiculous," he told him.

"No way," the jerk insisted. "It's a solid collar—she was driving on an expired license."

Seeing that he was determined to push this to the limit, I asked the desk sergeant to call my office, figuring that the cop looked a lot more stupid than I did now. I had really expected him to have the sense to back off once he got the satisfaction of pulling me in. But no—he actually locked me in a cell, away from the other incarcerees, some of whom might be spurred to violence by a law enforcement officer in their midst. I guess that was his idea of a professional courtesy. I was wearing a turquoise suede jacket, which I turned inside out and rolled up to make a pillow before I flopped on the hard prison cot, waiting for the call that would spring me.

Until it did, the big goon kept bringing his buddies back, one by one, to look at me, like an animal in the zoo. "Check it out," he delighted in saying. "I busted an agent. Look at her—the fuckin' feebs."

I wanted to bark like a seal begging for a fish, just to mock them. But I resisted the impulse, deciding it was beneath my dignity. I was soon sprung, but the goon would go on to pull the same stunt with a black male agent. It was obvious that he had a classic "white guy" problem, but I wonder what he had against the FBI. Maybe he was John Dillinger in a past life.

10

THE BAD GUY

Seth was always, as many boys are, mesmerized by my gun. When he was little, it was easy to keep it out of his reach, but now that he was getting older, I couldn't just take out the bullets and stash it in my purse high on a closet shelf. Guns and burgeoning testosterone in the house just don't mix. I knew of a cop who locked up his gun in a safe one Sunday while he and his wife ducked out for an hour to go to church, leaving their thirteen-year-old son at home, playing with a friend. When they returned, they found both boys missing and a trail of blood leading from their bedroom to the front door. The safe was open; the gun, short one round, lay near it on the floor; and there was a bullet hole in the wall. Can you imagine the panic they must have felt?

The cop had rarely allowed his son to see the gun and never let him touch it—which, of course, is a red flag to many kids. Forbidding them something makes them all the more desperate to get hold of it. These boys were so determined to see the gun that they somehow engineered their way into the safe. There were no trigger locks in those days, and one of them accidentally fired the gun point-blank right into the other kid's face. Mercifully, the bullet caught the fleshy part of his cheek and exited behind his ear, lodging in the wall. Though he was bleeding profusely, the other boy managed to walk him to the local hospital. With less than an inch's worth of difference, he would have been killed.

So I never left a gun in the house when I wasn't there. I trusted Seth but I couldn't assume that his friends would behave responsibly if they were in my home with, say, a babysitter. And rather than try to quash Seth's fascination with guns, I decided to deal with it head on. I made a deal with him—if he wanted to see the gun, all he had to do was ask me. He could see it as often as he liked, but only in the house, of course, when we were alone, and he was never to touch it at any other time. He never violated that. I would take out the bullets and let him hold it, showing him how to ascertain whether it was loaded and how to handle it safely, explaining that loaded or not, it must never be pointed at anything irreplaceable and certainly never at any human being. He would take it in his hands and make a shooting sound with his mouth, "Cwoo, cwoo, cwoo."

I even took him out to the firing range at times when no one but the instructors would be there, to let him try shooting a gun at a target. He was pretty good, even as a young child—more than once he shot a tighter grouping of bullets in the silhouette on the target than I did. I didn't think of all this training as deprogramming, exactly, but that was the effect it had. He soon recognized that a gun wasn't some glamorous and exciting toy but a tool that required constant, disciplined drilling to use properly. To this day, he has an entirely sane view of weapons and, interestingly, having learned to shoot as a child, is as opposed to hand-guns and the NRA as any cop or agent I know.

Every parent wants to shield a child from the ugliness of the world, and I worked closer to its sordid underbelly than most. I did my best to insulate Seth, but when the rapists and killers I was profiling made the news, becoming the talk of the kids at school, I had to explain—and I tried to reassure him by telling him of the progress we were making toward catching those "bad guys." I didn't want him to grow up fearful.

His father accused me of promoting just that by making Seth "compulsive about door locking." "Nonsense—that's just good sense," I insisted. "I don't care where you live." You'd be amazed how many assailants simply waltz right into unsecured homes. If they try a door or a window and find it locked, they just move on to the house next door, until they finally hit on someone who is easy prey. It's often people's own carelessness and stupidity, more than the perspicacity of criminals,

that makes them victims. But his father was convinced that I was robbing
Seth of his innocence.

I certainly never dreamed that I might actually, inadvertently con-
tribute to his loss of innocence through my police training work. At the
time I was teaching police department classes on Interpersonal Violence,
which was the Bureau's more professional-sounding name for its sex
crimes course. Humor was an essential part of these classes, for not only
were the crime scene slides horrific, the subject matter was somewhat
embarrassing, even for jaded cops.

Some segments of the class were focused not on crimes, per se, but
on sexual predilections, including perversions. I would introduce this
topic with a glossary of the clinical and law enforcement terms for the
various acts, illustrated with slides. Rather than entertain cops with a
"porno show," as Roger Depue called the class in the bad old days, I
got my laughs with the bestiality photos. I would show a picture of a
man having sex with a horse or a naked woman lying on her back, trying
to wrap a large pig in a romantic embrace. Then I would tell the class
to raise their hands, asking, "Now, who can identify the horse's ass in
this shot?" or "So, all you city boys, which one is the pig here, the one
on the bottom or the one on top?"

One day I was clicking through my slides, and when I reached the
right slots, I began, "Okay, now here we have some depictions of bestiality . . ." but only the image of the guy with the horse popped up. I
moved the carousel back and forth a few notches but got nothing. Evidently the shot of the girl with the pig was out of place. Thinking
nothing of it, I made my joke about the horse's ass, drawing guffaws
from the class, and moved on.

The police classes ran from nine to five, and at the midafternoon
break, I would always call Seth, who would just be getting home from
school. That day, after the usual chat about homework and what time
I would be home, I heard an odd pause at the other end of the line.
Then Seth said, "Mom, I found this funny slide under the couch. There's
a girl on it, doing something with a pig."

I felt blood surge into my face, and I am sure that I flushed beet red.
"Well, uh, why don't you, uh, just leave it there, right on the floor for

Mommy," I stammered. "Don't even pick it up. You hear me, Seth? Just leave it there."

I had no idea whether he could even guess what the slide was all about, and I prayed that he was still naïve enough to be confused.

Then he said, "It looks like she's trying to have sex with that pig."

Sex! I found myself cackling nervously. Good Lord, he did know. What kind of psychological damage had I just inflicted? I replayed his words in my mind, mentally checking their tone for any coloration of horror.

"Mom . . . ," Seth repeated, puzzled by my silence. "It looked like she was having—"

"I heard you, Seth," I quickly said, loath to hear his child's voice pronounce the words *sex with that pig* again. "Tell you what, just wait till I get home and we'll talk about it."

I wasn't going to lie to Seth about something like this—even if I could have concocted a credible story about the pig—but this was one parental talk that was going to take some rehearsing. It wasn't until I returned to the roomful of cops that it struck me that the babysitter might have been listening—maybe she'd even discovered Seth looking at the slide and had already reported me to the police. Today, surely I'd have been turned in to Child Protective Services. And what about my ex? If we were fighting about door locking, what would he make of sex-with-animals slides? This was definitely the kind of complaint that led to custody battles.

But even without my telling him, Seth seemed to intuit that this wasn't the kind of discovery to blabber about to his schoolmates or to his father. If the babysitter heard him on the phone, she never let on. And when we talked about the slide, Seth didn't seem traumatized but just giggled, finding the very idea of sex with an animal too silly for words. Thank God it hadn't been a crime scene slide. I was amazed and grateful at the maturity with which he took the experience in stride— and I was proud of him too. But from then on, I prepared my lectures in the office, never again at home.

Today Seth tells me that around this time I had periodic spells of rather overwrought protectiveness. Worried about his father's seemingly lackadaisical attitude, I urged him to lock doors with the story of a woman who took her laundry down to the basement, leaving the screen door unlatched (not that latching a mere screen would be sufficient, I explained), and came back up to find her killer waiting at the top of the stairs. I cautioned him about talking to strangers, even men who looked nonthreatening, with the story of Ted Bundy lulling his victims with a cast on his arm. I told him of a child who was dragged from a mall by an assailant and was later found decapitated in a ditch, but who never screamed out, even in a crowd, because his parents taught him to respect adults—any adult—too much. "So when you're around people, scream like hell," I told him. "Make eye contact with individuals, not the whole mass, who can retreat into anonymity, and beg those people, individually, 'Call nine-one-one!' "

And if a plainclothes cop ever flashed a badge and ordered him to come along, he was to refuse until the "cop" called me—his FBI agent mother—or radioed it in and he clearly heard the police dispatcher talking. Should someone he knew importune him, and for some reason he couldn't get to me, his father, or his sitter, he was to go directly to his school principal or to the police station. I even encouraged him to pass on these cautions to his friends, which he says he did, and luckily no parent ever complained.

Not that I was wrong, but in retrospect my warnings sound quite terrifying. Seth says that I made him realistic about the world, not unduly fearful, which seems true, for he is a fine, confident young man teaching and studying for his Ph.D. in political science—and I hope it is. Sometimes he tells me with exasperation of the foolish chances he sees other students taking, like running alone late at night, in deserted areas, with headphones on. Certainly that seems reckless at best these days, but there was plenty to be terrified about back when he was young too.

What had me so anxious about Seth were the cases I was getting involving children. According to Department of Justice statistics, some 34 percent of all sexual assaults involve children under the age of twelve (14 percent being under the age of six), roughly 70 percent of whom are girls and 30 percent are boys. Ninety percent of them knew their attackers, about half of whom were family members. Almost 15 percent of all sexual assault murders involve children under the age of twelve.

Nothing ever prepares you for the horror of such crimes, and the revulsion stays with you even after you've swept the vermin who commit them off the streets. They haunt you forever.

Melissa and Louise,* eight years old, lived in the sleepy rural Illinois town of Somonauk, about seventy miles southwest of Chicago. They were best friends and even looked alike, with dark brown hair and huge moppet eyes. One summer Sunday, they took a bike ride and stopped to chase butterflies by the side of a country road. A blue Gremlin hatchback passed them twice, then circled back and parked. A man got out and asked, "Which way is town?"

That frightened Louise, who had learned in "Stranger Danger" class in school that adults who asked children for directions were probably up to no good. Pointing wordlessly toward town, the girls backed away from the man—but not far enough. Suddenly he lunged forward and seized Louise around her tiny waist. With a few long strides, he reached his car and, dumping her in, commanded, "You stay there." He then went chasing after Melissa, which gave Louise the chance to scramble out an open window. Knowing she could never outrun the man, she hid behind a parked tractor. When she finally heard the car pull away, she peeked out. Melissa was gone.

Louise raced home on her bike to tell her parents, who called the police. An APB (all points bulletin) was immediately issued for the blue Gremlin with a dent in the driver's door that Louise had described. About an hour later, a county sheriff's deputy spied a blue Gremlin at a gas station in Mendota, a few miles from Somonauk. The driver claimed to have forgotten his license, offering his fishing license as identification instead. His name was Brian Dugan.

The deputy asked if he could examine the car, explaining that he was looking for a missing little girl, and was granted permission. But he found no trace of a child in the car. Feeling that he didn't have cause to hold Dugan—despite the fact that he was driving without a license—the deputy let him go.

Meanwhile, the Somonauk police department, which had only three officers, one for each eight-hour shift, called in the FBI and the LaSalle and DeKalb County Sheriff's Departments. The next day, thirty agents arrived in Somonauk, soon to be followed by thirty more—totaling one-fifth of the Bureau's Chicago division—to join the local and county authorities in one of the largest search efforts in Illinois history.

Assistant Special Agent in Charge Mike Wilson headed up the investigation, and Gerry Miller, a twenty-year Bureau veteran, took up the reins as case agent, working hand in hand with Tom Templeton of the LaSalle County Sheriff's Department. Because of my profiling school training on crimes against children and my background as a psych nurse, I was teamed with Jim and Joe, the two agents who had been assigned to Louise.

The investigators focused almost immediately on Brian Dugan, finding it too coincidental that a man so closely matching Louise's description, who happened to drive a blue Gremlin, should turn up in the area so soon after the abduction. When they discovered that his "forgotten" license was in fact suspended, they placed him under surveillance and were soon able to pick him up for driving illegally. It was a minor charge but it would get him off the street, at least, while they determined what had happened to Melissa.

A command post was set up at the local Catholic church rectory, a huge room where thirty new phone lines were installed. Or at least the room seemed huge until the Bureau investigators, computer operators, stenographers, dog handlers, search-and-rescue teams, topography experts, reconnaissance pilots, and even a media representative to handle the press, crowded into it. Local volunteers pitched in to support our staff and also joined the search parties, which were walking mapped-out grids of the farmland within a fifteen-mile radius of Somonauk. A plane, equipped for infrared photography, surveyed a broad area beyond the range of the ground search. But there was no trace of Melissa.

Her poor parents were always at the command post, hoping and praying for news. I could hardly bear to look at them when I was there, working or grabbing a bite from the lavish buffet of home-cooked meals that local ladies dedicated to the search effort. Cooking made them feel less helpless, and I often wished that my own contribution could be that concrete, to counteract my feelings of powerless frustration as the days passed without a break.

Every night when I got home, I hugged Seth so hard and long that he squirmed with annoyance. At first, not wanting to scare him, I told him nothing about the case except that we were looking for a little girl who was lost. So he would ask me, "Did you find the little girl today?" I would have to fight back tears when I told him "No, not yet."

Finally the day came when I couldn't hide the truth from him anymore. The abduction was front-page news in every newspaper in Illinois and in the surrounding states, all the way down to Kentucky 500 miles away, and was the lead story on every radio and television newscast. But thanks to the media blitz, we got another important lead. A young woman came forward to tell us that she had been overpowered on the street, taken to a wooded area, and raped, just days before Melissa's abduction. Her attacker had told her the name of the high school he had attended before he dropped out, and he had introduced himself as Brian Dugan. He had been driving a blue Gremlin.

She picked Dugan out of a lineup with no hesitation. Charged with rape, Dugan was held without bail as we worked feverishly to connect him to Melissa's kidnapping. As it turned out, that rape was just one of several in a spree that Dugan embarked on during a vacation from his factory job. After smoking marijuana and drinking beer in his boarding-house room in Aurora, thirty miles from Somonauk, Dugan had spent his vacation nights hunting for teenage girls. According to George Muller, LaSalle County's chief public defender, "He didn't do well on marijuana. Almost every crime he committed was while on some kind of substance abuse."

Dugan would later tell investigators that he had spotted a female jogger and, deciding to "get her," made a U-turn. But before he reached her, she turned into her driveway. Foiled, he headed back toward Somonauk and on the way came across Melissa and Louise.

Dugan had done nine months in the DuPage County jail for burglary, but had never before been charged with a sex-related crime. He was not one of the 225 registered sex offenders who lived—or so I was told—in or around Somonauk, a town of only 2,500 people! Today, under Megan's Law, their fellow citizens would have known that nearly 10 percent of the population had been convicted of sexual assault—and surely would have raised a tremendous hue and cry. How such a high concentration of sexual criminals wound up in rural Illinois is anybody's guess.

Now Jim and Joe faced the heartbreaking task of preparing Louise to confront her attacker again, through a one-way mirror, in a lineup. Her parents must have agonized long and hard about their decision to permit it. Throughout the investigation—unlike many children in her position who would have retreated into a shell, some irretrievably—Louise had insisted that she wanted to help. Her parents allowed it, fearful as they were about her emotional state, for to deny her might have suggested that there was something shameful about her actions or stoked her imagination with even worse fears. When you shut children out, what they conjure up in their minds is often much more horrific than what you are hoping to protect them from—not that much could be more horrific than what had already befallen Louise. But to come face-to-face with the assailant who had kidnapped Melissa would very likely be more traumatic than any other help Louise had already given us.

I was told that she sat quietly as the "suspects" filed in, each labeled with a number. A lot of children would have picked out someone, anyone, just to please her parents and the investigators, but Louise had more maturity than that. After studying them carefully, she said gravely, in her small voice, that she couldn't say for sure. Small wonder, since the clean-cut young man with his hair slicked back, wearing an orange prison jumpsuit, must have looked infinitely different from the bare-chested, sweaty, shaggy-haired, half-stoned, menacing man who had come after the girls. I still maintain that if the men in the lineup had come out bare-chested, in jeans, and then shaking their hair, had said, angrily and authoritatively, "You stay there," she would have picked Dugan out in a heartbeat. We all felt in our bones that he was the one.

Some two weeks after the abduction, Melissa's body was finally found. A sheriff's deputy got a nagging hunch that he should return to a place he had already searched, a small grove of oaks standing in an open field about a hundred yards from the road. A stream ran through there, choked with tall grasses and spanned by a small footbridge. It was there in the stream, her feet barely visible under the bridge, that he found Melissa.

Sometimes people do get uncanny flashes like that, which look almost clairvoyant. This deputy got out of his cruiser and, without even having to do much poking around, walked straight to the site. Some of my colleagues said, only half-jokingly, that the deputy should be compelled to take a polygraph test. It is not unheard of or even very unusual for a killer to insinuate himself into the search for a victim and to be the one to turn up the body, seemingly fortuitously, because he put it there.

Louise would have to be told of Melissa's death before the media got wind of the fact that the body had been discovered. Jim, Joe, and I talked over the prospect with Louise's parents, who were distraught at the news. How do you explain any death to a child in a way that can ease the pain of grievous loss, never mind a death at the hands of a monster who was already certain to haunt her dreams for the rest of her life? "Does religion have a place in Louise's life?" I asked. "Could that be a comforting way to interpret it for her?"

"Oh yes," her mother said. "Louise believes deeply in God."

We decided that we should couch the news in those terms. Louise's parents thought it might be least traumatic if they comforted Louise while one of us delivered the devastating message. Jim volunteered to be the one.

As Louise sat cradled on her mother's lap, Jim, a great Papa Bear of a man, knelt before her, taking her frail, tiny hands into his huge ones.

"Louise"—his voice cracked—"we found Melissa and . . . she's no longer with us."

Holding Jim's eyes, Louise asked sadly, sensing the truth, "Where did she go, Jim?"

"Well, God decided to take Melissa to heaven to get her away from that bad guy. He took her to heaven to be with Him," he said gently.

She said nothing at first. All the adults were stifling sobs, and I had to press my hand to my lips to keep them steady. I was flooded with grief and profoundly moved by the dignified sorrow of that little girl.

When she finally spoke, all Louise said, heavy-heartedly, without tears, was: "But, Jim, why didn't He take the bad guy?"

•   •   •

The FBI laboratory found hairs and fibers in Dugan's car and in the sleeping bag, proving that Melissa had been there. But it was not our case to prosecute. Since the body was found in Illinois, where the kidnapping took place, there was no longer a presumption that state lines had been crossed and so the Feds no longer had jurisdiction. To avoid going to trial, which might lead to the death penalty, Dugan cut a deal with the state that involved confessing to another murder.

A year or so before, Dugan had gone to a party, where he spotted an attractive twenty-seven-year-old woman named Donna, who was a nurse. She left for home about three in the morning, and he followed, pulling up alongside her car and trying to run it off the road. The next day the car was found parked on the shoulder with the keys in the ignition and the passenger door standing open. Beside it on the ground were Donna's purse and intact wallet, which ruled out robbery as a motive for the attack. Investigators surmised that the assailant had blocked the driver's side of her car with his own to trap her inside, then had come around to the passenger's door, demanding that she open it. When she did—there was no sign of forced entry—he reached in, and pulled her out.

Tragically, Donna must have been too frightened to recognize that her car was, in effect, a 2,000-pound weapon. As I tell my women's safety classes, if you are approached on the road, no matter what an attacker says—even if he threatens to shoot you through the window— never open the door or get out of the car. Quickly pick your best escape route, which might be behind you, and then step on the gas! Your chances of escape are far better in your car than on foot, when you may be easily overpowered.

Donna's body was later found three miles away, floating in a quarry lake. Dugan would tell prosecutors, "I pulled her forward and she lost her balance. I held her under water one or two minutes until she stopped struggling." She had been sexually assaulted and beaten before she was drowned.

It is still hard for me to accept that the state took Dugan's deal. "A bird in the hand is worth two in the bush," my colleagues told me. "The plea bargain at least ensures that he'll be locked up for life. You never know what a jury will do." Capricious as I know our legal system can be, that may be true—but it pains me that any slack at all would be accorded a vicious two-time rapist/killer, especially when one of his victims was a child.

This would be not be the last anyone heard of Brian Dugan. Less than a year later, he confessed to yet another murder, of a ten-year-old girl named Jeanine Nicarico, who had lived in Naperville, an affluent suburb of Chicago. She was home from school with a minor ailment, and her mother, who worked only a mile away, had just left the house minutes before, having come home on her lunch hour to check on her daughter. She had scolded Jeanine for letting in a utility man that morning, so when a knock came on the door, Jeanine answered but refused to open it. But that didn't stop the assailant, who kicked in the door and grabbed her. A few days later her body was found in a wooded area a few miles away. Her skull was crushed, and she had been sexually assaulted.

It all began, from what investigators could piece together, when Dugan's girlfriend tried to break up with him. After his release from prison on the burglary charge, he had met the girl of his dreams, a sixteen-year-old high school student named Annette.* Though he was twenty-six at the time, her parents accepted him and even allowed him to move into their basement. But Annette started resenting Dugan's controlling brand of love and wanted to end the relationship. Dugan was casing a Naperville neighborhood for burglary prospects, feeling angry and vengeful toward Annette, when he happened upon Jeanine Nicarico.

There was one big problem with Brian Dugan's confession to the murder of Jeanine Nicarico: Two men had already been convicted of the crime and were now on death row, awaiting execution. Dugan told prosecutors he would confess to the crime under oath, at trial, to free these men but only if guaranteed that he himself would be spared the death penalty.

What would motivate a prisoner to confess to a murder for which he was not even a suspect, for which others were already paying the price? Not altruism, exactly. It is possible that he thought it would enhance his status in prison—since he would be stuck there for the rest of his life— where child killers are reviled and shunned by other inmates, so many of whom were themselves abused as children. Just to cite one example I've heard, every prisoner in America knew of Richard Allen Davis, who in 1993 snatched twelve-year-old Polly Klaas from her Petaluma, California, home in front of two friends, who were sleeping over, and with her mother slumbering in the next room. He raped and strangled Polly, then had the temerity, just as his death sentence was being read, to turn to the girl's grieving father and contemptuously flip him the "double bird," two upthrust middle fingers. While in prison, he was allowed into the exercise yard with another inmate, to whom he swaggered over and said, with braggadocio in his voice, "Hi! I'm Richard Allen Davis."

To which his fellow inmate responded, "Hi, I'm Polly Klaas!" and knocked him out cold with one punch.

So Brian Dugan may have hoped that confessing and thereby springing two men from death row would make him a hero in prison. It's possible—but though the FBI was no longer involved in the case, a number of us continued to follow it intently, and I, among others, believed that Dugan was telling the truth. Dugan described the victim's home with incredible accuracy, right down to the pattern on the linoleum floor, the type of indoor/outdoor carpeting on the steps, and the design on the dish towel used to blindfold and gag Jeanine. The only thing he did not get right was the exact position of her body when it was dumped in the forest preserve. Skeptics saw this discrepancy as "proof" that Dugan was lying. Among them, apparently, were the prosecutors, who refused to accept Dugan's offer of sworn testimony in exchange for immunity from the death penalty.

The confession was enough to reopen the cases of the two defendants on death row, Alejandro Hernandez and Rolando Cruz. They had been convicted on largely circumstantial evidence in the midst of a firestorm of outrage—when a child is killed, the public wants the killer to be found and punished, fast. The pressure on law enforcement officials to come up with a suspect is intense; and juries, repelled by the crime, tend to convict whoever winds up at the defendant's table in the courtroom. It probably didn't help that Jeanine Nicarico lived in an upscale, predominantly white suburb and that Hernandez and Cruz were Hispanic.

Commander Ed Cisowski of the Illinois state police, whom I'd met during the Tylenol murder case, had been assigned the task of checking into Dugan's confession. He was a tough-minded, thoroughgoing, dogged investigator of incredible drive, but he couldn't seem to catch a break. He managed to recover the car Dugan said he had used in the Nicarico kidnapping, which was a perfect match for the one witnesses described, right down to its missing hubcap. But by the time Cisowski found the car, it had been washed so many times that no trace of evidence remained. Cisowski also tracked down Annette's mother and asked whether she had come across a tire iron—the murder weapon, Dugan claimed—that he had stashed behind Annette's parents' furnace. She recalled seeing it once, and Cisowksi's hopes rose, for there was a chance it might still bear fingerprints and traces of Jeanine's blood. But then she went on to say that during a rainstorm her basement had flooded and was now completely refurbished, with the waterlogged flooring torn out and a new furnace installed. The tire iron was nowhere to be found. The investigators even had Jeanine's body exhumed, in the hopes that further tests might yield a link to Dugan—with no luck.

For his pains, Cisowski would catch flak from Jeanine Nicarico's parents, in the form of a press conference at which they accused him of such improprieties as supplying Dugan with information to bolster his case. Their pain at seeing the case reopened and having to relive the nightmare must have been profound. Cisowski underwent a two-year investigation and was finally completely cleared.

Hernandez and Cruz were retried in new venues and reconvicted. It looked like Dugan's testimony was the only thing that might sway a jury in their favor. But he remained adamant that he would not talk without a deal, and the prosecutors stuck to their guns, refusing to ensure that he would be spared capital punishment. Some saw an element of self-interest in their refusal to deal—believing that with Hernandez and Cruz on the hook, the prosecutors didn't want the boat rocked, especially not in the absence of concrete evidence. Later, the DuPage Seven, as a group of investigators and prosecutors would come to be known, would actually be indicted on perjury, obstruction of justice, and official misconduct charges. They were acquitted, but Cruz later filed a civil suit that resulted in a $3.5 million settlement for the defendants.

Years passed, during which a handful of investigators and journalists continued to work tirelessly to establish Dugan's guilt in the Nicarico case. Eventually they won a new trial for Hernandez and Cruz—and this time, having served thirteen years in prison, the two were acquitted. Dugan has never been charged with the abduction and murder of Jeanine Nicarico, but in the minds of many, the case is "solved."

I wonder how the poor parents of Melissa Ackerman and Jeanine Nicarico ever managed to recover from their terrible losses. It seems impossible, but people do—the human spirit is more resilient than any rubber band—even finding the generosity to help others bear their suffering. Among those who have become advocates are Mark Klaas, Polly's father, who established the Klaas Foundation, as its Web site claims, to "stop crimes against children." John Walsh, the host of *America's Most Wanted,* lost his son in a kidnap-murder and went on to found the National Center for Missing and Exploited Children. There's real heroism in that.

Throughout the Melissa Ackerman case and long after it ended, I kept thinking of that bumper sticker on the wall at Quantico, in the office of a profiler who had seen far more of these harrowing murders than I had: IF YOU LOVE YOUR CHILDREN, NEVER LET THEM OUT OF YOUR SIGHT. During the time when Seth was in school, I let my mental guard down, but between three o'clock, when he got out, and five or six, when I got home from work, I felt hyperattuned, as if I were tracking him with a kind of mother's sonar, trying to sense whether there were any danger vibes around him. Like everything else, this became fodder for jokes at work. "Uh-oh, Mommy's antenna's up," the guys would tease. "Better put out that smoke, better hide that girlie magazine."

They knew that I would talk to Seth every day at three, either at home or at a friend's house, from which he would call me. So one of them would say, "Hey, DeLong, I talked to Seth. Everything's fine. But you're going to need a new microwave." Or, "The fire department called. They rescued Seth and they're taking him for ice cream. And don't worry—they got the cats out too."

"Very damn funny," I would reply.

11

COCAINE COWBOYS

For the fifty years that J. Edgar Hoover headed the FBI, he kept the Bureau out of the war on drugs. Legend has it that he considered the drug business to be so dirty and potentially corrupting that he was loath to put his agents, who were always to be above reproach, in temptation's way. His immediate successors upheld that policy until 1982, when the cocaine trade in the United States had ballooned into such a vast and sprawling business, with octopuslike reach into so many areas of the Bureau's oversight, from kidnapping and money laundering to organized crime, that it could no longer be ignored. But at street level, agents who had been schooled to think of themselves as above the chaotic fray of drug investigations deeply resented the new policy and resisted mightily when conscripted for the newly forming drug squads. So in Chicago in the late 1980s, the word came down from on high that every squad had to come up with a few lambs to sacrifice to the cause.

I probably looked more expendable than most because I was only a half member of the applicant squad, with the rest of my time dedicated to profiling and police training efforts that had still not attained the full legitimacy that they have today. So I was tapped and told to report for duty the following Monday on the squad that was concentrating on the Mexican connection. There was a drug pipeline that stretched from Colombia, which was the cocaine capital of the hemisphere, up through

Mexico into Texas, and from there to Chicago, which had a large Mexican population that dealers could blend into, and was a well-placed hub for distribution of drugs throughout the Midwest.

When I arrived at my new post, I was astonished to see that with less than ten years in the Bureau, I was one of the senior members of the squad. Clearly the more seasoned veterans were managing to wiggle out of drug duty. I was also the first female agent on the squad, and my presence did not sit well with the squad secretary. As in every other business, secretaries had an ambivalent relationship with the workforce, since their first loyalty was to the supervisor, for whom many of them were the eyes and ears. But in the FBI there was sometimes an extra level of complication. Many of the secretaries, invariably female, were troupers from the Hoover era, when there were no women agents. So they would sometimes be pressed into double duty—one day typing letters and answering phones and the next attending a mob function as an investigator's date or pushing a baby carriage full of money through a park, waiting for an extortionist to make his move. That kind of excitement was one of the perks of the job, which was snatched away from the secretaries once there were female agents to play those roles. Of course, many secretaries applied for admission to the Academy, but most didn't make the cut—and now and then, you'd come across one who was still nursing a grudge.

Once I got past that obstacle, I met my new supervisor, who directed me to check in with an agent I would nickname the Whelp, who had just caught a big drug case and was overwhelmed with work. The Whelp was fresh out of the Academy, with six or seven months on the job, and obviously thrilled that he had happened to reel in a promising informant. "I've got the ticket on the biggest case on the squad," he told me. "Lot of offenders, lots of dope."

He then handed me a five-inch stack of phone records and told me to enter them in the computer, which would analyze them for patterns. "This phone search could break the case wide open," he declared. "Your role here is critical."

You self-important little brat, I thought. Asking a squad member obviously many years his senior, new or not, to do his scut work—and with a transparently patronizing pep talk, no less, on how it was "critical"— was positively brazen. Who did he think he was kidding?

In case I hadn't reached the right conclusion on my own, behind him, two of my new squadmates started sticking out their tongues and crossing their eyes. One of them stood up and, crisscrossing his hands in front of him, shook his head, mouthing, "No, no," then twirled a finger at his temple to signal "He's out of his mind." The message was loud and clear: This arrogant kid had already alienated everyone on the squad, and what he was billing as a major case was, in fact, small potatoes.

I was about to march in to my supervisor to complain when I spotted him standing at his office door, observing my interaction with the Whelp—and, to my disgust, smirking approvingly. Every time I started to feel secure in my job, with a network of trusted colleagues both inside and outside the Bureau, including Chicago cops, I seemed to trip over a rock and turn up one of these worms. Clearly I'd get no help there.

Since it was my first day, I didn't see much choice but to swallow my pride and do the job. Soon, when I figured out what the drug scene was all about, I'd be pulling my own cases out of the hat. There is a measure of boring clerical work in every drug case, mostly checking phone records. When a suspect was arrested in a drug case, we would get a court order to allow us to examine his telephone records in hopes of finding correlations that might lead us to his drug supplier or even higher. In those days, cell phones had just come onto the market, and drug dealers were among the first to take advantage of the new technology. For a while, the word on the street was that calls made from cell phones were harder to trace than those made over conventional phone lines, which was completely untrue. But cell phones did offer the advantage of being more disposable than fixed telephones, so to throw the authorities off their scent dealers would change their cell phones every month. They did create a vastly greater workload for us—more court orders, infinitely more numbers to be input by hand for computer analysis. Mercifully, with today's telephone technology, the process is much easier.

No one was more relieved than I was when we finally got a break in the case that would get us out of the office. The informant had set up a meeting with a high level drug dealer and was to go in wired, under our surveillance, after which we'd move in for the arrest. We expected a decent score. Consumer-level drug dealing was the responsibility of the police, for whom a kilo or two was a fine catch. But since the Bureau only got involved with drug deals that intersected our areas of broader oversight, such as interstate commerce, the fish we caught tended to be bigger and the scores larger—often hundreds of kilos.

The Whelp was bursting with self-congratulation as he gave us our assignments. He handed me a slip of paper. "Candice, go to this address and wait there for further orders," he told me.

"Where is it that I'm going?" I asked.

"It's the informant's house. You'll be told what to do when you get there."

I was delighted to receive what seemed like an important assignment—maybe I would even be the one to drive the informant to the meeting. I regretted the dark thoughts I'd had about the Whelp and the times my colleagues and I had laughed at him behind his back. Assured that there was nothing I needed to bring, I set off for the address, which turned out to be a high-rise on the near West Side.

An Asian man in his thirties answered the door. We introduced ourselves and then he showed me into the living room, telling me to make myself comfortable on the couch.

"I don't think there's time for that," I said. I hadn't been told to bring a body recorder, so I figured he still needed to get wired up. "Isn't the meeting pretty soon?"

"Right, okay," he replied. He handed me a folded paper and then started to walk out the door.

"Whoa, wait a minute," I protested. "Let me go first."

"You can't come with me," he said, sounding surprised. "Everything is right there on the paper."

He was gone by the time I got it open. It said, in effect, that I should wake the baby if he wasn't up by 4:30 and that his bottle was in the refrigerator. My role in the bust was to babysit for the informant's kid.

Needless to say, I was livid. If it hadn't meant abandoning a helpless child I would have been out of there. As it was, I had to sit there stewing until he returned—just a few hours, luckily—before heading back to the office to exact my revenge.

When I walked into the squad area, the Whelp and his cronies burst out laughing. It was pull-the-girls' pigtails time at the nursery school.

"You useless little piece of shit," I couldn't help saying, much as I hated to give them the satisfaction of seeing me angry. "I will never, ever work with you again."

I went in to my squad leader, only to find him chuckling too. "Come on, Candice, it was just a joke," he said. "Be a good sport."

Some joke. Today no one could pull a stunt like that at any government agency, and no supervisor could laugh it off. Even back then I could have filed a complaint. I know plenty of women who would have, and who can blame them? But women who did were branded tattletales, troublemakers, and women "on the rag." That wasn't how I wanted to be known. So far, I had always fought my own battles on the job, and I planned to now, the same way I always had—by taking the initiative and developing my own cases, so I wouldn't be at the mercy of swell-headed kids like the Whelp.

In the meantime, I found myself some new allies. One was a new female agent on the squad, who was nicknamed the Ice Woman, because with her long, lean, blond good looks, she could have passed for a fashion model from some frigid Nordic land. But her personality was more spirited and adventurous than chilly. Just out of the Academy, she had the same wide-eyed enthusiasm and eagerness to please that I'd had as a fledgling agent. The guys were taking advantage of it, essentially using her as a secretary. So I took her under my wing, warning her, "Don't let them do that. They'll make you a doormat if you give them half a chance."

My other allies were on a different squad, which had its cluster of desks a few yards away from ours. But they were different in another way too—they weren't FBI but were agents of the DEA. The DEA was on the floors below us in the federal building, and that year the brass decided that we should work together as a task force, with agents from both groups on the same squads. It was like trying to mix oil and water. As I heard one FBI agent snipe: "DEA—doesn't that stand for 'Don't Expect Anything'? Or is it 'Drunk Every Afternoon'?"

The DEA agent shot back: "FBI—doesn't that stand for 'Famous but Incompetent'?"

But the conflict ran deeper than just my-badge-is-bigger-than-your-badge competition. There were major cultural differences between the agencies, which had long been highly suspicious of each other. Unlike the FBI, which required applicants to have both a college degree and some kind of managerial work experience or an advanced degree in law, accounting, or computer science, the DEA took its agents right out of college. They would work only a few violations, primarily drug offenses and money laundering, while the FBI worked more than two hundred different crimes. They even dressed differently, tending more to jeans and leather jackets—street fashions—than to the FBI's suits and ties. So FBI agents felt superior and looked on their counterparts in the DEA as cowboys—reckless gunslingers, constantly in shoot-outs, immersed in a brutish underworld—while DEA guys regarded FBI agents as effete, desk-bound "sissies." The FBI's attitude toward the interlopers, even among some of the squad leaders, was, "Don't talk to the DEA guys. Don't work with them. We don't want them here, and if we freeze them out, maybe they'll go away."

But I found the DEA training course impressive. After half a century of working drugs, the agency obviously knew the business inside out—better than we did then, having come so recently to the field. Unlike the male agents, many of whom were threatened by the DEA guys' more-macho-than-thou swaggering, I was attracted, not repelled, by a little swashbuckling flair. And like the cops I had worked with, for the most part they did not see themselves as playing on the same field as female FBI agents and so were inclined to think of us as an interesting and potentially advantageous novelty. There were a few jerks, of course, but overall I found the DEA agents welcoming and open to working with women and less likely to put us through the girls-have-to-prove-themselves rituals than some of my own male colleagues.

I encountered two new DEA pals my very first day of working drugs. One, Tony Ryan, was about twenty-five, nice-looking in an Irish way, and though not much taller than me, was like a sparkplug carved out of solid moxie. He had a *Miami Vice* wardrobe—deck shoes without socks, skinny leather ties—and more mouth on him than virtually anyone on the floor. His profanities, especially about drug dealers—"those fucking jackoffs"—would echo throughout our squad area. He was hilarious and great fun.

Tony's partner, Rick Barrett, was closer to my age and a fifteen-year DEA veteran. Born into a Chicago cop family, he had recently returned to the city after three years in Paris, where he had been working drugs with Interpol, as well as law-enforcement groups from various European countries. With his impenetrable calm and deep, gravelly voice, he was like the opposite of Tony, though also very funny in a more subtle, clever way—and tough to the bone.

So I was thrilled when Tony and Rick asked me to come along as a "date" on an undercover intelligence-gathering mission at a nightclub and recruited the Ice Woman to make up the fourth member of our team. She was surprised, having already been indoctrinated with the us-against-them attitude of the squad. "Are you really going to work with them?" she asked. "I hear that those guys are bad news."

"Sure, I am," I told her. "We're supposed to be working drugs, and these are the guys who really know the ropes. Why not?"

But the rivalry between the agencies was such that even my supervisor took a dim view of the plan, especially when I told him that the Ice Woman and I needed the afternoon off to shop for nightclubbing attire. With so few women around, however, he could hardly refuse to let them borrow us, even though we would be fraternizing with the enemy.

So that night, the Ice Woman and I—wearing a silk slip dress and a skin-tight black spandex tube, respectively—met up with Rick and Tony at Binyon's, a famous federal watering hole that was hidden down a dark alleyway, a stone's throw from the Loop. I had never been there before, for it was more of a hangout for the brass than for mere mortal street agents. Finding my way to the door of Binyon's in the gloom of the alley, where I could almost imagine the fog of Dickensian London rising from the cobblestones, set a cloak-and-dagger tone for the evening, which intensified as I moved incognito among the judges and prosecutors I recognized from the courts. Rick introduced me to John

Peoples, the second in command of the Chicago DEA, who was an old friend of his, and I spotted some of the Bureau's top guns, my uber-bosses, bellying up to the bar.

From there we grabbed a cab to the hottest nightclub in the city, where Rick's informant was going to introduce us to some high-level dealers. Outside, an FBI surveillance team would be standing watch, for agents working drugs never meet contacts alone. The reason is that the drug world is an ultravolatile criminal environment—far more than old-fashioned organized crime, with its careful apportionment of turf, strong lines of allegiances, and internal policing mechanisms. The Mafia has traditionally been more focused on running businesses and establishing rackets—prostitution, extortion, and the like—that bring in a steady income over time than on making quick, huge scores. But in the drug world, obscenely large sums of money are always changing hands in individual transactions, so the risk of a rip-off—a buyer or a seller simply blowing away the other party and making off with both the money and the drugs—is very great.

Then too, drug dealers are more likely than other criminals to try to shoot their way out of arrest situations. The federal government has established a mandatory minimum twenty-year prison sentence for any-one caught with ten or more kilograms of cocaine (about twenty-two pounds. Each kilo is about the size of a brick and, depending on its quality, is worth $15,000 to $30,000 today; a kilo of heroin is worth several times that, roughly $70,000 to $90,000). There's no plea bar-gaining, no chance for a judge to go easy on an offender, and no early release on parole. Twenty years behind bars seems like a long enough time to make it worth risking your life to resist. There's an axiom in law enforcement to the effect that the surveillance backup for an un-dercover drug agent is really just an ambulance on standby. A drug dealer who gets spooked will be too quick on the trigger for the surveillance team to intervene, so its chief role will be to rush the agent to the hospital—and, of course, to apprehend the shooter. Not many drug dealers who shoot federal agents under surveillance tend to walk away from the scene of the crime.

Nothing that dangerous was likely to go down at the nightclub. Rick had told us that the bust in this case was probably a year off. This was simply a night out to meet the players, and indeed his informant did seem to know everybody in the place. As I looked around at all the flashy clothes and the beautiful bodies gyrating to the music, it struck me that drug crimes were the only kind I would ever work that were so much the province of the night. Though I had worked undercover before, going to mob parties as agents' dates—and, of course, I had met Clay Carlson, the boyfriend who had recruited me into the FBI, at a disco where he was tailing a mobster—those were isolated evenings in the typical investigation. But as a so-called dope whore, as agents who worked drugs were called, once I cultivated my own informants and starting making my own kilos of coke fall from the skies, scenes like this would be my world. Instead of checking records at my desk all day long, I'd be home when Seth got out of school and set off for work after I had given him dinner, dressed not in a suit and pumps but the way I was now, in spandex. For the first time I began to see that being assigned to a drug squad wasn't necessarily exile to Siberia—that it might actually be fun.

Before long, there was an opening on the same drug squad as Rick and Tony, and I was able to transfer in. Its supervisor was a woman—the first and only one among the twenty-five in the division. Elaine Smith was half of one of the Bureau's first "double agent" couples. She and her husband, T. D., had grown up in Chicago and attended the University of Illinois at Champaign-Urbana together. Legend had it that she used to sit on T. D.'s back, smoking a cigarette, while he did push-ups in his dorm room. I could believe it. She was a head-turner, an always beautifully turned-out woman who loved clothes. T. D. was known as the "iron man" of the fugitive squad. He was once shot in an accident on the firing range and, with an injury so severe that he would need extensive surgery, managed to run to the hospital. As he once explained it to me: "Candice, I knew if I stopped and lay down I might not get up. So I just kept running."

But Elaine didn't achieve her position by riding on her husband's coattails. She was famous in her own right for her tremendous skill at developing informants and would often guest lecture on the subject at

Quantico. One of her triumphs involved cultivating a prominent gangster who had been shot in the head and left for dead by the mob. Over
the years, seven or eight FBI agents had tried to recruit him, to no avail.
Despite the truism that no one in the Mafia would ever deal with a
woman, Elaine went to see him in the hospital, managed to persuade
him to become an informant, and through him, sent a lot of mob guys
to jail. As you might imagine, some insecure guys, who couldn't bear
to give a woman her due, said, "Well, sure, Elaine was able to turn
him—he had a bullet in his head."

That was unfair—and untrue. Elaine had been cultivating him before
he was shot, and when he got ready to talk he chose her over all the
other agents. No one could deny that Elaine had the magic touch. Even
as a new agent, she had made a multimillion-dollar securities fraud case.
I once asked her the secret of her success and she told me a story: She
was assisting on a massive arrest, and amid the entire hullabaloo, she saw
a black woman being handcuffed and placed in a car. Elaine went over,
opened the car door, and sat down beside her in the backseat, asking
whether there was anything she could do to make the woman more
comfortable. They started talking, and a few days later, the woman called
her from jail to say, "Can you come over here? I'd like to talk to you."

It wasn't even Elaine's case, but she rushed right over, and what the
woman told her cracked the case wide open. "Why did you pick me?"
Elaine asked, certain that the woman had already stood up to hour-
upon-hour of interrogation. The woman answered, "Because you were
the only one who was really, really nice to me."

That was a lesson I never forgot, and more than once in my career,
it has worked for me too. When I train new agents, I always pass it on.
Once, when I was acting supervisor of the Child Abduction Task Force
in San Francisco, I told a young agent who was up in Eureka on a child
murder case, trying to get information from a woman who had known
the suspect for years, "After your first meeting, send her flowers with a
note saying, 'Thank you for your time.' You just might be surprised."

Sure enough, at her next meeting, the woman not only told her
everything we wanted to know but also volunteered leads that helped
us tie him to other crimes against children in the past. No one had ever
sent her flowers before.

Informants are the lifeblood of FBI cases. Sometimes we ferret them out, but often as not, they come to us, to "work off a beef"—help us make a case against their henchmen in exchange for reduction of the criminal charges or penalties they are facing—or out of fear, because some criminal confederate is subjecting them to threats or extortion; or to get revenge, the strongest motivator of all. Some drug figures become informants because they need money—the DEA pays valuable inform-ants quite well and even offers bonuses based on the number of kilos recovered. In exchange, they require their informants to testify against the people they turn in, which the FBI doesn't do. But because the DEA operates closer to the street than the FBI, their informants are usually criminals, while Bureau informants are often concerned citizens. Now and then, we even encounter a principled whistle-blower. For example, in 1994 an Arab terrorist group planned to blow up the Lincoln Tunnel and the New York Stock Exchange, but one of their members couldn't morally justify the loss of innocent lives. So he came to us with infor-mation that enabled us to raid their bomb factory, actually catching them in the act of mixing up a vat of precursor chemicals for explosives. The plot was foiled, and eleven terrorists went to jail in what was thereafter known as the "witch's cauldron" case.

While I was working drugs in Chicago, one of my FBI colleagues was tipped by an informant that a major dope shipment would be ar-riving in a white truck at a certain place and time. Agents staked out the location, and when the truck showed up, they actually guided it as it backed up to the loading dock. The driver just assumed that the guys on the ground waving him on were the drug buyers' henchmen and was utterly shocked when they whipped out their badges and placed him under arrest. Inside the truck, stacked in bricks, was a ton of coke.

So every informant an FBI agent develops is a medal on his or her chest, and the number you "open" each year is a measure of your ef-fectiveness on the job. Once I started working drugs, they seemed to start popping out of the woodwork. I quickly learned that it never paid to use the word informant, because even the ones who approached us hated to think of themselves as "rats." So instead I would say, "What help can you give us on this case?" or "Look, we can help you get the guy who screwed you."

One productive informant of mine was a prisoner in Cook County jail, which has notoriously bad conditions. He was doing time for murder, having beaten a stranger to death with a pipe because he had happened to cross him. When he was arrested, the drug dealer he worked for promised to look after his wife and child, but after a few months stopped paying her rent. So Steve* called us, offering to give him up, in exchange for support for his family and transfer to a less overcrowded and oppressive federal prison. We accepted his terms—and because he was too cheap to cough up a pittance of his sizable black-market income to uphold his end of the bargain, a drug dealer would ultimately go to jail.

My partner on that squad was a wild and brilliant DEA agent named Dave Tibbetts. Through his bosses at the drug agency we were handed an informant they were bringing up from Louisiana, whom they wanted us to plant in Chicago's largely Mexican Pilsen neighborhood on the near South Side. Elaine and I flew down to met him in New Orleans, and then we installed him in a nice Chicago apartment and turned him loose. He was incredibly effective. One night I went undercover as his date at a salsa bar, which we had heard was a drug world hangout. I was the only Anglo there, but that didn't seem to draw any suspicion to my informant, who worked the room more effectively than Miss America in a fraternity house. By the time we left at one or two in the morning, his pockets were stuffed with business cards and phone numbers of drug dealers, opening up dozens of new targets for us to investigate. He could walk the walk and talk the talk that well.

One of the people he got hooked up with was a female drug dealer who lived in a huge cattle ranch south of Chicago. She had been in business for decades but was so wily and untouchable that she had never spent a day in jail. The informant represented himself as a drug dealer who wanted to establish a partnership, and to make him look credible, we had to give him all the trappings of a drug kingpin. That meant flying him in to Miggs Field, a small airport right on the lake in downtown Chicago, serving private planes, on a Learjet that he passed off as his own.

That halfway convinced her that he was on the level, but to cement his credibility, he threw a party at a bar the woman owned in the Pilsen neighborhood, through which she ran her drug transactions. The plan was for him to introduce her to his drug connections, but in fact many of the guests were FBI agents. So they would look the part, the Bureau brought in tens of thousands of dollars' worth of jewelry (seized from other drug dealers) to deck them out—solid gold Rolex watches, diamond necklaces. The government spares no expense when it comes to impressing drug dealers. And the gambit worked.

Most of the cases the informant was opening up for us in Chicago involved cocaine, or its cheaper, smokable, even more highly addictive spin-off, crack, which was ravaging American cities in the late 1980s and early 1990s. But when he got a line on a Mexican supplier of heroin, Dave and I snapped to attention. In the drug hierarchy, heroin occupied the very top rank.

At the bottom of the pecking order was methamphetamine or crank, a crude stimulant that was relatively easy to manufacture, so it tended to be found in places like Idaho and Montana, which were far afield from the regular drug distribution channels. It was a biker drug with its own subculture that, unlike the conventional drugs of abuse, rarely intersected with middle-class life. Its users could get so hyped up that they were capable of committing horrible crimes, and because the home labs that produced the drug varied wildly in their quality control, it could be dangerous to use. It could also be dangerous to work, because meth labs were often booby-trapped to keep out intruders. Although the FBI didn't handle methamphetamine investigations, we would periodically get DEA warning bulletins about the latest diabolical device to be found in the amateur labs. One, I remember, was a crumpled ball of aluminum foil that would be left lying around the lab for an unsuspecting person to pick up. When he opened it, a chemical inside would explode, blowing away his fingertips or his corneas. A number of DEA agents have been killed or maimed while trying to investigate methamphetamine labs.

On the rung above crank was marijuana. The FBI might get involved if there was some enormous shipment coming in to a city, but the guy next door growing a patch of pot in his backyard we left to the local police or the DEA.

Next on the totem pole was cocaine and above that heroin. Although cocaine was much more of a middle-class drug and more widely available, heroin was much more expensive and had the mystique of being a derivative of opium, one of our oldest drugs of abuse. It also had a longer history as a crime drug than the others. Though robberies related to crack addiction were skyrocketing, it was still a relatively new drug, whereas for decades, heroin addicts had been known to steal to feed their desperate cravings.

One of our informant's contacts had offered to set him up for a heroin deal, which would take place in a bar in Mexico, just over the U.S. border. Dave and I, disguised as tourists, were to observe the deal from nearby seats at the bar. But the plot came together so fast that we had to jump on a plane immediately to the border city, where we hooked up with the local arm of the DEA and then went shopping for tourist attire. Both to save the taxpayers money and so our clothes wouldn't scream "new," we settled on a Goodwill store. We entered looking like federal agents and came out utterly ridiculous in shorts and Hawaiian shirts, an ensemble I completed with thongs on my feet and a big straw hat. When we looked at each other, we couldn't stop laughing.

But when we crossed over to Mexico, our attire was no longer funny. There were no tourists within miles of the place. Two Anglos materializing out of nowhere and plunking themselves down in a tiny bar in a one-horse town seemed certain to draw suspicion. But we were there, and the deal was about to go down. All we could do was trust in our DEA surveillance backup and pray that our getups looked silly enough to make us seem like the kind of people who were likely to have lost their way.

There were booths in the bar, and our informant was already seated in one with his connection when we arrived. We took the booth abutting theirs, and since I spoke Spanish, I was positioned with my back to them trying to listen in. The slang they used was hard to understand, but by concentrating hard, I was able make out enough to know that there was potential for a big score here. The goal of the meeting was to have our informant get at least a sample, so we would know the connection had the goods. He kept asking, and the other party kept bringing up every other possible wrinkle of the deal. This was shaping up to be the longest, most torturous meeting in the history of law enforcement.

It's hard to take more than an hour to eat, and you can only nurse a drink for so long. So Dave kept ordering beer after beer, hoping that we seemed like a couple of drunks who had settled in for the duration—there was no other conceivable reason for us to linger there for hours. Suddenly a figure burst through the door of the place and headed straight for our table. It was the DEA agent who had been stationed outside as our backup surveillance. He even looked like a federal agent, in his jeans and shirt, with his beeper on his belt. I broke out in a cold sweat—something must have gone terribly wrong for him to risk blowing our cover that way. But what he said was, "Can't you two hurry this up?"

I started gasping for breath. Dave's face flushed beet red. I fully expected the gates of hell to open and a hand to emerge, yank me out of the booth, and drag me off into the Mexican countryside, where my body would never be found. Were we really all about to get killed because some jackass got impatient and wanted to go home? I couldn't have said a word, so it was Dave who choked out, "Yeah, we will, pretty soon. Now get the fuck out of here."

The talking behind us stopped. I signaled to Dave with my eyebrows, *Anything going on?*

Dave just shook his head and muttered, "Amateur night."

Fortunately our quarry seemed to assume that the agent was just some guy who was there with us for some other reason. It was a classic case of "aren't you glad they're stupid"—thank God. Their meeting lasted about another twenty minutes, then Dave and I had to sit there awhile longer, to keep up the ruse. When enough time passed that we could finally leave, Dave confronted the surveillance agent. I thought he was going to rip his head off. But the agent had nothing to say in his defense and shrugged off Dave's anger, snorting, "Well, half of these deals are bullshit anyway."

He wasn't wrong—but he was wrong about this one. My informant would come out of the deal with a pound and a half of pure opium. But when we got back to the states all I could do was float in the pool of the hotel for a day decompressing and thinking, *I'm alive, I'm alive.*

Some agents would say, "Well, what do you expect, working with the DEA? They're cowboys."

But every organization has its solid, true-blue constituents, who are fortunately in the majority, and a few slackers who, as we say in law enforcement, care only "where their next doughnut's coming from." The experience didn't sour me on the DEA at all, but it left me wary of ever again working anything as treacherous as a drug deal without backup I knew I could rely on, whatever its source.

The sizable opium score made us believe that we had tapped into a new Mexican heroin supply line. Before long, however, the informant, who had been opening up cases for us left and right, "went sideways," in Bureau parlance—meaning that he spun out of our control—and vanished from sight. That is always the risk with a drug dealer informant. Every lead he opens up for you is a potential new business opportunity for him; and ours had seemingly found a better employer than the FBI.

By that point Dave and I had invested three or four solid months in him, along with tens of thousands of dollars of the taxpayers' money. He had identified dozens of new bad guys for us to watch but had failed to hand us a new head of the drug hydra. By their very nature, criminal informants are unreliable, and drug dealers are even more so. Since the world began, there has probably never been a drug deal that was consummated on time—"three o'clock" means "five o'clock at the earliest"—or before noon, and a high proportion of them never go down at all. That's why, if you ask a cop or a DEA or FBI agent working drugs what his current hot case is, your answer is likely to be the classic law enforcement expression "AFDD"—"another fuckin' drug deal."

Today Seth tells me that there were only two periods in my career when he was terrified about my safety—when I was undercover in Montana tracking the Unabomber and during the three years I worked drugs. He was old enough by then—in his early teens—to have a sense of the risks, but I think it reassured him somewhat to get to know my colleagues on the drug squad. He was especially drawn to Tony Ryan, who would entertain Seth with tales of jumping through windows to catch bad guys and other wild exploits. When Seth was assigned to write a paper for school on someone he admired, he picked Tony Ryan, describing his leather ties and his superhero achievements—knowing Tony, I'm sure that at least some of those stories were absolutely true.

The Ice Woman was equally fascinating, if for different reasons, to a teenage boy. For a while she lived nearby and would pick me up when we did nightclub crawls to work informants. I remember that one night Seth invited some friends over for what I suspected was the express purpose of ogling the Ice Woman in her club regalia. Standing in my kitchen in our short miniskirts and tight tops, with our red lipstick and big hair, we definitely had their attention, so the Ice Woman and I decided to give them a little drug education show. Even today when I hear the two words "legalize drugs" in the same sentence, it makes my blood run cold, and back then when I had daily exposure to the ravaging effects of drugs on our society, I was rabid. Beyond the damage drugs can do to an individual—crippling addiction, toxic psychosis, and even death—drugs and alcohol, according to U.S. Department of Justice statistics, figure in roughly a third of violent crimes. Just to cite one example from my own cases, Brian Dugan, who abducted Melissa Ackerman, was high on marijuana at the time he committed all his rapes and murders.

So we gave the boys a stern lecture and extracted the promise from each of them never even to experiment with drugs.

I wish that all of Seth's friends had been present that night and taken our advice to heart. A few years later, one of the kids he grew up with, then a freshman in college with a 3.9 grade-point average, was robbed of his future and eventually his life by drugs. He made a typical kid's mistake one night, trying a hallucinogenic "designer" drug that had been concocted by a friend, and had a psychotic reaction. He began exhibiting the symptoms of paranoid schizophrenia, seeing visions and hearing voices. Even the best treatment and the loving support of his family could not ease the pain of his frightening ordeal. Finally, at an age when most kids are finishing college and have their whole lives before them, he ended his suffering by lying down in front of the local commuter train.

When I heard the news, I immediately called Seth to tell him of the suicide. He was devastated. He flew home from college and spent the night before the funeral trying to console the boy's grief-stricken mother. "What should I say to her?" he asked me.

I had to tell him just to be there—that there was nothing anyone could say or do to relieve the anguish of parents who were confronting such a senseless loss.

How I wish I could have spared him that.

12

GIRL TALK

The DEA is one of the few federal agencies that do not cost the taxpayers a dime. Its operational budget, which runs just under $2 billion, comes from forfeitures and seizures of cash and property, as the law provides, used in furtherance of a drug deal (a car with a kilo of coke found in the trunk, say) or purchased with the "ill-gotten gains" of drug dealing. If John Q. Citizen, who has no visible means of support and hasn't paid taxes for years, suddenly plunks down $3 million in cash for a house or $75,000 for a sports car, he's going to have some explaining to do about where he got the funds. If he can't easily account for the money, and the government has good reason to believe that the money was obtained illegally, it can seize the property. He will be given the chance to reclaim it in court, where the burden of proving that it was obtained legally will be on him, for this is a civil, not criminal action. More often than not, he won't show, preferring to forfeit the property than risk giving the government enough information to charge him (rightfully) with a criminal offense.

One of the benefits of working drugs was the chance to trade up from our standard-issue Hoover blue cars to the much more stylish vehicles that were de rigueur in the drug community. In 1988 my official car was a top-of-the-line Mercury station wagon loaded with accessories, which had belonged to the wife of a drug dealer. He had paid cash and put the title in her name, believing that since she wasn't personally tied to any criminal activity, the government couldn't seize the car. He was wrong. At one point I was even assigned a bright red Ferrari, which had owners fastidious enough that our usual methods didn't detect the presence of drugs. Then the FBI lab suggested that we vacuum it with a Dustbuster lined with a coffee filter—and sure enough, the filter was permeated with cocaine. I loved driving that car, but considering its maintenance bills, maybe the joke was on us.

One day we seized a shiny, black, new Ford Bronco that had been doing double duty as a drugmobile, and Mary Ellen Moore,* the forfeiture clerk, and I went down to the impound lot to do the paperwork. We were almost finished when the "previous" owner, a thug with two huge bodyguards, showed up to harass us. "Who the hell do you bitches think you are?" he snarled. "I never heard of no forfeiture laws."

I told him to call his lawyer with more courtesy than he deserved—he had made his own tough luck—but he continued to badger us, puffed up with anger and firing off ever more colorful salvos of invective. I had to laugh. In my entire career, none of the roughnecks who called me names could ever hold a candle to the Cursing Granny. I couldn't resist blowing our bedeviler a kiss as Mary Ellen, trying to swallow her own laughter, hustled me out to the station wagon before my mouth, as I used to say, "wrote a check that my badge couldn't cash."

We were still giggling over some of his expressions as we peeled out of the lot. "How nice of him to say I had a 'bony ass,' " I told Mary Ellen. "That's a first!" We were heading north on Lake Shore Drive when suddenly a voice somewhere in the car intoned: "I want to eat your pussy."

We both whipped around to check the backseat. It was empty. "What the hell?" I began, and then we heard the voice again: "I want to fuck you all night."

For a moment, we panicked, thinking that the thug had taken revenge by somehow booby-trapping our car. I was about to pull over when the voice said: "I want to fuck your eyeballs out."

We then realized that the voice was coming from the car's two-way radio speaker, under the front seat. But the FBI had its own special radio frequency, and no one would dare use such language on the air. Where was our dispatcher? The only explanation was that someone was broad-casting from a Handy-Talky, or "H-T," one of our handheld portable radios. About the size of a pencil box, they were very expensive and were supposed to be safeguarded carefully at all times—either kept on the agent's person or secured in the trunk of a Bureau car with a lock and chain. No one would ever leave a Handy-Talky lying around where someone might make off with it. Obviously, however, at least one Handy-Talky had fallen into the wrong hands!

"What's your name?" I heard Lynn, the dispatcher, ask. Agents' names and identifying factors are never given over the radio because no transmission can ever be 100 percent secure. Then it struck me that if Lynn could hear the guy, he was also broadcasting to hundreds of agents on the street, all of whom were lying low. Nobody wanted to tip off the thief that he had the Feds on the line.

Back at headquarters, we found Lynn hemmed in by men, all laughing uproariously. No administrator was bothering to coach her through the situation. Instead she was left dog-paddling, trying to parry Loverboy's lewd remarks; and with every response she managed to squeak out, her audience would wink and poke shoulders and slap one another on the back. Poor woman! To make matters worse, the Lothario was too smart to call from anywhere, such as the subway, where the background noise might tip us off to his whereabouts. On one level, the situation was hilarious, but it was horrible for poor Lynn and also potentially tremen-dously embarrassing to the FBI.

Someone had to take charge. But this was the kind of operation that had "career buster" written all over it. If it blew up and exposed the Bureau to public ridicule, anyone linked to it would become a sacrificial lamb; and since there was nothing tangible at stake, like someone's life, everyone could justify backing into the shadows. The agents watching Lynn struggle wouldn't hesitate to confront a sniper or a terrorist wrapped in dynamite, brandishing grenades, but a political stink bomb—that was too hot to handle.

I had a brainstorm that I knew my supervisor at the time was too much of a "company man" to let me try. With him it was always better to ask forgiveness than permission if you needed to get anything done. But I wanted some kind of official blessing before I put my head on the chopping block—I wasn't completely suicidal—so I sought out Lane Crocker, aka the Crocodile, an ASAC who was my boss's superior and also one of the most creative and dynamic managers in the Bureau. Highly personable, he actually knew most of the Division's employees by name. He stood a trim six feet three inches and had a shock of white hair that always reminded me of Santa. He wasn't afraid to make decisions.

When I got to his office, I found Ron Dibbern, one of my favorite agents, who made his reputation on the fugitive squad, already there discussing the radio problem. The longer it went on, we all agreed, the more likely it was that the press would get wind of it, with humiliating results. They told me what had happened—some poor agent had left his Handy-Talky in the car overnight after parking on a street in exclusive Lincoln Park, where he assumed it would be safe. He awoke the next morning to find the car stripped of everything fenceable, including thousands of dollars' worth of FBI camera equipment. If he was in hot water before, he was boiling now.

Still, no one had a plan. Mine was simple. "All he wants to talk about is sex," I pointed out. "If he wanted money, he'd be trying to sell us the radio. So why not trap him in his own snare? If it's sex he wants, let's give it to him."

They both looked at me wide-eyed, so I quickly filled them in on the rest of the plan. I would go on the radio as the madam of a prostitution ring, whose "girl" had left the radio in the car he had robbed. I would tell him that the radio had a special "police-free" frequency—he seemed unsophisticated enough to buy that—so I needed it back and would pay for it. When we met to conduct the exchange, we'd grab him.

Both men laughed. The Crocodile offered me whatever support I needed to pull off the plan, and Ron definitely wanted in on it. I asked him to line up ten female agents whom I could radio periodically when, for the sake of verisimilitude, I needed to talk to my "girls." Then I went back to the radio room to tell a grateful Lynn that I was relieving her at the switchboard. Suddenly the temperature dropped in the room, and there was nothing wrong with the thermostat. Agents who had been reluctant to stick their necks out were now twitching with resentment that someone else was stepping into the ring, with the blessing of management. The case was a hot potato, to be sure, but there would be great kudos for the agent who succeeded in breaking this embarrassing standoff. Since they had been too nervous to try, a lot of them were willing me to fail. "Bureaucracy!" I snorted, only half to myself.

At this point our Lothario had gone silent for an hour, so to smoke him out, I started checking in with the "girls." We were all going to use our real first names, and for the sake of the cause, I revived the nickname that no one in my adult life had ever been permitted to utter: Candy. I placed my first calls to Cindy Linden* and Linda Swanson because both had charmingly feminine Southern accents. I gave Cindy her "assignment," and she signed off by saying, "You got it, Candy-girl!" Linda pretended to copy the address of a "high roller on Lake Shore Drive who likes basic black, with a single strand of pearls," and closed with, "Okay, I read you, Candy-Mama."

Both times I cringed. I hated to be called Candy, but the name certainly seemed suited to this job—not the profession, I'm sure, that my parents had in mind when they named me Candice.

Though I had waited a decent interval between my calls to Cindy and Linda, there was still no word from Loverboy. Had he tired of his game? Was he contemplating some more diabolical use for the stolen Handy-Talky? Had the batteries gone dead? I was starting to worry as I checked in with my third "girl," the Ice Woman. "What's up, Can-do Candywoman?" she asked. "Do you have something for me?"

I later learned that she deliberately called me "Can-Do Candy-woman" as an expression of the confidence the female agents in the call-girl ring had in me. The moniker cheered me tremendously. "Yeah, I've got a hot one for you," I told her, deciding I might as well try to have some fun. "It's Big Daddy Fun Bucks again."

That was a goofy name my brother Keith jokingly called himself. It was lucky that I had the mike keyed off when the laughter erupted around me. I shushed my listeners, evidently a little too sternly for some delicate souls, for I heard someone leave the room, murmuring, "Bitch."

"Big Daddy Fun Bucks!" the Ice Woman squealed. "Mm-mmm . . . He knows how to have a good time!"

Just then I heard another voice on the line: "Eat me, not him. Eat me . . ."

The Sweetheart of the Radio was back, as debonair as ever.

"Who is this?" I asked. "Are you the guy who stole my girl's walkie-talkie?"

Silence. It looked like I had scared him off. Long minutes stretched into an hour, plenty of time for me to question my sanity for ever climbing out on such a visible and shaky limb. The entire division was listening to me make a fool of myself. I tried to raise the guy a few times on the radio with no luck. Then John Furren* slid in beside me. He was a fine agent, a tall drink of water at six feet three inches, and a trusted friend. "I'll keep you company, Candywoman," he said.

It was the boost I needed. John urged me to have Loverboy call me on the phone, so we could trap and trace him. Otherwise we'd lose him when the radio batteries faded. "And he will call, Candice," he assured me. "Your scam is going great. Who do you think he is?"

"He sounds young to me and possibly nonwhite—maybe Asian or even Hispanic," I said.

Now Ron joined us—just in time to hear our Lothario return, with the "seductive" whisper, "I want to eat you."

"I want my radio, we'll eat later," I told him. "And who am I talking to, anyway?"

"Who the hell are you?" he countered.

John passed me a note. "Get him to call on the phone! The battery!"

"I'm Miss Candy. Look, Mystery Man, I don't like talking on the radio. Call me on the phone at—"

"Fuck you, bitch," he said, and then he was gone.

It was the third time I'd been called a bitch since I arrived at the impound lot, six hours ago. It was getting old. I punched the button as if he hadn't signed off. "Look, your batteries are about to run down," I said. "Then we can't reach each other. So call me at"—I gave him a number—"and let's make a deal. You get a girl for the night and cash for the radio and camera stuff."

He heard me. "What's the name of your outfit?"

"The Candy Store," I blurted out. I could see from the look on John's face that I had just made myself major joke bait. I repeated the phone number and he clicked off again.

Illinois Bell had rigged the phone to trap and trace the call, but 1980s technology being what it was, I'd have to keep him on the phone for a full three minutes—if he called. As we waited, I kept placing calls to the "girls," in case he was listening. At one point, a supervisor pulled Ron out of the room, and I caught occasional traces of arguing from the hall, with Ron saying, "No, no," and "I disagree—she's doing fine." It was only later, after I badgered him, that Ron finally told me that the supervisor, along with a few others, were mounting a campaign to convince Lane Crocker to let them take over the case—not that they had come up with any better idea. "He's a jerk," Ron said. "So I just told him to screw off."

When the audience started to trickle away, I looked up and saw that it was six o'clock, time to head home to dinner and families. *Good,* I thought. *The fewer witnesses to my downfall, the better.*

The phone was silent until, finally, at 6:45, he called. Thank goodness!

"So what do you want?" I asked.

"I want eight hundred dollars and the Ice Woman," he demanded.

Now I knew I was dealing with a kid. The radio alone was worth over a thousand dollars and the camera equipment three times that. But to keep him on the phone, I dickered about the cash and insisted that the Ice Woman was busy. We hadn't quite worked out which female agent would come along because we had no way of knowing when or how the deal would go down.

At the three-minute point, John gave me a thumbs-up—it was long enough for the trace to go through (though as it turned out, we wouldn't need it). My caller was driving a hard bargain, standing firm on the cash and the Ice Woman, and now insisting that his friend get a woman too.

"No deal," I said. "One of my girls can handle both of you."

But who? It was pushing seven o'clock. I hoped there was another woman somewhere around the office whom I could press into service. All of a sudden there she was, in tight black pants and a pink satin camisole with spaghetti straps. In her high heels, she looked six feet tall. The Ice Woman. She had wanted to help out enough that, just in case she was needed, she had gone home to change. At that moment she became my friend for life.

I made dinner plans at a restaurant in Chinatown with Loverboy, and when I hung up, everyone in the room burst into applause. I had been at the switchboard for six straight hours. When I had placed my daily three o'clock call to Seth, I had apologized for being out late and promised to make it up to him with a good story. Now it looked like he would get one.

We then moved into Phase 2 of the operation. One of the guys from the surveillance squad cased the restaurant, and on his advice, the Ice Woman and I sat at a booth near the door. Once the exchange was made, I was to take off my white straw summer fedora and place it on the table, which would signal Ron and five other male agents to move in and make the arrest. Even though we believed we would be dealing with kids, it didn't pay to take chances. Teenagers could be even more dangerous than adults, for they were likely to get "hinky" and start shooting in situations that more experienced criminals would have the confidence to navigate without bloodshed.

We arrived early and watched Ron and the guys order an impressive array of food. Then our "clients" appeared—two young Chinese men, neither of whom even weighed as much as I did. For this I had laid my career on the line and was putting in overtime? We introduced ourselves and ordered a few dishes as a cover. Then they tried to act tough. "Let's see the money," one of them said.

Below tabletop level, I fanned my stack of $100 bills. "Now what about my stuff?"

They showed me the Handy-Talky and the camera equipment, and we surreptitiously made the swap. The Ice Woman then played her role to the hilt. "What about me? What am I getting out of this?" she protested, to distract our companions until I could signal Ron and get the show on the road. The way they were looking at her, I thought they were about to drag her off by the hair like cavemen.

I swept off my hat and laid it on the table, as if I were exasperated to have to argue with her. Just then, however, the waiter brought our order, blocking Ron's view of our table—if he had been looking. I stole a glance at the guys, who were absorbed in chatting and circulating dishes of steaming aromatic food. Some backup!

I put my hat back on, so I could signal again when the guys seemed to be paying better attention. The Ice Woman understood and shifted gears, now working on promising the boys a wild time after dinner. We ate uneasily, with the kids shifting restlessly, staring at us, looking at the door, until I decided I had better quickly set the arrest plan in motion again, to forestall trouble. Once more I took off my hat, waiting for all hell to break loose. Nothing happened. I shot a suggestive look at Ron's table, and the kid across from me caught it. "Hey, what's going on?" he yelped, jumping up.

Rising out of my seat, I grabbed his two wrists in my hands and slammed them down on the table, pinning them down with my body weight. The Ice Woman followed suit. "What's up is, you're under arrest," I shouted. "FBI!" adding, "Hey, Ron, join in any time now."

Ron dropped his fork, and the men swarmed our table. As the others subdued our suspects, he said, "Jesus, DeLong. What's the rush? Don't you like Chinese food? I was trying to enjoy a nice dinner on the 'G' [the government]."

"I couldn't wait. They were too antsy," I told him. "Something's up—they kept looking at the door."

He and I strode quickly to the restaurant entrance and through the glass spotted three more young men getting off motorcycles. They were heading our way, hands shoved in their jackets, either to check on their friends or to "roll the whores."

Big bad FBI men from the surveillance squad moved in to stop them. "Rumble in Chinatown," Ron laughed, as we stepped outside. A Saturday night special went flying in the scuffle and skittered under a car. They were armed.

All those guys didn't need my help to mop up, so I headed back to the office to collect my things. Before I left there, I stopped by the radio room to make one last broadcast to any diehard fans who might still be listening. As it turned out, there were plenty. I would later learn that a substantial proportion of the division had eaten dinner in their Bureau cars that night, sitting in their driveways with the radio on, just to keep up with the unfolding Candy Store drama.

"This is Candy Mama," I announced. "Suspects in custody, no shots fired. Time to go home."

"Way to go!" The clerks and agents in the radio room applauded me. Then the phone rang. It was Lane Crocker, whom someone must have called about my broadcast. "Well done, Candice," he bellowed into the phone. He was calling from Binyon's, where a retirement party was in progress for, of all people, the Grinch, the squad leader who had made my life as a fledgling agent miserable. Between the irony of my succeeding on the very night that the Grinch was being ushered out the door and the generosity of Crocker, taking time out from a party to congratulate me, I couldn't stop smiling all the way home.

Then, the next morning, when I arrived at work, my fellow agents clapped and cheered. Someone shoved a newspaper in my hands. There it was, in big, black letters: FBI USES HOOKER SCAM TO BUST ASIAN BURGLARY RING.

It seems that our little gang of six had grown rather notorious for their "smash-and-grabs," breaking into cars and fencing the contents for cash. The police were able to link them to dozens of such thefts and recovered thousands of dollars' worth of stolen property. So the taxpayers got their money's worth—the Chicago cops were delighted to have the gang behind bars—and the FBI was spared the embarrassment of being tyrannized by a teenage potty mouth. What a different story might have run had we been unable to apprehend our young Lothario.

I would be known as Can-Do Candywoman for years.

The biggest payoff for me from the Candy Store caper was personal: It cemented my friendships with the Ice Woman, who remains one of my closest pals to this day, and with Ron Dibbern. Ron and I had known and liked each other for years—his son had even been one of Seth's occasional babysitters—but it wasn't that often that we got to work directly together on a case. Our next big one, oddly enough, would also involve an office political contretemps; and again, Ron would have to come to my defense. It would turn out to be a classic case of "No good deed goes unpunished."

The FBI never sleeps. Twenty-four hours a day, seven days a week, there is a duty agent at the switchboard, fielding calls from agents in need, cops, and the general public. It's not a job entrusted to a telephone operator because at least some of the calls will require urgent action, even if 90 percent of the late-night callers are cranks. We rotated this duty, which in a Bureau the size of Chicago's meant that each of us had to serve only once every couple of years. I'm not a night owl, so I was probably fighting to stay awake when a call came in at 4 A.M.—things tend to pick up after the bars close. But this caller didn't sound particularly drunk. "There's this guy I met," he told me. "We've been hanging out for a couple of days, and he's got a load of cash. He says he robbed some armored truck in San Francisco."

The more he talked the more convincing he sounded. Bogus tips don't usually come with a lot of detail. He gave me a full description of the guy, as well as the places he seemed to hang out, and then clinched his credibility by giving me his name and number—often a sign that a call is legit.

There was nothing we could act on that night, so the next day, I wrote up my report and took it over to the fugitive squad, which is responsible for chasing suspects like an armored car robber on the lam. I tried to deliver it to an agent known as Goober, who was a genuinely nice guy but whose judgment was sometimes nutty. "Candice, this is bull," he told me. "Nobody just drops a dime on a Class A fugitive."

At this point I wasn't a rookie. I was a trained field profiler, a well-regarded interviewer, and known for doing good work developing informants on the drug squad. I might have been wrong, but I deserved to be heard. And if I was right, apprehending a Class A fugitive—the most dangerous category, an offender known to be violent—would be a crowning achievement in any agent's career. I could well be giving Goober the tip of a lifetime, but he blew me off. "Look," he said, "I don't have time to go chasing down this stuff. Why don't you go call San Francisco, and if it turns out to be anything good, you can bring it back."

I must have gaped at him in disbelief. Drugs were my responsibility, as he knew full well. I may have caught the call, but other agents didn't do the legwork for the fugitive squad. It was his job to pursue the tip, and it was arrogant of him even to suggest that I run down a lead for him—not to mention lazy and, must I say it, sexist? I was getting mighty tired of hitting the pink wall between "what women do" and "men's heroic work."

But all I said was, "Yeah, sure," thinking, *If it is anything good, you'll be the last to know.*

When I called San Francisco, the tip checked out. An armored car had been robbed of $250,000, and the driver had been shot. Just to tie a bow on the gift wrap, in Chicago the suspect was using the very name that he was wanted under in San Francisco. Another case for the "Aren't You Glad They're Stupid?" file!

I took my findings to Elaine, my supervisor, explaining that I had been turned away when I tried to present them to the fugitive squad. "So it's my case now," I told her. "I want to set up the caller as my informant, and I want to make the arrest."

Elaine lit up like a Christmas tree. It would be a triumph for the whole squad if one of us managed to collar a Class A fugitive. "But we can't just snatch him from the fugitive squad," she said. "You and I still have to work in this office. We'll share the case with them, but you'll work the informant and you'll head the arrest team. That's the deal I'll cut with"—she said his name, but I always thought of the fugitive squad leader as the Blue Flamer. In Bureauspeak, a blue flamer is someone trying so hard to rise in the hierarchy that he has blue flames shooting out of his ass. A Blue Flamer never rocks the boat, toadies to the brass, and will stop at nothing—including subterfuge and case stealing—to get ahead.

"Get the deal in writing," I urged Elaine. But she demurred. "Don't worry. We'll work it all out."

The Blue Flamer was irate and subjected Goober to such a scalding public dressing-down that I actually felt sorry for the poor guy. But he had to accept our terms if he wanted to get in on the case. Ron Dibbern was on the fugitive squad, so he became my liaison, helping to pull together the arrest team. In the meantime, I made a plan with the caller. On a certain morning, he was to lure the robber to his house, where at eleven sharp, we would ring the doorbell, walk right in, and arrest him.

That day I woke up tingling with excitement. When I got to the office I tried to work but was too restless with anticipation to concentrate for long. I was practically counting the minutes till it finally came time for the fugitive squad arrest team to pick me up. They were five minutes late, then ten minutes late, and I started to smell a rat. I ran over to their squad area and found the desks empty. I swung by the radio room and tried to reach them over the transmitter. Nobody answered. I stomped back to the drug squad, where I told my partner Dave, "Damn those bastards! They're stealing my collar. Let's go get him."

We jumped into Dave's car, pulling on our bulletproof vests as we tore out of the parking lot. By the time we reached the house, the arrest had already gone down. The guys had the fugitive up against a car, cuffed, with shotguns pointed at his head.

"Hold it right there, you pricks," I said.

Sweeping aside their shotguns, I seized the suspect's handcuff chain. "Hi there," I greeted him brightly, "I'm Candice, and we'll be going in my car."

"What the fuck?" he protested. "Who the hell are you?"

But I just marched him away, with the fugitive squad clamoring behind me like three-year-olds in a sandbox: "Wait, he's ours." "We got him!" "It's our arrest!"

A few of them came after us, and Ron got in the middle, trying to cool things down. They cursed him out, and I ignored them all until I got the suspect to the cars. Then I turned around to face them. "What the hell were you trying to pull?" I demanded. "We had a deal."

"We couldn't find you," one of them whined.

"You're on the fugitive squad and you couldn't track me down at my desk, fifty seats away from you? Where was your seeing eye dog?"

To Ron, I added, "I thought we were friends."

I got ready to leave, but Ron insisted on driving me back, trying to be conciliatory. I was furious at him, but I sensed that he wasn't to blame. The betrayal reeked to high heaven of the Blue Flamer, his boss.

I rode in the backseat with the fugitive. "So, how you doing?" I asked him. "This all must seem a little abrupt. You want something to drink? A Coke?"

He did, so I offered him the one I had been saving for myself in my bag. Since he was handcuffed, I fed the suspect little sips as I read him his rights, then quizzed him, "So what did happen back in San Francisco? Was it for the money?"

"Yeah, I needed the money," he admitted; and then it all came out: holding up the armored car, stashing the money under the stairs—he gave me the address—shooting the guard. "I probably shouldn't have done that," he acknowledged, which underscored his confession. "How is he, by the way?"

"He's alive," I told him. "But you're still in a lot of trouble, I'm afraid."

"You're so nice," he said. "I thought those guys with shotguns were going to blow my head off."

"From what I know of those guys, you're lucky they didn't. We're trying cut down on that as much as we can."

He laughed. By the time we got back to the office, we were on more cordial terms than I was with the fugitive squad. After his fingerprinting and mugshots, we even had our picture taken, side by side, with the suspect pointing as if to say, "She got me."

When it all shook out, because the fugitive squad made the technical collar, they got credit on paper for the arrest, while I got the assist, instead of the other way around, as I had been promised. It was still a great professional victory for me. Besides, everyone knew the truth—including the Blue Flamer's boss. When the Blue Flamer came by the SAC's office to crow about his squad's latest conquest, the boss dismissed him out of hand, saying, "Oh, come on. That was Candice DeLong's arrest."

Elaine had gotten there first. She knew how to play the game. It was an embarrassment the Blue Flamer would nurse for years, and a decade later, when he became my boss—that's the danger with blue flamers—I think he punished me for it, though of course I couldn't prove it. I was acting supervisor of the Child Abduction Task Force in San Francisco but had been promised a full-time profiling position as soon as a replacement could be found. San Francisco needed a full-time profiler, and there was no one else around with my experience and track record. (Years before, I had even turned down an offer from Roger Depue to join the profiling staff at Quantico, because Seth was still at home and needed contact with his father.) But then the Blue Flamer was transferred in and welched on the bargain, decreeing that I could do profiling only 20 percent of the time. So he got his petty revenge.

It still killed him after all those years—I guess I can take some satisfaction from that! And to this day, some of the fugitive squad won't even talk to me. Darn the luck.

•   •   •

As for the Ice Woman, she would go on to reprise her Candy Store role in a number of other stings, notably the bust of the madam of a real high-priced call-girl ring on the South Side of Chicago, which had a number of prominent judges and politicians among its clientele. The case agents, George Huston and Ross Rice, needed an undercover operative to go in "wired," ostensibly to interview with the madam for a job, and turned to the Ice Woman, whose blond surfer-girl looks made her possibly the most credible top-tier hooker in the division. But before the madam agreed to an interview, she insisted on seeing photos of the prospective candidate—pictures her male colleagues were only too eager to take. Instead she asked me to do the honors. "Only if you wear a bikini," I said. "I'm not taking any centerfold shots."

"Of course not," she said, horrified.

Even in a bathing suit, she was very bashful until I plied her with wine to loosen her up. But when I saw the Polaroids, I shook my head. The Ice Woman looked even more glamorous in pictures than in person. "You definitely have nothing to be bashful about," I told her. "But you do have two things to worry about. One, women who see these will consider you unbeatable competition and want to kill you to get you out of the gene pool; and two, once your fellow agents on this case get a look at them, they're going to be all over the division. The guys won't be able to resist passing them around."

I urged her to demand that the case agent destroy them once the madam had seen them. He was a decent guy, and he agreed. Sure enough, just as planned, the pictures piqued the madam's interest enough that she requested a personal interview with the Ice Woman.

It takes phenomenal courage and self-possession to wear a wire—to play a part without breaking character, knowing that all the while on your person is a machine that irrefutably marks you as a traitor, which may well get you killed. In those days it wasn't all that physically easy to wear one, either, even the FBI's state-of-the-art, reel-to-reel recorders called Nagras, less than half an inch thick and about four by six inches in size. For one thing, Nagras had to be taped onto the body, and over long periods, they could run too hot and burn the skin. For another, at the end of the tape, they could click, faintly but still audibly enough to alert a wary target. Today's devices are far superior.

But the Ice Woman had the guts to brave the interview with the madam with her Nagra taped to her thigh. Not only was she hired as a hooker, but she also won the madam's confidence, and what was to be brief "face contact" stretched to an hour and a half. The madam told her all the in-and-outs of the business. The girls were driven to their assignations by limousine, and they shunned the usual Frederick's of Hollywood-style "hooker" garb for business suits, even carrying brief-cases on their calls. It appalled me to hear that at the height of the AIDS epidemic, when there was no viable treatment, a john could have sex without a condom for an extra $100—a mighty cheap price for a human life. Apparently the madam wanted to impress the Ice Woman, for she didn't stop at describing the call-girl business but went on to fill the tape with accounts of a broad range of criminal activities. It was enough to send her away for a long time.

Just how dangerous the Ice Woman's role had been became apparent when the madam started to suspect that someone in her employ was talking to the Feds. She confronted her office manager, a woman, fright-ening her so much that she actually confessed to being an informant. At gunpoint, the madam forced the woman into her car, tied her up, and drove to Indiana, where she planned to kill her. Luckily, the madam stopped en route at a convenience store, and while she was inside, the office manager was able to slip her bonds and break free. She found a cop, who checked her story with Ross Rice and George Huston, who in turn rallied the troops. The agents tracked down the madam and her henchmen in Indiana, with a new kidnapping charge to top off her laundry list of crimes. A life was saved—and five criminals were swept off the streets and into prison.

This case was developed into a TV segment for the show *FBI, the Untold Story,* and the Ice Woman was recruited to appear. The day she went for the taping, she arrived in the office in one of the ugliest suits I have ever seen. It was boxy and pink and gray. I couldn't help saying, "What have you got on? I mean, that's not really 'you.' " She just smiled enigmatically.

Later in the day she came over holding a snapshot of a frumpy brunette with an unflattering hairdo wearing the same suit. "Guess who?" she said. We all burst out laughing. To conceal her identity, the show's makeup artists had transformed a woman beautiful enough to be a television actress into a homely matron. "They even bought me this suit," the Ice Woman informed us.

"Ugh!" I said. "Give it back!"

The Ice Woman was nine years younger than me, so I started out as her mentor before we became partners on the drug squad and then close friends. She was a real go-getter, one of the finest agents I have ever had the pleasure to work with, making incredible cases, like the bust of the madam, when she had only three or four years in the Bureau under her belt. It was rare for women to team up, except on the occasional case, simply because there were still so few of us. Even as recently as the late 1980s, there were only about 30 women out of some 400 agents in the Chicago division.

Unfortunately, our scarcity in itself did not breed sisterly camaraderie. We were all struggling to maintain our footing among the men. For some female agents, the ongoing battle to be perceived as equal seemed to necessitate shunning other women—as if being "one of the girls" would drag them down. There were some who were hyperconscious of other women's potential to fail, as if all the rest of us in the division would be tarred with the same brush. When I was in the midst of the Candy Store caper, trying to persuade our radio Lothario to call on the phone, one of the female agents listening in contacted me to say, "You know, you're not a trained negotiator. I am—why don't you let me take over? Here's how you need to talk to him . . ."

"What I'm doing is working," I had to point out. "Why should I shift gears now?"

She was as nervous about my screwing up as if there had been an entire church-bus-tour's worth of little old ladies' lives at stake. And where had she been all day? The hard part was just about over by the time she called.

Some women had an unhealthy sense of competition with others, reflected in the "queen bee syndrome." Early in my career, I worked briefly on a squad where not one but two women were already entrenched. How grateful I would have been had either of them deigned to take me under her wing. I had no role models to speak of, no one who could help me navigate the often confusing male bastion of the FBI. Instead, while they had made common cause with each other, to them I was a threatening interloper.

There was a coatrack in the squadroom, where we would all hang our wraps, and on the hook on top of mine, I would stick my fedora du jour. I happened to look up from my work one morning, after I'd been in and out of the room a lot on various tasks, and saw that my hat had been crushed flat then stuck back on the hook. "What happened to my hat?" I asked.

Everyone suddenly got very busy. I scanned the twenty desks, waiting for an answer. No one would meet my eyes. Then I saw one of the women, who was pretending to be writing—I had privately nicknamed her the Boll Weevil—let a slight smirk cross her face. I felt like I was back in junior high school.

Looking at her, I asked, "Do you have any idea how my hat got crushed?"

"No," she said, with her eyes still glued to her desk. She didn't even bother to fake an excuse, like it had fallen down and she'd hung it back up but hadn't straightened it. Too exasperated to pursue the matter further, I just let the question—and her lie—hang in the room.

Later one of my squadmates confirmed that she was indeed the culprit. When I was out of the room, she had put on my hat and strutted around, playing for laughs by making fun of me. Then, as her grand finale, she sat on my hat, squashing it, and hung it back up so I would see it, just as a gesture of contempt.

There's a "Bureauism," an innocuous-sounding expression that is in fact the ultimate put-down one agent will give another: "Well, I wouldn't want to work with her . . . ," delivered with a flick of the wrist, waving the subject off as unworthy even of discussion. That's certainly how I felt about the Boll Weevil, and so I didn't work with her long. I very quickly moved on to more welcoming—and much more interesting—pastures, leaving that petty little fiefdom to her.

That's why it meant so much to me, after the Candy Store caper, when I was told that the Ice Woman had called me "Can-Do Candy-woman" to attest to the faith that all the female agents involved had in me. Only one other time in my career would I have the chance to work with another all-woman team. Appropriately enough, it was on a sexual harassment case that the Department of Justice was trying to prosecute under the housing discrimination laws. The offender was a landlord, a sixty-odd-year-old Russian immigrant who relentlessly demanded sexual favors from the female tenants in his low-income apartment house. He even kept what was called the "rent bed" in his office for rent collection days.

Like most sexual predators, he had a voracious appetite. According to one of his victims, he was "good for several times a day." If the women he importuned complied with his demands, he would give them breaks on the rent, but those who didn't he evicted, sometimes without warning, or harassed. He would spy on the recalcitrant tenants; and when they had male visitors, he would have a thug with a Chicago Police badge tow their cars or even bang on their doors and threaten to beat or arrest the men (many of whom lived close enough to the fringe to want to dodge trouble with the cops).

Finally some female tenants banded together and went to a not-for-profit legal agency, seeking legal recourse against the landlord. Represented by attorney Zeva Shuba, they filed a complaint with the city and in federal court with the Chicago Commission on Human Relations. The case wound up in the hands of a U.S. Department of Justice attorney, Barbara Kammerman, who had a strong track record of prosecuting civil rights cases. What she needed in this case, however, were witnesses who were willing to testify against the landlord.

I went door to door in the apartment house, as well as in buildings the landlord owned in the past, trying to find women who would talk to me. Most were too afraid. Finally, I came across Jeanette,* an attractive African-American student at Northwestern. A pipe in her apartment had burst, but the landlord had refused to fix the damage that it had caused unless she had sex with him. Rather than comply, she gave him notice that she planned to move out. "I love you, you're so beautiful," he told her. "You'll never get out of here. I'll keep your security deposit and give you such bad references that no one in this community will ever rent to you."

At the time I met her, Jeanette was trying to scrape together the money to move, even if it meant forfeiting her security deposit. Like the other women I talked to, she was terrified not only by the landlord's direct threats but also by the tales of retribution she had heard. "What if we got you out of here now?" I asked her. "Would that make you feel more able to take the chance?"

She said yes, and within a matter of days, we had her installed in a new apartment in a better building, with her security deposit, first month's rent, and moving expenses paid. Thanks to her testimony, we nailed the guy we had jokingly code-named "LL," for "Lecherous Landlord." He was found guilty, ordered to sell his building, and barred from operating any rental properties for the next four years. He was given two weeks to clear out and, until the building was sold, had to turn over its management to an outside firm. He was permitted to enter it to check on things only twice a month and then only in the company of the managing agents. Finally, he was directed to pay a penalty of $150,000 to six female tenants.

That should have been the end of it. But the landlord had so little respect for American law that he simply ignored the order. Hauled back into court, he was again upbraided by the judge, who told him that to his ensure his compliance with the ruling, he would be monitored and reported to the FBI if he so much as sneezed in a tenant's direction.

He learned that day that I was the agent who had made the case against him. On the courthouse steps, standing at his lawyer's side, he stabbed his finger at my face. "Keep away from me and my building, you bitch! You better not let me catch you there," he growled.

His lawyer was apoplectic, pulling at his sleeve. I grabbed the poking finger. "You better take your client home," I said. "I think he's trying to book a room at the federal Hilton."

As he was dragged away, I indulged myself in a parting shot that gave me a wicked satisfaction. "And don't forget, it was a bunch of women who took you down!"

13

"A LITTLE DOSE OF CANCER"

Buying the house in LaGrange seemed like a smart move, though I would have reason to doubt it. In the mid-1980s the Chicago real estate market started going wild, and faced with the prospect of handsome profits on their houses, everyone I knew was "trading up." I did it myself, twice, once to a slightly larger bungalow and then to a big, ramshackle hundred-year-old Victorian. My income level being what it was, I could never afford a house that was pristine and instantly habitable. But I was too naïve to realize that the previous owners' taste—painted-over oak moldings, "John Wayne" swinging doors here and there—might betoken bad judgment elsewhere in the house, choices that would cost serious money to rectify. Home owning transformed me from a person with ordinary debt—a few hundred dollars on credit cards here and there—to a penniless scrounger, always teetering on the brink of financial ruin.

The cosmetic work on the houses I did myself. I got quite handy at painting and wallpapering—some of the layers I scraped and steamed off walls had been cemented there for thirty years—laying tile, sanding and finishing floors, and even doing simple plumbing repairs. By the time I bought the Victorian house, Seth was thirteen, and I hired him and his friends to help tear down some of the walls dividing it into a warren of tiny, dark nineteenth-century rooms. I'd give them all hammers and helmets, space them three feet apart, and let them smash away at the plaster—what could be more fun for teenage boys?

When trouble struck, I turned to my Bureau family for advice on how to fix things or to borrow tools, like the special $30 drill bit for installing deadbolt locks that Brian Ott* loaned me. Not wanting to impose, I'd ask for step-by-step instructions rather than expect anyone else to do the work—and I wanted to learn. But for problems requiring muscle or special expertise, like the buckling and cracking of my basement floor, fellow agents were incredibly generous. One of the SWAT team snipers, Bobby Parr,* helped me and Seth tear it up with pickaxes. We'd swap skills. Colleagues would call to say, "I heard you rehab houses"—not by choice!—"so how do you fix a sink U-joint?" or "How would you strip the paint off old oak molding?" Before long, I knew the answers.

Even so, I got in way over my head. One rainy November day, I flicked on the light switch in my dining room, and the ceiling fixture started crackling, throwing off huge sparks, and then burst into flame. I called the fire department, who arrived in minutes and extinguished the blaze. "I'd say you've got a roof leak, lady," the fire captain told me. "When water gets into the wires, you've got problems." As if that wasn't devastating enough, he added, "You know, in a lot of these old houses, the wiring isn't up to code. You better get it inspected." Dan Kentala, my profiling partner, who had built an entire house with his own two hands, crawled around in my attic and confirmed his diagnosis. So I called the cheapest roofer I could find to repair the leak, but his estimate was still shocking. I just didn't have that kind of money to spare. Fortunately, the house's previous owners had left an old tractor lawn mower in the garage, which I could never see using on my tiny patch of grass. The roofer took a shine to it, and so I swapped it for his services. Saved!

But then winter came, one of the coldest on record, which in Chicago meant 25 degrees below zero, with the windchill dropping it to −40 or −50. It was then that I discovered just how old and decrepit the furnace was—so incapable of standing up to the cold the whole house shook when its fan was running. With the house's poor insulation, whatever warm air it managed to generate seeped out through the roof. Finally, in the middle of one night it heaved a great groan and conked out, leaving us at the mercy of the elements. To keep warm, Seth and I camped out on the kitchen floor in sleeping bags, huddling near the open oven. But when the stove started heating up, a nasty odor filled the air, which I traced to the rarely used broiler pan. It seems that Seth's pet rat, Pavlov, had been seeking refuge there from the cold and left it littered with droppings. To add insult to injury, our heating bill that month was almost the size of my mortgage payment. I had run through my savings getting the furnace repaired, and winter was just beginning. Threatened with having the heat cut off, in abject humiliation—being a professional in my thirties, raising a child—I had to ask my parents for a loan.

It was a profound relief to "flip" that house for a profit, but I hadn't lost my uncanny knack for picking lemons when it came to homes. Not only was the wiring in the Victorian house shot, but a repair to its eccentric elderly plumbing nicked the toilet "stack" or disposal pipe, which was of a porcelain variety that probably went out of style with the zoot suit. Rather than have sewage spew into my walls, I had to tear it out and replace it. Reconstruction projects like these were not for amateurs—they called for building permits and inspectors and professional contractors who inevitably took twice as long and cost twice as much as planned. I had to sell my car to raise some of the money and went back to driving the now-antique Whisperjet—fortunately, it was working better than anything else in my life.

With all the construction going on, I sent Seth to stay with his father, who was now living nearby, because I didn't want him exposed to so much plaster dust. But since I had to keep tabs on the contractors, I continued to live in the house. Before I crawled into bed, I would swat my pillow to release a blast of pulverized plaster. I was working drugs at the time, busting cocaine dealers, so I was breathing, eating, and sleeping gritty white powder. In my dreams I was Lot's wife, overcome not by a pillar of salt but by mountains of noxious plaster dust and cocaine.

One night I came home to a pitch-dark house because the contractors had ignored my pleas to leave a light on. I grabbed a bag of garbage sitting by the door, planning to switch on a lamp then take it out to the cans. But as I blindly shuffled my way across the room, I hit a gaping hole in the floor that the contractors had left and went crashing down into the basement. The garbage bag shot out of my hands, and as I lay aching on the cold cement, with the wind knocked out of me, I heard cat food cans clattering across the floor above me. That's what told me I was still alive.

The last straw was the discovery that the roof was rotting through in places. All those Victorian pitches and eaves, which gave the house such charm, jacked the price of installing a new roof sky-high. Now my SWAT and DEA colleagues came to the rescue, tearing off the old roof to spare me some of the cost. They spent an entire weekend clambering over the roof with pitchforks, stripping and flinging off the old, decaying shingles so fresh plywood could be laid underneath. For two days, it was raining nails. The only payment my heroes even dreamed of accepting was a constant flow of pizza and beer. I could have cried with gratitude.

I was starting to feel like Job. At one point during these travails I confided my despair over my impoverishment and ravaged credit to an old friend from University. "Candice," she said, "you know, you're still a nurse."

At first I thought she meant that I should quit the FBI. "No, no," she explained. "But there's such a terrible shortage of nurses that you could easily do some weekend and holiday pickup shifts. You could make extra money and you could also do some good. Think about it—you're trained in self-defense and you carry a gun. You could work in places that scare lots of nurses, like inner-city emergency rooms; or better yet, doing home health care. You speak Spanish, right? Well, there are plenty of people in the barrio who need house calls from nurses. What about all those people with AIDS?"

What she said made a lot of sense. I needed the money desperately, and it was true that neighborhoods that might daunt some nurses wouldn't intimidate me, since I had grown used to them as an agent. I could work on the weekends Seth spent with his father. But there was one big catch—moonlighting was forbidden in the FBI. Even agents who weren't on "reactive" teams like the violent crime or fugitive squads were expected to be available, armed, and "fit for duty"—not intoxicated, for example—at all times.

"How would they know?" my friend asked. "Who would you be

hurting? If you did get called for emergency duty, you could always come up with an excuse to leave the hospital, like a crisis at home. It happens. And let's get real—millions of people in this country work second jobs once in a while, like when they've got kids going off to college. Aren't cops always moonlighting as security guards on the weekends?"

Thus began my life of crime. Now and then, whenever I was in a terrible financial jam, I would hire myself out as a nurse. I started by taking shifts in the roughest emergency room in the city, which could be standing room only at ten o'clock on a Saturday morning, with only one doctor and three nurses to carry the load. I can't even count how many times I said, "Don't take that out!" meaning, "Leave the knife or broken bottle that's embedded in you alone! It's probably stopping you from bleeding to death."

But joining the Bureau had made me such an adrenaline junkie that I loved the crisis intervention aspect of the work. And Catholic girl that I was, I prayed that my hard labors in a place where obviously I was so desperately needed would morally counterbalance the possible wrongdoing of breaking the Bureau's rules. I also prayed that while I was moonlighting, I would be spared from ever running into a fellow FBI agent.

This second prayer the Almighty chose to overlook. One day I looked up to find an agent I knew making straight for the nursing station. I actually crouched down and hid behind the desk until he passed. I thought I had escaped, but later, when I was bent over a stretcher tending to a patient, I suddenly heard, "Candice! What are you doing here?"

Flustered, I started begging, "Please don't tell anyone, okay? I need this job to pay my heating bill. Please don't get me in trouble!"

"Oh, no, I won't," he assured me. "I forgot you were a nurse. It's kind of cool that you're working here."

The next time it happened, I was better prepared. A different agent spotted me in the same emergency room and said, "Hey, what's with the uniform?"

"Keep going," I said, sotto voce, "I'm undercover."

"Whoa, I feel like a dope," he replied. "Sorry, I should have guessed that."

I never told any of my hospital co-workers the truth, but one supervisor figured it out when I was working home health. "Are you some kind of cop?" she asked. "How come you always work these neighborhoods?"

"Well, the other nurses don't like to, so I can get a lot of jobs at the times I want," I told her.

She was dubious. "You're a cop, aren't you?"

"Look," I said, "I'm not out to bust any of our patients. But I guess you could say that I am, kind of—just between you and me."

The neighborhoods I worked were some of the poorest in the city, where I sometimes saw more cockroaches in the refrigerator than food. That put my own financial woes in perspective. I always wore my stethoscope around my neck while walking from my car to patients' homes, and no one ever tried to rob me or bother me—people understood that I was providing an essential service. In the rowdier buildings, I would call ahead to have someone meet me at the door and escort me upstairs—that is, if my client had a phone. I had one patient named Julio whose blood sugar had to be checked at seven o'clock in the morning, but his doorbell didn't work and I couldn't get into the building. I waited on the street, hoping that some neighbor would come out but finally had to resort to throwing stones at his window, calling, "Julio! Julio, es la nursa, la enfermera! Abre la puerta, por favor! Pronto, pronto! Julio!"

Finally he peeked his head out the window and came to let me in. But the whole time I was down on the street screaming, "Julio!" I was terrified that I would be overheard by some unexpected FBI surveillance team, thinking, *Oh man, I'm gonna get caught, I'm gonna get caught.*

One Sunday, I was assigned to call on a bedridden paraplegic, a dying man in his sixties, to dress his terrible, raw bedsores and change his urinary catheter. These were tasks so familiar that I could do them in my sleep. But his regular nurse, whom I was relieving, called to warn me that the patient had anatomical problems that could make catheterizing him a challenge. She tried to give me instructions—insert the tube four inches, twist it this way and that way—and though I wrote them down, I marveled because it is usually very straightforward to catheterize a man.

So after I did his wound care, I gingerly inserted the foot-long tube and was surprised to find that with only minimal fiddling, it slipped in about ten inches. It had to be in his bladder—there was no place else for it to go, or so I thought. I injected saline into the tube to inflate the balloon at the end of the catheter, which holds it in the bladder, then waited for urine to trickle out, which would show that the catheter was working. Nothing happened.

Ten minutes passed, then fifteen. I massaged his abdomen to stimulate the flow, with no luck. I decided to remove the catheter and start all over, but when I tried to draw the saline out of the balloon to deflate it, I couldn't. So I told the man, "I'd like to go call your doctor about this."

I was sitting on the edge of the patient's large double bed, which was jammed into such a small room that there was only enough clearance on its sides for two nightstands. I got up and had just made it past the foot of the bed, on my way to the door, when behind my back I heard him say, "Don't worry. I'll take care of this."

Instantly my psychiatric nurse's antennae went up. I whirled around and found him rolling onto his side with an arm outstretched, lunging for something in the nightstand drawer. I knew in my bones that he was grabbing for a gun, that he was going to kill himself. Now my FBI training kicked in, and leaping into the air, I dove onto the bed, slamming down onto the man's back and pinning him flat. Sure enough, in his hand was a black semiautomatic pistol.

Although paraplegics cannot use their legs, they often have tremendous upper body strength. With the man bucking and writhing beneath me, I fought to stay astride him, with my two hands clutching his forearm, trying to shake loose the gun. He had a death grip on it. He was screaming, "Let me have it, let me have it," while I shouted, "No! No, let go!" and hollered for his wife to come and help me.

But when she reached the bedroom door, she just shrieked and wrung her hands. "Grab his arm," I said. "Help me get the gun!"

"Police!" she wailed. "I'm calling the police."

"No, no cops—there's no time!" I shouted. "Help me! I can't hold on." But the thought racing through my mind was, *You can't call the cops because they'll write this up and I'll be reported to the FBI!*

My elbow was close to the man's face, and as I'd been taught at Quantico, I began jabbing it into the side of his head. He still clung to the gun. "Drop it!" I said. "Drop it now!"

He was beginning to get winded, with perspiration beading on his face. "Okay, okay. Just get off me and let me up."

"Oh no," I said. "Not until you give me the gun."

Finally his grip loosened and I yanked it out of his hand. "Get this out of here," I told his wife. "Go hide it someplace."

"Don't take it away," he yelled. "Put it back. I won't do it again. I'm sorry. That was stupid. Just give it back."

"No way," I said. I rolled off his back and took the gun away from her, telling her to go call the doctor.

The doctor came over and fixed the catheter himself, while scolding the patient for his suicide attempt. The couple's adult son, who arrived with the doctor, promised to take the gun out of the house. The man's eye was swelling, and I knew I had blackened it. *Well, better that than death,* I thought.

My heart was pounding and my hair was matted with sweat from the struggle and the fear that he would kill himself—and possibly me—but even more, I have to confess, from the fear that he might get off a shot, rousing the neighbors to call the cops, which would expose me and cost me my FBI job. That's what really had me panicked. I also worried that if the nursing service found out that I was an FBI agent, I'd be fired from that job too.

I reported the incident to my home health supervisor. The next time I went into the office, the nurses all gathered around and had me repeat the story several times, staring at me in amazement as if I were Wonder Woman. If they only knew where my strength had really come from— abject fear! A couple of months later, I asked the man's regular nurse how he was doing and was told, "He's dead. He kept asking for the gun, so they gave it back. They didn't think he was serious, but he got it back and he shot himself."

He had just been too defeated to go on. I felt sick.

. . .

If I happened to be moonlighting around holiday time, I made it my Christmas observance to bring a five-course dinner to my neediest patients, along with a bottle of Christmas wine from a Michigan vineyard, if their health permitted. I would precook everything at home then pack up the hot and cold dishes in insulated bags, thermoses, and coolers, along with a microwave. When I reached each place—wearing my red and white Santa Claus cap—I would load up the plates in the car and carry them upstairs, then bring up the microwave to warm the entrées and set up the patient to eat before moving on to the next stop. I loved this ritual, which seemed to me to be as fitting a celebration of Christmas as going to church.

I became heartbreakingly aware of how much it meant to some of my patients when I arrived later than planned at one house and found my patient sitting alone, eating Campbell's soup straight out of the can. That would have been his Christmas meal. "I was hungry," he told me, with tears in his eyes. "I didn't think you were coming."

I realized then how very often people who live in poverty have been let down—so much so that they no longer believe that anyone will come through. After that I was careful to arrange my route so that my first stops would be the patients without phones, whom I couldn't reach if, for some reason, I got delayed.

My schedule was hard to predict because carting the food and the microwave up and down stairs was a big job for one person. It wasn't always easy to find friends who weren't too encumbered with their own family Christmas obligations to come along. Seth would spend Christmas Eve with his father and have Christmas dinner with me, but I didn't think it was fair to require him to sacrifice his Christmas mornings to my mission. Once, when he was in his late teens, I made a point of bringing him because I wanted him to see another side of life—to know that the whole world didn't have dishwashers and shop at malls. He fit right in, I'm proud to say, and I realized that in the past, by underestimating his maturity, I had probably needlessly deprived myself of help. But soon I got another right-hand man, John Gray, the man who would become my fiancé.

. . .

The Ice Woman was the one who introduced us. One Friday she and I hooked up at Ranali's after work because there was someone she wanted me to meet—a new boyfriend of hers, I assumed. The place was packed, but we managed to get a table, and then she spotted him and waved him over. He had been her firearms instructor at Quantico before he transferred to Chicago. John sat talking and drinking and laughing with us for an hour, and when he got up to go to the men's room, I asked, "So, is something happening between you two?"

"Not with me, Candywoman. I had him in mind for you."

"Oh baby, oh no," I said. "I'm definitely not up for that."

I was at a point in life when I almost doubted that relationships were worth the trouble. Civilian men were too intimidated by my job, so from the time of my epiphany in the bar at Quantico, when it suddenly struck me that I was bobbing on a sea of attractive men, I had been dating badges, mostly cops. Profiling, doing police training, and working drugs brought me into contact with scores of men in law enforcement. Inevitably some were scared off by the fact that Seth and I were a package deal, but once I started throwing off the right sparks, I had no shortage of suitors. Cops and DEA guys loved female agents, whom they saw more as a charming novelty than as emasculating competition—I can't speak for their view of the women in their own ranks—and seemed to appreciate how free the give-and-take could be with someone in a similar line of work. And they were certainly a lot more fun than the average computer jockey or financial analyst. They were everyday heroes, men whose lives were always on the line, and so most of them lived large and played hard—lots of drinking and wild high jinks. Their theme song could have been "Let's Party Like It's 1999."

Of course, there are plenty of staunch family men in law enforcement. But the ones who are available in their thirties and forties tend to be single for a reason. More than in other fields, it seems, cheating comes with the territory—which is why some of my female colleagues went through men like pantyhose, then finally gave up on badges altogether. Not me, I'm afraid—many women are drawn to "bad boys," and I was no exception—and I paid a steep price over the years.

I still remember the day, around that time, when I was driving to work and happened to tune in a female talk show on the radio. The subject was "The Best Places to Find a Husband." The commentator opened by reading a list of the top ten potential-husband-harboring lines of work from one of the women's magazines. The number one field was law enforcement—and the number one job was the FBI. I almost crashed the car.

Law enforcement is a target-rich environment, to be sure. Definitely a field where you can find a lover—and probably have the wildest, most passionately romantic affair of your entire life. But to find a husband— someone faithful, devoted, and home- and hearth-building, with whom you could spend the rest of your life? You'd probably stand a better chance of winning the lottery. People do it, but not very often.

So I was especially disinclined to risk getting mixed up with John, a fellow agent. But we really clicked, and when the Ice Woman left for home, we decided to get a bite to eat. Seth was with his father, and I thought to myself, *Why go home to Lean Cuisine in front of the tube? Why not make an evening of it? It can't hurt to have a little fun with this man.*

I knew a great place called Blue Chicago, a bar on the North Side, that featured a wonderful, down-and-dirty, blues-belting diva and some of the best pizza in town. We took in a couple of sets, and then I dropped him off at home. The next morning my phone rang at nine. It was the Ice Woman, who, before she even said hello, asked with a self-satisfied snicker, "So, is John still there?"

"Of course not," I protested. "I just met him. But if you must know, he's coming by to see the room I'm thinking of renting"—another one of my debt-reducing notions—"and then I'm going to show him around town a little. But it's not a date or anything."

"Yeah, right," she said. "How much do you want to bet that you wind up with him?"

"No bets," I told her. "It wouldn't be right for me to rob you."

But one afternoon led to another, and before long John and I were spending every spare moment together. When Christmas came it was so much easier having a big strong man haul my turkeys and hams and vats of mashed potatoes and bottles of wine out to his commodious Pathfinder and then drive me all over town to make my rounds. I was afraid to tell John the truth that I moonlighted as a nurse—at first because I was still living in terror of being caught, and later for fear that if I were found out, he might be dragged down too by some Bureau regulation that required him to blow the whistle on me. So I lied, explaining my Christmas calls were an outgrowth of my weekend "volunteer work."

John bought my story, and it was gratifying to see how much he enjoyed delivering the meals to my patients. When I brought him upstairs, the clients got a kick out of meeting him too, for a lot of them were curious about my personal life and had been asking whether I had a boyfriend. "Sort of," I would say. For a while I was still too gun-shy to commit.

Our last stop that Christmas was the home of Jerry and Gerry, an elderly man and his grown daughter, who had been wheelchair-bound from birth. I was caring for Jerry, who was recovering from a heart procedure and had just lost his wife, Geraldine, the third Gerry in the family. We set up their dinners on their TV trays, and they begged us to stay and join them. "No, no, this is your Christmas dinner," we said. As we left, Jerry followed us out onto the steps to say good-bye and just broke down in tears. He said, "This is the nicest thing anyone has ever done for me."

My heart ached for him, knowing that as grateful as he may have felt about the dinner, his tears probably sprung from the pain of facing that first Christmas as a widower. I was worried about him—so often with my older patients, when a husband or wife died, the spouse would also be gone within a year. Indeed, two months later Jerry would have a stroke and pass away. Most of the patients who need home care are close to death, but this loss would hit me especially hard. I felt certain that he died because he missed his wife so much.

When I left him that Christmas day, saddened as I felt, something in Jerry's grief seemed to shore up my shaky faith in marriage and relationships. I could see that John had been deeply moved too. That drew me to him—and I now tentatively began to allow myself to envision a future with him, the kind of lifelong partnership my parents had or that I imagined Jerry and Gerry had enjoyed. Sharing my Christmas ritual with John was like some kind of acid test. It shifted the equilibrium of our

relationship and intensified my feelings for him, strengthening and deep-
ening the bond between us. Within a year we were engaged.

For Christmas dinner I always roasted a big beef tenderloin, a special
treat too expensive to indulge in the rest of the year. Before I went out
on my Christmas mission, I would have most of the other food prepared,
so all I had to do was pop the tenderloin in the oven. One year, when
Seth was home for the holidays from college, we had a near disaster. I
put the tenderloin in the oven, and Seth and John joined me in the
kitchen, where we all sipped glasses of Christmas wine. We were talking
and laughing when Seth happened to notice a lever on the stove.
"What's this?" he asked, as he slid it across its slot.

It was the lever for the self-cleaning feature of the oven. I so rarely
used the oven that I had never tried it. When I tried to slide it back, it
wouldn't budge. I tried every maneuver I could think of—jogging it up
and down, shaking it, pushing it in and out—and eventually had to get
out the manual. That's when I discovered it had a safety lock—that to
self-clean, the oven got so hot that it would be hazardous to open it. So
a ratchet mechanism sealed it shut, which would not unlock until the
full cleaning/cooldown cycle was complete. Fortunately, there was an
override procedure, which I immediately tried to implement, with no
luck.

"Let me try that," John said.

I stood aside and watched him run through the instructions several
times. That didn't work. Clearly something was broken. He got a butter
knife, which he tried using to jimmy the lever, without success. Then
he started poking the knife around the edges of the oven door in case
there was a latch that could be tripped. He was growing red-faced with
frustration.

Seth, meanwhile, was getting agitated, pacing around, convinced that
he had ruined our Christmas dinner. When his pacing took him out of
earshot, John said exasperatedly, "Why the hell did he do that? What
was he thinking?"

Never having raised children, John hadn't developed the nerve-
deadening capacity that protects parents from short-circuiting.

"Shush," I told him. "Seth likes you and he respects you, so don't
rag on him. He feels bad enough."

But I could see that he was still stewing. Seth returned and propped himself against the kitchen counter, trying to offer suggestions that John rebuffed. He apologized over and over. Inside the oven, the tenderloin was crackling, and I could see through the window that it was getting nicely seared. John was testy, Seth was miserable—I couldn't see that I had too many options. We could let the roast incinerate and go out to dinner, but a buffet at one of the big hotels downtown—probably the only places that would be open—wasn't my idea of holiday fun. There was nothing in the house that I could whip up on top of the stove that would seem festive enough for Christmas dinner. Spaghetti or grilled cheese or bacon and eggs weren't going to soothe John's annoyance or ease Seth's distress. Maybe if we could get into the oven, we could rescue the roast, which by now was definitely done.

I got a hammer and handed it to John. "The hell with this. That roast is coming out of there," I told him. "There's only one way to do it."

"You mean break the window?" he said.

"Why not? I have to get the oven fixed anyway. Don't slam it because we don't want glass in the meat. See if you can just crack it gently."

So that's what he did, and that $50 piece of meat ended up being a $200 piece of meat because the new door cost $150. But it was the best tenderloin I ever cooked. More important, the break-in salvaged our Christmas by making an absurd situation as funny—as opposed to cranky and recriminatory—as it deserved to be.

It was my patients who were teaching me to focus on what mattered, and to let the rest go. So many of them led impossibly difficult lives, with terrible disadvantages of every kind, grave illnesses, heartbreaking losses, dire poverty. Most of them managed to muddle through with a modicum of dignity, and even grace under fire. They had to—the only other choice was the way out my paraplegic took when his family gave back the gun.

So if my roof was falling in or I had to scrape together Seth's college tuition money, which was my immediate problem then, it didn't torment me anymore. I had a new DeLongism: "You need a little dose of cancer"—meaning, whatever someone like me was going through, it was nowhere near as bad as things could get. "Is anybody hurt?" I'd ask myself. "Is anybody dying? Well, then, what is there to get upset about?"

14

SHARK BAIT

The FBI is less a place to work than a way of life. Unlike the police, who are "off duty" when their shifts are over, FBI agents are required to be armed, available, and "fit for duty" at all times. That means that we must carry our guns everywhere, even on vacation, and there's no quick dashing off to the cash machine at the bank, leaving your gun at home. If a bank robbery went down in your presence and you were unarmed, you'd have some explaining to do. "Available" means that you must always be within two hours of the office unless you are on some officially approved leave, such as a vacation. But even then, you are required to file an itinerary at the office with CBR ("can be reached") numbers. The Bureau's arm is long.

Those are fairly straightforward requirements. But the "fit for duty" provision is thornier, since it encompasses such a wide range of physical and even "moral" conditions. Every year agents are required to "qualify" both on the firing range, meaning that they must shoot at least an 85 percent, and at physical training, running a mile and a half and passing sit-up, push-up, and stair-step tests. (However, since the physical training requirement isn't strictly enforced, many agents wriggle out of it.) Until recently, being overweight would make you "unfit for duty," and there were rigorous standards. If you exceeded them at your annual physical, you would get a "fat boy" or "fat girl" letter, giving you a

deadline and requiring you to weigh in monthly until you got the weight
off. If you didn't, you could potentially be fired, and I do know of people
who were demoted for being too fat.

These days, the standards have been relaxed, after legal challenges—
and, according to Bureau gossip, thanks to some high-ranking officials
who had trouble keeping their own weight down. Many agents don't
applaud these changes. Who wants a partner who has to wrestle his or
her belly out from under the steering wheel? And do you really want
your backup waddling and huffing and puffing through an emergency
situation? If you are pregnant, you can be assigned to light duty (and the
Bureau has one of the most generous family leave policies around), but
there's really no such thing as a desk job in the FBI.

Having more than one or two drinks, even on weekends, will make
you "unfit for duty." In major cities, there are "reactive squads" that
respond to emergencies such as bank robberies and kidnappings, whose
members are "on call" and must be clearheaded at all times. Agents will
do reactive duty in weekly rotations, so no one bears the onus of constant
demands. But in smaller satellite Bureau offices, agents don't have that
luxury and must always be alert and ready for action.

Agents are expected to be model citizens. Every five years, investigators will call on the people who live nearby to ascertain whether you
are a "good neighbor." If you fall behind on your rent, your landlord
knows that he can call and get you reprimanded by the Bureau. Association with anyone who has a criminal record is forbidden; any roommate of more than thirty days and anyone you plan to marry will be
subjected to criminal record checks. Any contact with law enforcement—a moving violation while driving, a visit from the police if you're
playing the stereo too loud at a party—must be reported to your supervisor. You are obliged to list any traffic tickets you have received on
your five-year "reinvestigation" forms.

The more intrusive investigations are aimed at discerning whether
you are vulnerable to bribery or extortion. Every five years, you must
undergo a credit check to prove that you are solvent enough to resist
temptation (as if missing a few Visa payments would make you turn to
espionage). Lest you be subject to coercion or blackmail, you must be

legally and morally aboveboard. Legend has it that in the Hoover days, unmarried agents might be placed under surveillance. A bachelor spotted coming out of a woman's house early in the morning would be called on the carpet for "conduct unbecoming an FBI agent," and be told, "Marry the girl."

Over the past fifteen years, agents have been allowed much more privacy in their personal lives. Cohabitation—never mind an occasional sleepover date—is far too common to raise eyebrows anymore. I don't know of any female agents who have borne children out of wedlock, but presumably that would no longer be a violation of the rules. There was an uproar in the mid-1980s when a married agent couple was accosted by a robber outside a sex club, and in the ensuing struggle, the wife was badly wounded and her husband killed the robber. What got them in trouble was not the killing but not quite coming clean on what they had been up to beforehand. The press would have a field day with jokes about agents dressed in superhero costumes with their private parts exposed flitting around a sex club. As punishment, the couple was fired but sued for reinstatement and won. In the old days, such infractions might be punished by compulsory transfers, a disciplinary measure rarely used anymore, but should an agent become embroiled in a serious intra-office scandal—such as publicly taking up with another employee's spouse—that rendered him or her ineffective in a division, relocation might be strongly suggested.

Homosexuality remains somewhat dicier. Even today—given that the Bureau is an 85 percent male, paramilitary organization with members who are, for the most part, politically conservative and religiously observant (there's even a sizable faction known as the Mormon Mafia)—few men openly profess to be gay. Women tend to be less intimidated. Recently, two lesbian agents fell in love and asked to be transferred so that they could live together as a couple. The Bureau complied with their request, though it continues to require heterosexual couples to marry in order to qualify for "togetherness" transfers. The FBI is no longer allowed to ask about sexual orientation, but should the question come up, you can't lie to conceal it. Because gayness is still viewed as a potential blackmail issue, the Bureau will ask whether an agent's parents

know of his or her homosexuality—that's the degree of openness believed to make coercion unlikely. To be sure that the parents know,
investigators will follow up.

Any breach of the Bureau's myriad rules—from piddling offenses to
felonies such as heroin-dealing, selling classified documents to foreign
governments, and murder (all of which agents have been known to
commit)—can lead to an investigation by the Office of Professional
Responsibility, a so-called OPR. One of the worst violations an agent
can be accused of is "lack of candor," which encompasses the full spec-
trum of dissembling, from outright lying to failing to confess transgres-
sions of the rules. Big discrepancies, say, between the number of traffic
tickets an agent claims and has actually received will prompt an inquiry
to determine whether "lack of candor," a much more serious offense
than the tickets themselves, was the cause. If the "lack of candor" involves a more significant transgression than traffic tickets, the agent may
be asked to take a polygraph test and be suspended without pay for a
time or even dismissed.

Few agents make it through an entire career without a few OPR
reviews. In *Mindhunter* John Douglas describes one that he received for
giving an FBI-sanctioned interview—talking to the press without permission would have been a major violation—that resulted in a newspaper quote, taken out of context, that the Bureau didn't like. After
being "raked over the coals"—his words—he escaped with a letter of
censure. Many agents jokingly refer to these letters as "red badges of
courage" and hang them on the office walls, on the notion that screwing
up in the line of duty means that you are doing your job—as opposed
to being RIP, the Bureau term for a slothful agent, meaning "retired in
place."

I got my first OPR for a careless mistake I made while traveling to a
profiling conference in Oklahoma City. Agents are supposed to carry
their guns aboard planes on their person, after doing paperwork to be
delivered to the pilot, or else pack them (unloaded) in baggage to be
checked. I was running late to the airport due to a storm, so after checking my bag, in which I thought I had packed my gun, I made a mad
dash to the gate. When I got to the security point I placed my small
carry-on bag on the conveyer belt. There was an immediate flurry of

alarm. As guards raced to grab the carry-on and restrain me, I held up my hands, saying, "Wait! I'm an FBI agent. What's going on?"

Then it struck me that I had packed my gun not in the suitcase I had checked but in my small carry-on bag. In my hurry, I had forgotten where I had put it. When a guard spotted the gun on the X-ray scanner, he called in the troops. "Oops, you got me," I said cheerily, as one law-enforcement agent to another. "Gee, you guys are really good."

But that's not how the airport security people understood my remark. A letter wound up on my ASAC's desk, maintaining that I had deliberately tried to carry my gun onto the plane as a test and then "ridiculed" the guards when I got caught. An OPR investigation was opened and my supervisor was asked to confirm that I had reported this brush with the law (I had, luckily, lest I be charged with not reporting "an incident") even before I, the suspect, was brought in to tell my side of the story. In those days, an agent could be under OPR investigation and not even know it until summoned to testify, a morale-dampening practice abolished by the FBI's current director Louis Freeh. Then, under oath, I delivered my account, which was typed up for signature and became the SSS (signed, sworn statement) reviewed by the brass, who would judge the charges to be unfounded, founded-but-minor, or founded-and-serious and take disciplinary action. Mine were ruled founded-but-minor, and I received my first "red badge of courage."

A great many complaints leading to OPR investigations originate not outside the Bureau but within—from agents informing on other agents, sometimes anonymously, which allows for the proliferation of minor, bogus complaints. The rules require anyone who knows of a criminal act or a policy violation by an FBI employee to turn in the offending colleague or risk suspension without pay ("time on the bricks," in Bureauspeak). Of course, knowing that someone has stolen money, is sleeping with a Russian spy and passing on classified secrets, or using or selling illegal drugs—anyone should feel compelled to report that colleague. We are, after all, sworn officers of the law. But there are supervisors who will routinely report their own people for violations most would consider minor, just to look like they're on top of the activities of their staff. There are also, inevitably, agents who will tattle to the OPR just to make trouble for others—a practice so common that there's even a term for it in FBI slang: "jamming." All such reports must be taken seriously, so countless man-hours and, no doubt, vast sums of money are spent each year on unfounded and minor complaints agents plant to "jam" others. There's an entire drawer on jamming in that imaginary file cabinet I label "If the Taxpayers Only Knew . . ."

There was one character in the Chicago division whom I nicknamed SG, for Spiteful Gossip, who spawned a number of complaints against fellow agents. I always believed that he was behind two ridiculous ones filed against me and my boss on the drug squad, Elaine Smith. Elaine's alleged crimes included leaving work early every other Friday to get her nails done and funding an investigation with her own money. The latter allegation harked back to a remark Elaine made the night of the party staged to help my drug-dealer informant impress the rancher drug queen. Elaine had told someone that she'd brought along $100 just in case there were any last-minute expenses, to make sure everything went smoothly.

Just hearing that charge made me laugh. Not long before, the division had hit one of its seasonal budget crunches, when the money allotted by Congress fell short, so our beeper service was temporarily cut off. The slackers accepted the situation, but the more conscientious agents— loath to be out of touch with their informants—went out and bought their own beepers. They had to, if they were to work drugs effectively. Would the taxpayers really want to see us penalized for that?

My supposed violations included running a home-renovation business from the office and hauling lumber in my Bureau car, which at the time was a station wagon. It was a roomy station wagon, admittedly, but still far too tiny to transport the building supplies I was running through for the Victorian house. My lumber had to be delivered by flatbed truck! My purported remodeling business was concocted out of thin air and a few calls from the contractor working on my house that came in during business hours. I was borrowing money, not making money on the one rehab job I was doing—on my own house. But my "concerned" colleague SG had added two (home renovation plus Bureau station wagon) and two (contractor calls plus office phone) together to make seven.

For both Elaine and me, all the changes were determined to be unfounded. Preposterous as they were, they had to be investigated. What a waste of everybody's time and energy!

This is the kind of intramural terrorism that tends to go on in closed systems like academia, the military, and the FBI. Academic tenure—or in government jobs, the pension you're guaranteed if you last twenty years—is too good to make quitting an attractive option, even if you're unhappy. It's not like you can jump ship and go work for the competition, and your skills are too specific for most other lines of work. So, while jockeying for power, backstabbing, and slacking off are all rampant in the private sector, they become recreational for some people in jobs that nobody leaves. In an environment like the FBI, where secrecy reigns, rules are ironclad, and the culture not only gives you myriad opportunities but actually requires you to turn on others, unhealthy kinds of rivalries can develop. Adrenaline junkies who aren't generating enough excitement in their own work—it's not the busy, productive agents who prey on others—will often whip up waves. Harpooning colleagues can become their gladiator sport.

But there would come a time when I faced an OPR review so serious that I kept my attorney on speed-dial. I was almost KMA (Bureau slang for "kiss my ass," meaning eligible for retirement, so you don't have to take any guff), but I was threatened with the loss of my pension—twenty years of service down the drain. And, I'm sorry to say, the charges were founded. I was busted for moonlighting as a nurse.

Just how my offense came to light remains in question. One Friday my current San Francisco supervisor and I were summoned to the office of the ASAC, who informed me that an OPR investigation had been opened up on me for "unauthorized violation of the secondary employment rule." I had stopped moonlighting after leaving Chicago until I got caught in an unexpected bind—I risked coming up short on Seth's college tuition because my engagement had dissolved, sticking me with an expensive lease for the house I had shared with my fiancé. To make ends meet, I had resumed working as a nurse, and someone had gotten wind of it.

What's more, I later learned, the person had placed a copy of a nursing agency time card and a patient report signed "Candice DeLong, R.N." on my supervisor's desk. I had had the documents in my briefcase so I could leave them at the drop site on my way home from work.

"So I had to turn you in," my supervisor said. "You know that."

I was surprised that the supervisor hadn't even discussed it with me first, for I was the primary relief person, the right hand on the squad. I had just been recommended for an award for "consistent and unfailingly exceptional performance of my duties." Not that I expected any special treatment, but I would have appreciated the heads-up.

I couldn't help asking, suspiciously, "Who would just drop something like this on a supervisor's desk?"

"There's no way for us to know that," I was told. "Could it be some revenge thing, like over your broken engagement?"

The idea that my ex-fiancé would ever jam me was beyond ridiculous. Not only was our parting amicable, once the dust settled, but I wasn't even sure that he had been paying enough attention to realize that I had been getting paid for my "volunteer work." The supervisor pointed out that everyone had enemies or perhaps had misplaced trust in friends, but I knew that none of my friends could be responsible. Though I had one enemy that I knew of, it was hard to imagine anyone, however bent on jamming a colleague, rifling someone's briefcase in search of evidence.

The full roster of charges against me would include the classic "car violations," a very common offense. In my case, the accusation stemmed from the fact I sometimes signed out of the Bureau at 5 P.M. and then signed in at the same time, 5 P.M., on my nursing time card. In fact, there was a five- or ten-minute interval between jobs, when I would drive home, drop off my Bureau car, and switch to my own car for my nursing calls. But in the Bureau's view, the five minutes it took me to drive home constituted misuse of my Bureau vehicle, for technically, during that time, I was "on call" for the nursing agency.

To address the charges, I decided to get a lawyer. Louis Freeh, the current director of the FBI, is well respected by agents both for his background—he's a onetime federal judge, the prosecutor of New York's famous "Pizza Connection" mob case, and unlike most directors since Hoover, a former special agent himself—and for bringing a new fairness to the FBI. In the past, agents facing OPR charges were denied due process and not even permitted legal representation. As John Douglas writes in *Mindhunter*: "When I went to headquarters to appear before OPR, the first thing I had to do was sign a waiver of my rights. Upholding justice in the outside world and practicing it inside are not necessarily the same thing."

But Freeh reformed the OPR process to make it fair, not only by allowing agents to hire lawyers but by making precedent, not caprice, the basis for punishment. All too often in the past, white men who were part of the old-boy network were let off easy, while they might throw the book at women and minorities.

My lawyer, Richard Swick of Washington, D.C., an expert on Bureau disciplinary procedure, is kept on retainer by the FBI Agents Association (FBIAA), which is like a trade guild or a union for agents. Even he, who had seen countless OPR investigations, considered the timing of my case to be "mean-spirited." With his backing, I requested that my case be tried at FBI headquarters in Washington, which is every agent's right. The enemy I suspected of setting me up in San Francisco was well connected and, if indeed responsible, might conceivably influence the outcome of my adjudication. I wanted to be sure that the hearing I got was impartial.

I knew that I had to tell the absolute truth. Fortunately, there were precedents for my situation, and the fact that other agents hadn't been fired for moonlighting and car violations established that these offenses weren't in themselves cause for dismissal. But "lack of candor" was something else—for since 1994, when Louis Freeh created his Bright Line policy, you could possibly be sacked for that.

Determined as I was to tell the truth, I was still terrified when I was asked to take a polygraph test. A completely innocent person who has no knowledge of a crime might stand a chance of passing a polygraph test (and then so might a psychopath, with no emotional connection to his acts). But for those of us in between, the likelihood of passing is uncertain, which is the reason why polygraphs are not admissible in court. Polygraphs measure signs of stress—sweating, increased heart and respiration rates—which tend to develop when you are telling a lie. I never said I was innocent, but having charges dredged up against me when I was a mere few months shy of retirement, with my income for the rest of my life hanging in the balance, I was so stressed out that I could have set off the bells and whistles just by walking past the machine.

Then too, there were gray areas where I could go astray, things I doubted I'd be able to remember and charges like the car violations, which could easily trip me up. Since the automobile was invented, there has probably never been an agent who perfectly followed the rules governing the use of Bureau cars. If I went five blocks out of my way to pick up my drycleaning going to or from work, that was technically a violation. And there was my ingrained Catholic guilt. When Seth was a child, I always thought that if he went missing and the police should question me about it, I'd never be able to pass a polygraph test. I would be so riddled with guilt for ever letting him out of my sight that the needle would be swinging wild.

But to refuse to take the test would suggest I had something to hide. So I agreed. If the situation hadn't been so dire, it would have amused me that the polygrapher used all the standard tricks for grilling a suspect that I myself had learned at Quantico; even trying to get me riled up, hoping that if he flummoxed me I'd change my story. It seemed like just one more intimidation tactic when, at the end of the test, the polygrapher left me hooked up to all the gear. I took it off myself and said simply, "This interview is over."

Just as I feared, I flunked the polygraph. But the lead investigator would later tell my lawyer that he believed that I had been completely candid in my interview. In my day and a half of questioning, I explained the financial problems that had beset me over the years, including the need to raise Seth's college tuition money. I wanted to add, "For three of my twenty years in the Bureau, I worked drugs. If I were really corrupt, I had every opportunity to take a payoff from a dealer or to get hooked up to deal myself. With a single kilo of coke I could have scored a lot more money—and a lot more easily—than I could make being vomited on and exposed to AIDS as a nurse."

I pointed again to my good record—before the trouble started, my supervisor had just put me in for an "incentive award," a cash acknowledgment of merit. I told them of my dedication to the job, that I had erred out of need, not to flout the rules. "I love the FBI," I said, and it was true.

One of the investigators, a woman, was understanding and generous enough to offer, "I hope things work out for you."

Ultimately, they found me guilty of moonlighting—as indeed I was—and because I had done it for so long, they decided to throw the book at me, probably as an example for others. They would recommend my dismissal within thirty days, just six weeks shy of my retirement. The severity of the ruling was astonishing. In one case I knew of, and which my lawyer confirmed, a male agent facing criminal felony charges—not policy violation citations, like the ones I was facing and which represented the vast majority of OPR complaints—had his case held in abeyance for an entire year, so that he would not risk conviction before his official retirement date, which would cost him his pension.

Thanks to Louis Freeh's new rules, I had the right to appeal the decision. I had just begun the appeals process when my father became gravely ill and passed away within a month. When my lawyer advised the adjudication division of my situation, they told him, "We're not monsters, you know."

Rather than force me to go through the appeals process, they gave me a technical out. They couldn't just drop the charges—I was, after all, guilty. Instead they scheduled my hearing for the day after my official retirement began, when I would no longer be required to attend. I would retain my full pension.

For all the anxiety of those months, I did have one consolation—the fact that unlike most crimes, mine had accomplished some good in the world—or so I hoped. I still felt a spark of gratitude to the patients I had served as a nurse—painful as the outcome had turned out to be—for they had enriched my life immeasurably. For that, I had to feel lucky.

15

THE BEAST

In 1995, when I got the chance to transfer from Chicago to San Francisco, I jumped at it. My parents now lived there, and since Seth was away at college, there was no reason for me to stay in his father's vicinity. I loved San Francisco, and so did John, my new fiancé. The feelings sparked when he had accompanied me on my Christmas dinner visits to my neediest patients had in time developed into a serious commitment, of the kind that I had never expected to make again. We had begun living together in Chicago and decided to marry. By now John was in FBI management, and he even stepped down, returning to street agent status, so we could move together to the West Coast.

However, neither of us was the least bit keen on the case that was creating a crying need for agents in San Francisco—the Unabomber investigation. Having consumed millions of dollars and hundreds of thousands of agent-hours, the case was considered to be a black hole, no closer to being solved than it had been in 1979, when a bomb detonated in midair on American Airlines flight #444 from Chicago to Washington, D.C. Fortunately, rather than explode, downing the plane and killing everyone on board, it fizzled in its mailbag, filling the cabin with smoke and forcing an emergency landing. Nobody was seriously injured, but twelve people were treated for smoke inhalation. The bomber would record in his diary that he was "pissed off" at the failure.

Investigating the near disaster, the Chicago FBI took a closer look at two recent bombings in the area. The first had occurred in 1978, when a nine-year-old boy, walking home from school with his mother, found a shoebox-size package on the ground. It bore the return address of a professor of engineering at Northwestern University's Technical Institute, Dr. Buckley Crist, and was to be sent to Professor E. J. Smith at Rensselaer Polytechnic Institute in Troy, New York. But when the boy's mother called Crist, he was puzzled, claiming to know nothing of the package. They agreed that she would have it delivered to his office. When it arrived, a campus security guard, Terry Marker, brought the suspicious package upstairs and opened it.

Under the wrapping paper was a crude pine nailed-together box with a large black arrow drawn on it, pointing to a latch. As Marker moved to open it, Crist backed up, an action that would later make him a suspect in the case. But whatever instinct inspired him to do it was correct. The package exploded. Fortunately Marker escaped with only minor burns.

A year later, John Harris, a civil engineering graduate student at Northwestern, opened a taped-up cigar box in a study area, and it blew up. He too suffered only moderate injuries. Both of these early bombs seemed amateurish enough to be the work of rather malicious and destructive pranksters and so were not brought to the attention of the FBI. But in retrospect it would be apparent that with each new device, the bombmaker was honing his skills.

The bomb on Flight #444 was his most sophisticated yet, but FBI examiners were able to connect it to the others by his "signature." Once a bombmaker hits on the right materials and effective techniques to assemble critical elements of his device and, especially, his fusing mechanism, which trips the explosion, he tends to keep using and refining them. Bomb scene investigators are trained to recognize pieces of these mechanisms and other elements in the debris of a blast and so can often match up the device with its designer. All three of these bombs had technical similarities, contained wooden elements, which was unusual, and used the kind of materials that might clutter any home tool bench or utility drawer—string, flashlight batteries, nails, plumbing parts, and later on pieces of scrap metal. His first nickname was the Junkyard

Bomber. There was a method to his madness, however—all the components of his bombs were so commonly available as to be virtually untraceable.

His fourth bomb upped the ante. In the late spring of 1980, he sent a letter to the president of United Airlines, Percy Wood, telling him that he would be sending him a book of "great social significance." It arrived on June 10 and proved to be a novel, *The Ice Brothers*, by Sloan Wilson. When Wood opened the book, it exploded, riddling his hands, face, and upper legs with shrapnel, but he survived. In the debris investigators found a metal disk stamped with the letters FC, which had been designed to withstand the explosion—it was as if now he was literally, as well as figuratively, affixing a signature to his bombs.

So now the bombmaker had a trademark, and he also got a new name. Instead of the Junkyard Bomber, he became the Unabomber, after the FBI code name for the case, chosen because the targets had been two universities (UN) and two airlines (A): UNABOM.

There would be three more bombs planted in the next two years. One at the University of Utah at Salt Lake City would be detected and defused. Another arrived on the desk of Professor Patrick Carl Fischer, a computer scientist at Vanderbilt University, when he was away. It would be opened by his secretary, Janet Smith, who would suffer severe lacerations from the blast. It bore the return address of Leroy Bearnson, a professor of electrical engineering at Brigham Young University, whose middle name was Wood—like the United Airlines president and like some of the components of his bombs—prompting speculation that wood was somehow part of the puzzle. Two months later, in July 1982, Diogenes Angelakos, a professor of electrical engineering at Berkeley, picked up a strange canlike device in Cory Hall and was badly injured.

For the next three years, the bomber went underground, only to reemerge with a vengeance in 1985. In May, a package postmarked Oakland, California, arrived at a Boeing Aircraft plant in Auburn, Washington. The bomb inside was safely defused. Around the same time, Cory Hall was the site of a second incident, when John Hauser, an electrical engineering grad student who was also a U.S. Air Force captain, opened a plastic file box that blew up, tearing off parts of his fingers and damaging one of his eyes. Then in November, a bomb was mailed to University of Michigan psychology professor James Vernon Mc-Connell, a behavioral modification expert who had recently been featured in the *New York Times*. The blast would cause him partial hearing loss and seriously injure his young assistant, Nicklaus Suino, who had opened the package. A month later, on December 11, Hugh Campbell Scrutton picked up what looked like a bag of construction debris in the parking lot of his computer rental store. When it exploded, its shrapnel pierced his heart, killing him. The Unabomber had now become a murderer.

Two years later, he would strike again at another computer store, CAAMS, Inc., in Salt Lake City, badly wounding its owner, Gary Wright. Then he disappeared again for six years, raising hopes that he had been caught and jailed for some other offense or even possibly had blown himself up. No such luck. There was speculation that he might have been flushed out by the February 1993 bombing of New York's World Trade Center, which he could have seen as upstaging him. Whatever the reason, he resurfaced in June 1993, again targeting professors. Charles Joseph Epstein, a renowned geneticist and the recent subject, like James McConnell, of a *New York Times* profile, was seriously injured by the explosion of a "jiffy bag" that had been sent to his home in Tiburon, California. A few days later, a similar padded envelope exploded in the office of a prominent Yale computer scientist, David Gelernter, who managed to lurch outside—streaming blood from his face, chest, abdomen, and hands—trying to get to the campus health center down the block. He was rushed into surgery at Yale New Haven Hospital and survived, though the attack would leave him permanently maimed, deaf in one ear and blind in one eye.

Thomas Mosser wasn't so lucky. On December 10, 1994, when the well-known New York advertising executive opened a package, which a former employer had forwarded to his suburban New Jersey home, he was decapitated and died instantly. Then, on April 24, 1995, Gilbert Murray, president of the California Forestry Association in Sacramento (a timber-industry lobbying group), unwrapped a parcel addressed to his predecessor, William Dennison, and was literally blown to bits. The attack took place just a few days after the bombing of the Murrah Federal Building in Oklahoma City, which had killed 168 and wounded more than 500 people—another tragedy that had robbed the Unabomber of attention.

It was obvious that he yearned for attention—like most serial killers— because he had begun to communicate with the press. Right around the time of the Epstein and Gelernter bombings, he wrote a letter to the *New York Times*, introducing himself as "an anarchist group calling our-selves FC"—the letters with which he "signed" his bombs. He would go on to establish a regular correspondence with such newspapers as the *Times*, the *Washington Post*, and the *San Francisco Chronicle*, and would even write to David Gelernter, his victim:

> People with advanced degrees aren't as smart as they think they are. If you'd had any brains, you would have realized that there are a lot of people out there who resent bitterly the way you techno-nerds are changing the world and you wouldn't have been dumb enough to open an unexpected package from an unknown source.

The return address on that letter was "FBI Headquarters, Washington, D.C." But because so many of the bombs and letters had originated in California (most allegedly coming from real or fictitious professors and students at various universities), the center of the investigation now shifted from Chicago—the "OO" (Office of Origin) at the time of the American Airlines bombing, which had closed the case during the Una-bomber's long stretch of inactivity—to San Francisco. A UNABOM Task Force was set up—comprised of agents from the FBI, the U.S. Postal Inspection Service, and the Bureau of Alcohol, Tobacco, and Firearms (ATF)—to work out of the San Francisco FBI offices. The task force was divided into three squads: the suspect squad, to investigate any possible Unabombers we turned up (close to 2,000 of them, ultimately); the project squad, to undertake specific investigative initiatives; and the administrative squad, to process all the paperwork and to provide logis-tical support.

I arrived in San Francisco in May as a temporary extra pair of hands and then joined the project squad in September 1995. All the agents on it had at least ten years in the Bureau, so we all had what was known as "the attitude"—a certain cynicism. But once I got established there, I came to enjoy the work and stopped seeing UNABOM as an agent's graveyard or a rabbit hole, down which so many had disappeared. There's an FBI expression for doing a job that might not be so great, but you like it anyway—"the best work in the Bureau"—and that's what I had stumbled into here.

The initial reward for information leading to the arrest and conviction of the Unabomber was $50,000, but within months of the Epstein and Gelernter bombings, the amount on offer increased to $1 million, more than half of which had been raised by the academic and scientific communities. A hot line was established for tips: 1-800-701-BOMB. With a reward that large, whenever the case made the news, we would be deluged with calls, most of which fell into the my-spouse-isn't-paying-his-alimony or the my-professor-flunked-me-and-he's-a-weirdo category. Still, anything not obviously dismissable had to be checked out, which kept the fifteen agents on the suspect squad hopping, checking into dozens of leads a day.

At least in this case, unlike the Tylenol murders, which might have been committed by anyone, we could rule out women and nonwhite men, as well as Caucasian men under thirty-five and older than fifty. At the time of the CAAMS bombing in 1987 (which was the last placed, as opposed to mailed, device), an eyewitness had told us that the man who planted the bomb, which looked like a piece of wood, in the parking lot was white, in his late twenties, and of average height and weight, with a protruding jaw, thin, light-colored mustache, and blond curls, possibly from a wig, just barely visible between his dark sunglasses and the hooded sweatshirt he wore pulled around his face. This description was the basis of the first Unabomber sketch, and others would follow, including one by the famous Jeanne Boylan. Unfortunately, despite all of them, having concealed his head and eyes, the bomber would be hard to recognize.

Among the project squad's tasks were tracking down the unfamiliar orange Fiat the CAAMS eyewitness had reported seeing in the parking lot, checking out suppliers of old typewriters like the one on which the bomber was composing his letters, and trying to find Nathan R. One of the first letters the bomber had written the *New York Times* bore the faint impression of a message that had seemingly been jotted on some paper lying on top of it: *Call Nathan R Wed 7 P.M.* Thousands upon thousands of Nathans whose last names began with R were dug out of Department of Motor Vehicles records and such computer databases as Lexis/Nexis; and then agents in each division were dispatched to interview every one of them, reporting their findings to San Francisco for evaluation and, if promising, follow-up. Despite the countless agent-hours dedicated to the Nathan R search, nothing ever panned out; and to this day, we don't know what the inscription means. The Unabomber isn't talking.

I was put in charge of the Dungeons and Dragons project, which was born of the second bombing, the cigar box planted in the student lounge at Northwestern, back in 1979. Oddly enough, I was working as a nurse at University Hospital the day the injured student came into the emergency room. A year later I became an agent, and here I was, sixteen years later, investigating that very incident.

We had determined that back then, a small group of young men would gather periodically in a room directly across the hall from the study area where Harris found the cigar-box bomb to play Dungeons and Dragons. "D&D," as it was known, was a video game with a medieval theme, in which the players assume the roles of fantasy characters and are assigned tasks to perform by the Dungeon Master. For any number of impressionable young men, the game became an obsession; and for some, the line between their fantasy tasks and their real-world equivalents would blur. Since the advent of the game in the 1970s, more than a hundred murders and suicides have been attributed to Dungeons and Dragons.

In one dramatic D&D murder case, a female museum guide was killed in a gallery displaying medieval suits of armor. She was discovered seated on the floor with her legs outstretched, her ankles well apart, and her head slumped forward, as if she had fallen asleep sitting up. What held her in that position was a four-foot sword that had been plunged into her back near her right shoulderblade and had exited below her right breast, with its tip embedded in the floor between her knees. She was fully dressed, and there was no evidence of sexual assault.

This bizarre crime fooled even the FBI profilers, who surmised that the guide had been killed by a schizophrenic with voices in his head that ordered him to stage such a strange scene. The conjecture made sense to me, having worked on a maximum-security psych ward for all those years. However, when the murderer was caught, he turned out to be not a full-blown schizophrenic but a misguided teenager, a D&D devotee who had taken his role a bit too seriously. The poor innocent young woman had become a prop in his game.

So agents on the D&D project tracked down the members of the game-playing cadre at Northwestern—some of whom had been students there or at other prestigious universities, and others who had been hangers-on who never attended college—and surveilled them, searched their garbage, and interviewed their families and friends. The investigations revealed that some of the players' activities and habits of mind corresponded in certain ways to the Unabomber's (or at least what we knew of his). These correlations seemed clear even to the players themselves, who began pointing the finger at one another. One of them was so convinced that, when the real Unabomber was arrested in 1996, he called the UNABOM task force in Montana to insist, "You've got the wrong guy! Kaczynski wasn't even in our group."

Some of our more arduous efforts were the airline projects. The one focused on the former Western Airlines, a carrier based in Salt Lake City that had been bought out by Delta, would occupy twelve to fifteen agents full-time for four solid months. The theory behind the investigation was that since the Unabomber had hand-placed two devices in Salt Lake City, sometimes using it in his bogus return addresses and cover notes, and had also targeted airlines, he might be a disgruntled former employee or related to someone who had lost his job after the buyout. The capper was that Western made runs to both Chicago and San Francisco, the Unabomber's other chief stomping grounds.

So the personnel records of all former employees, pilots, flight attendants, mechanics, and so on of Western Airlines were subpoenaed and delivered to the task force in a huge truck. They filled 118 large boxes, which formed a wall some twenty feet wide by nine feet on the San Francisco Federal Building's thirteenth floor. Not only did the thousands of records—which may have once been alphabetized but were no longer—have to be checked for biographical resemblances to the Unabomber, but any typed matter (since all the Unabomber's communiqués were typed), such as the employee's original job application, had to be pulled out for scrutiny by an FBI laboratory typewriter specialist whom I thought of as St. Henry, for his painstaking work.

Document analysis is an art, and those with highly specialized training can tell the difference between handwriting and old-fashioned typewriter samples and often even between word-processed and photocopied specimens. The FBI laboratory will analyze the inks on the document, comparing them to the vast range of samples from around the world that it keeps in its library. It will determine the composition of the paper used, as well as its point of origin and date of production, and examine it for indentations, impressions, and the presence of foreign elements. If you spill a fine French wine from your personal cellar on a ransom note you're composing, the FBI can track it to its home province and possibly its vineyard, its importer, and the liquor stores that stock it. And if you used a credit card to purchase it, you might soon be fitted for an orange jumpsuit.

The project was already under way by the time I joined the squad. All of us would gather at the big table in the windowless room where the files were housed, and in the long, tedious weeks that we perused them, we developed an uproarious camaraderie. Our king of comedy was Bert O'Connor from Boston, with Darin Werking from Newark running a close second. Bert loved to regale us with top ten lists about the project—"The Top Ten Reasons You Know It's Time to Take an Early Retirement" to "The Top Ten Reasons This Project Is a Loser"—to break the monotony.

Finally, we got down to the last box, jubilant at the prospect of escaping into the light and air and more active duty. But at the end of the final day, we were summoned to a briefing by St. Henry himself, who by then had been studying UNABOM typewriter samples for fifteen years. I had a bad feeling about this, and I could see that my fellow team members felt the same trepidation. We could feel the tentacles of the octopus I was starting to think of as the Unabeast reaching out to wrap themselves around our ankles.

St. Henry held up two templates, clear plastic eight-by-eleven-inch sheets with black markings or "spacers" on them corresponding to the letter patterns on the two typewriters that the Unabomber had been to known to use over the years. The templates were to be placed over the typed document, and if the typed characters fit perfectly into the minute grid on the template, they stood a chance of being a match for the Unabomber's. They would then be subjected to a letter-by-letter examination. There were certain letters on the Unabomber's typewriters that had unusual characteristics—for example, the lowercase T had an umbrellalike hook at the top, and the uppercase M had an especially distinct V at its center. We would find that perhaps one in every twenty of the hundreds of documents to be examined fit the templates and then we'd have to do individual naked-eye comparisons to the letters on the unusual-characteristics list.

Exacting and tiresome as the work was, it did offer the occasional cliff-hanger. You would be sitting with your stack of "likely" documents, the ones whose letters fit the templates, checking them against the unusual-characteristics list. Letter after letter would match, and your pulse would race, as you thought, "This is it!" But then you'd hit on the one "wrong" letter that didn't match up and would knock the document out of consideration. Each of us had our hopes repeatedly dashed. But we did turn up three documents that matched on all counts—eureka!

Word that the Western Airlines project might have hit pay dirt shot a thrill of excitement through the whole San Francisco division and its outlying satellites. We felt like we had won the lottery. But when St. Henry took the three documents back to Quantico for more rigorous analysis, it was no go—they didn't match. After weeks and weeks of punctilious work, we were foiled again.

Another airline project focused on United, since the Unabomber's fourth target back in 1980 had been Percy Wood, president of the company. Wood had begun his career as a mechanic and risen through the ranks—surely, the reasoning went, stepping on a few toes along the way. The notion that a vengeful United Airlines employee might be the Unabomber gained even greater credence when the National Transportation Safety Board, at the behest of the FBI, examined the bomb remnants and determined that some of them bore drill marks specific to airliner machining. So, with utmost discretion—it was critical both to our investigation and to the carrier's business that the public not know that we suspected a United employee—we procured personnel records of likely current and former workers and embarked on a months-long hunt for the snake in the woodpile. We couldn't rule out mechanics from other carriers either, since they would use the same drill techniques, so we also quietly began to check out every airline maintenance facility in the Bay Area.

Our squad supervisor, Max Noel, also known as Mad Max, always encouraged agents to propose their own ideas for developing leads. Two of my resourceful female colleagues, Joanie Kvech and Connie Seibert, cooked up their own airline project, which he gave them the green light to pursue. Every San Francisco airport worker (and other vendors cleared to enter nonpublic areas) carried a photo ID, a copy of which was kept on file, so Joanie and Connie decided to check the file copies against the sketch of the Unabomber, to see if they could score a match. That meant reviewing tens of thousands of photos, for as it turned out, a huge proportion of the airport workers were white males in the right age category. We wouldn't see Connie and Joanie for a long, long time.

But while the airline projects, including Connie and Joanie's, would yield dozens of potential suspects, all of them would come to naught.

Another major venture was the scrap metal project. The former Junkyard Bomber had continued to craft his devices out of untraceable, recycled materials, but the lab thought there was a chance that the alloys found in certain metal shards might be trackable to some particular scrapyard. The UNABOM case agent at the time, Sven Holmes,* had an engineering background and so he personally prepared the set of questions, or protocol, for us to use on our sample-collecting forays into every scrapyard in the region. Not only did we come up empty on the scrapyard project, but the press managed to get wind of it. Suddenly there were headlines about the search and scrapyard owners claiming their fifteen minutes of fame on the nightly news. If we had been able to develop a promising lead, it might well have been scuppered by all the media attention. I could only wonder what there could possibly be in the scrapyard project that the public had such a compelling need to know.

"Little cases, little problems; big cases, big problems" (some agents subscribe to the motto, "No cases, no problems," and make avoiding them a fine art). With so many intensive efforts going on, during its last two years, the Unabomber investigation ballooned beyond the management capacity of any one case agent. Sven Holmes had fought the beast longer than most, so now two supervisors, Max Noel and Lee Katz,* took over to co-run the investigation, which would be spearheaded by San Francisco's SAC Jim Freeman.

All of us were feeling frustrated by the dead ends and blind alleys we kept hitting, not to mention the sheer, exhausting volume of data it was necessary to process in hopes of finding a killer who had been clever or lucky enough to elude detection for seventeen years. People ask me whether the task force was close to catching the Unabomber on its own, whether he would ever have been apprehended had he not slipped up. Obviously no one can answer that question, but what I can address is the nature of detective work—it's at best 10 percent inspiration and insight, and 90 percent dogged persistence. Few of us can always reliably second-guess the people we live and work with—never mind a complete stranger, known only by his deeds. How can you begin to find a needle in haystack? You have to keep pushing on any front that seems possible—our airline, scrapyard, D&D projects, and all the rest—hoping to winnow down the possibilities, instead of waiting for a break that might never come. You have to expect that most of your efforts will come up dry.

What very often tips the case for investigators, fortunately, is the offender's own need to call attention to himself, an impulse that the Unabomber had resisted for more than a decade. But once he succumbed to the desire for recognition, he would become almost garrulous in his need to explain himself. He would write to the *New York Times* that he had killed Thomas Mosser because he had once worked for Burson-Marsteller, the public relations firm that had helped Exxon rehabilitate its image after the accident of its tanker, the *Valdez*, which had caused widespread environmental damage, and "on general principles" because he was in the business of "manipulating people's attitudes." Justifying his actions wasn't enough, however. The Unabomber was also bent on delivering a message to the world, one that was so important that he would "permanently desist from terrorist activities" if it were published in a prominent news organ, such as the *New York Times,* the *Washington Post,* or the magazines *Time* and *Newsweek* and—grandiose enough to believe that his ideas would kindle impassioned public debate—if he had "the right to publish . . . for three years after the appearance of our article . . . three thousand words examining or clarifying our material or rebutting criticisms of it."

There were good reasons not to capitulate to the demand—for one thing, it would be submitting to extortion by a terrorist, and for another, it would set a precedent for the many disaffected groups who already believed that violence was the most effective way to publicize their cause. But on the plus side, there was a chance that publishing the Manifesto would spark someone's recognition of the Unabomber. In fact, that is exactly what would lead to his capture.

The Manifesto was a dense treatise on the evils of scientific progress and social organization, calling the Industrial Revolution "a disaster for the human race" and blaming technology for "permanently reducing human beings and many other living organisms to engineered products and mere cogs in the social machine." The only solution the Unabomber saw for the myriad problems caused by this "disruption of the power process"—including a "tendency to depression" leading to "insatiable hedonism," "sexual perversion," "eating disorders," and more—was the destruction of industrialized society and a return to "wild nature." To get his message before the public "with some chance of making a lasting impression," he explained, still hiding behind the façade of his imaginary anarchistic group, FC, "we had to kill people."

With the blessing of the FBI, the Manifesto was jointly published by the *Washington Post* and the *New York Times* on September 19, 1995.

The press on the Unabomber had already been nagging at Linda Ka-czynski, a philosophy professor living in Schenectady, New York. Her husband, David, a social worker working with troubled teens, had a brother she had never met—Ted had cut off contact when David decided to abandon the "natural" life in the Texas desert and get married. It was evident that Ted had a few screws loose, and Linda knew that he had frequented the same places—Chicago, San Francisco, and Salt Lake City—that were the reported ambit of the Unabomber. But the Manifesto was the clincher, for David had told her how much Ted loathed science and technology, though he himself was a math prodigy with a Ph.D. from the University of Michigan, who had been an assistant professor at Berkeley.

The couple was traveling, however, when the Manifesto was published, so it was not until October that Linda got hold of it and urged her husband to read it. When he did, the truth was inescapable: The ideas, the style of reasoning, the language—right down to specific turns of phrases, such as the inverted expression, "They can't eat their cake and have it too"—echoed the letters Ted had written over the years. Heartsick, David and Linda approached a private investigator they knew for advice on the "hypothetical" problem of possessing letters suggesting that "a friend" was guilty of a serious crime. The investigator, Susan Swanson, quietly began to check the dates of the bombings against the "friend's" known whereabouts and also confidentially passed on the letters to Clint Van Zandt, a retired FBI hostage negotiator and profiler. Van Zandt had them analyzed by two independent teams who placed the probability that the letter writer and the author of the Manifesto were the same at 60 to 80 percent.

Anonymously, via Swanson, David now contacted a lawyer, Anthony Bisceglie, who gave a few of the letters, with identifying marks carefully removed, to an FBI agent he knew. Before he could even figure out what to do, David had to know if his suspicions were warranted. As it turned out, the typewriters didn't match, which must have given him a momentary sense of relief. But then when he was cleaning out his mother's house, preparing her to move to Schenectady so she could be near him and Linda, he came across an essay Ted had written and tried unsuccessfully to publish in the early 1970s. It was the stunning piece of evidence that we would later call the "Ted Document"—an undeniable precursor to the Manifesto.

When Jim Freeman saw it, he knew we were on to something and opened the lengthy negotiations of the terms under which David might be willing to talk to the FBI. For David, the question was a matter not only of ethics but of potentially saving his brother's life—letting him be captured in a controlled situation, rather than in what we call a "severe arrest," and lobbying for Ted to be spared the death penalty. Not that his brother would be grateful: Theodore Kaczynski would maintain in *Truth versus Lies* (as cited in *Time* magazine), the book he wrote to refute the claims by David and others that he was mentally ill, "[David] knows very well that imprisonment is to me an unspeakable humiliation and that I would unhesitatingly choose death over incarceration."

I can only imagine the agony it must have been for David Kaczynski to decide to inform on the brother he had long idolized. David would later tell *Time*, when asked if he felt guilty: "Guilt suggests a very clear conviction of wrongdoing, and certainly I don't feel that I did wrong. On the other hand, there are tremendously complicated feelings not just about the decision itself but a lifetime of a relationship which one brother failed to help protect another."

To my mind, David Kaczynski deserved to be named Man of the Year.

I still recall how I first became aware that an anonymous person, through an attorney, had contacted us because he suspected that his brother was the Unabomber. I was "sitting the desk" for Max Noel on the project squad—working as primary relief supervisor and so "moving the paper" and handling operational questions that came up when he was not around—when a copy of Bisceglie's letter reached Max's "in" box. We had so many people dropping dimes on their friends and relatives that I didn't pay it much heed, but the fact that these were brothers, not warring ex-spouses or cranky neighbors, struck me. Then a few days later the entire task force and support crew was summoned to a meeting in the conference room. There were many stifled yawns when it was announced that we had a new Unabomber suspect, the umpteenth one. But there was a new intensity and excitement in the ASAC's voice as he told us of the lawyer's letter and the anonymous brother-tipster, with whom two San Francisco veterans would be meeting that Saturday, in the company of the attorney and the Washington field office agent he originally approached, Molly Fienes. This was a major break, the ASAC said. "We're turning the ship."

I was off that Saturday, but unable to stand the suspense, I stopped by the office while running errands. Max wasn't there, but the desk of Tony Muljat, the U.S. postal inspector/supervisor who sat next to him, showed signs of life. A ten-year veteran of UNABOM, Tony even got his "mandatory" retirement date postponed so that he could see the case through. He was a big, kindly, humorous man who endeared himself to the task force grunts by often treating us to ice cream bars while we were slaving on the Western Airline project or the UNABOM hot line. Thinking I'd wait for Tony, I glanced down at his desk for a clue as to where he'd gone, not really meaning to snoop. But what I saw there grabbed me and, before I could help myself, I was reading it.

On a yellow legal pad, Tony had jotted notes on what David Kaczynski had told the investigators in Washington earlier that day. In 1969, after the clash between student protesters and the National Guard in People's Park, Ted had resigned his Berkeley professorship, claiming that math "wasn't relevant for the times." Back home in Chicago, he told his brother, seven years younger, all about his campus life, including a caper that he thought was funny. He had written a bitter and threatening letter to a colleague he didn't like and sent it with another professor's name. The story reminded David of an incident in grammar school, when Ted had written a similarly hostile letter to a female classmate and signed another boy's name to it.

That made the hairs on the back of my neck prickle. I knew we had our man. It was the same modus operandi that the Unabomber had used throughout his career—signing the letters accompanying his mail bombs and filling in the return addresses with the names of other, mostly real, people. He had even planted a note in the bomb that injured Diogenes Angelakos reading, *Wu—It works! I told you it would. RV*—seemingly trying to implicate two men who, it would later turn out, had been his former colleagues at Berkeley, Hung Hsi Wu and Robert Vaught. This was a classic "passive/aggressive" tactic—to perform a surreptitious hostile act, duck the blame (in this case, by pinning it on someone else), and then sit back to watch the fireworks. But then what could be more passive/aggressive than planting a bomb and sneaking away or sending one through the mail?

·   ·   ·

Now that the "ship" was "turning," John and I both expected to be put ashore. With a suspect to focus on, there would be no more massive undertakings like the airlines projects and, consequently, far less need for hands on deck. We had been on the UNABOM task force for just a few months, and the agents who had been on the case for years would be the ones to see it through. Personally, I was glad to leave UNABOM behind and was looking forward to a new slot on the Child Abduction Task Force, working under the legendary supervisor Gordon McNeill.

But John, who had been the surveillance squad (SOG) chief back in Chicago, had been discussing the Unabomber suspect with Jim Freeman, who told him that Ted Kaczynski lived near Lincoln, Montana. After doing some research, John presented Freeman with a packet of information on Lincoln, a small town just thirty miles west of the Continental Divide. It would be very difficult, John explained, to do surveillance in such a sparsely populated area, where strangers would be sure to attract attention. Only a small team, working discreetly over time, could effectively insinuate itself into the community, ferret out the Unabomber without being made, and keep an eye on him till we had gathered enough "probable cause" to make the arrest.

Evidently Freeman and the other members of the "Breakfast Club"— the worker bees' name for the management, who spent their entire mornings locked in meetings—were impressed. Later that day John grabbed me. "Candice," he said excitedly, "they want us in Montana— you and me."

If we wound up doing surveillance in Lincoln, a couple would look much less suspicious than lone men roaming around town. I knew of a few husband-and-wife teams who sometimes worked cases together. There was a "double-agent" couple on the Bronfman abduction case in New York. An heir to the Seagram's fortune had been allegedly kidnapped—and later accused of helping engineer the snatch, to get back at his parents—and a surveillance team spotted the suspected abductor's car. When they tried to radio the couple to close in, what they heard, according to Bureau myth, was a heated argument. The double agents had accidentally left the mike open, apparently, and though no one could break through to them, all the other cars were treated to a veritable three-ring circus of a marital spat. If the tale was true, it must have taken the couple years to live that one down.

Nothing like that would ever happen to John and me, I was certain. For one thing, we would be a trio, not a duo, teamed with another veteran agent, Dave Weber, who had grown up in Montana. For another, since this would be our first case together, I was sure that we would be ultrasolicitous of each other. Finally, we were both still new enough to the case to find it invigoratingly fresh. We felt thrilled and tremendously privileged to be chosen for such a critical and delicate mission.

When we got home that night, I checked with the weather service to see what we should pack to take to Montana. Though it was late winter, the temperature in San Francisco was hovering pleasantly, if damply, in the sixties. But in Montana, spring was just a distant memory and an unimaginable future—it was 23 degrees below zero.

Some privilege!

16

BLUE EYES

John and I were to leave for Montana that Sunday, just a day or two away, and there was no telling how many weeks or even months we would be gone. So we spent the weekend in a fever of activity—arranging for the care of John's dog and my cats, lining up people to handle our bills and check the house periodically—and finally met my parents and my brother and sister-in-law for dinner to say our good-byes on Saturday night. We couldn't tell them where we were going or why. My parents had never known anything about the cases I was working until they were over, when it was too late to worry. But now they sensed that we were up to something big, which excited them and, I think, frightened them a little. "Be careful, Candice," my father urged me. Then he said to John, rather sternly, "You watch her back!"

All the cold-weather clothes I had needed in Chicago were still packed up in boxes, but I managed to pull a reasonable assortment together. At the last minute, though, with the taxi waiting outside to take us to the airport, I realized that I had neglected to excavate a warm jacket. "Tell the cab to wait," I told John.

Racing back down to the basement, I tore open a few more boxes and finally came across a black and red ski parka. It was Seth's, but it fit me well enough. I shoved it under my arm.

We flew into Great Falls, Montana, and transferred to a small commuter plane for the trip to Helena, the state capital, an hour's drive from Lincoln. The weather was fierce, and as the tiny craft bucked hard in the winds I clung to John and Dave. "Put her in the worst neighborhood in Chicago and she's okay," John teased. "Have her stand up to terrorists or drug dealers—no problem. But a bumpy plane ride, forget it. She's a wreck!"

The next day we awoke to a driving blizzard that overmatched my (Seth's) parka, ski hat and goggles, and long underwear. Uncle Sam would have to treat us to a whole new class of cold-weather gear. But through it all, I felt exhilarated, confident that we were finally hot on the trail of a killer who had been clever enough to elude capture for seventeen years. I wanted to be the one to run him down to the ground.

As in any investigation, before the action started there would be lots of legwork and intelligence gathering to establish "probable cause." At this point all the FBI really had on Kaczynski was suspicions—strong ones, admittedly, owing to the highly suggestive linguistic comparison of the Ted Document and the Unabomber Manifesto, but nothing solid enough to make an arrest or even to get a search warrant. Our one shard of hard evidence was, unfortunately, not definitive. The Unabomber had slipped up and licked the stamp on one of his letters, allowing us to test for DNA and compare the results to the DNA on a stamp licked by David Kaczynski. The two samples were convincingly similar and shared a fairly rare "marker," found in only 3 percent of Caucasians. But 3 percent of the white population of the United States was still a few million people—far too many to make a persuasive legal case.

So in the absence of irrefutable links, we would have to assemble a strong foundation of circumstantial evidence to establish Ted Kaczynski as the Unabomber. In San Francisco, a team of intelligence research specialists, aided by Mary Lou Felder from Quantico, was hard at work on a "timeline" tracking Kaczynski's movements from 1978 to the present. It was painstaking work that involved scouring bank, hotel, Department of Motor Vehicles, and other records, and plotting every piece of data uncovered, as well as reported sightings of the suspect, on a chart spanning the full seventeen years. For example, from bank records, we learned that on a certain date, Kaczynski had cashed a check at a Missoula bank. A mark was then placed on the timeline indicating his presence in Missoula that day. As the timeline grew increasingly dense with information—eventually it would stretch to nine feet long—it was repeatedly checked against the dates and places that bombs and letters had been planted or mailed to see if there were any irresolvable conflicts. If, say, Kaczynski had been cashing the check in Missoula the same day that the man was spotted leaving the bomb in the CAAMS parking lot in Salt Lake City, we would have been hard pressed to show that he was our man. Fortunately for our case, though there were a few close squeezes, there were no absolute physical impossibilities.

John helped out with that. We knew Kaczynski didn't have a car so we surmised that he might have traveled by bus to the Bay Area and Sacramento, where a number of the bombs had been mailed. John discovered that the bus trip would take from twenty-four to thirty-six hours, depending on the route, which made us doubt the prevailing belief that the Unabomber was motivated to mail his last bomb—postmarked in Oakland on April 20, 1995—by the April 19 explosion of the Murrah Federal Building in Oklahoma City. The timing just didn't add up.

In any case, John now set about interviewing bus drivers who in recent years had driven routes running through Lincoln, stopping at the Rainbow Café. Using the cover story that he was working a drug case, he showed them a photo of Kaczynski, without revealing his name. None of the drivers was positive, but a few believed that they recognized Kaczynski as a former passenger. Soon those impressions would be confirmed.

Meanwhile, two specialists from San Francisco, Bill Hagle and Rick Ethridge, were trying to accomplish a task we were told couldn't be done—set up a communications transmitter covering the area around Kaczynski's cabin. Although the mountains were supposedly too dense and high to permit radio communications, Bill and Rick determined that a solar transmitter could do the job. "Get it yesterday," Jim Freeman told them; and using John's undercover credit card, Bill procured one from an electronics supplier in Idaho. But Bill's technical wizardry did not extend to snowmobiles, contraptions as exotic and unfamiliar as space satellites to guys from California. The first day out, the snowmobile hit a tree and survived, but it would ultimately perish in a 400-foot plunge down a steep, rocky ravine into a frozen stream. Bill managed to jump off at the last minute and lived to get our radio transmitter safely installed. It took him and Rick weeks of hard labor in the biting cold.

It fell to me and Phil Gadd of the Helena Bureau to try to pull in any scrap of information that might tie Kaczynski to the Manifesto or the bombings. We hit every car rental agency, chemical supply house, and hobby shop within two hundred miles of Helena, using the same drug-investigation cover story as John, but no one could place him. One of our other tasks was a library project. The Manifesto had referred directly to four books: *The True Believer* by Eric Hoffer, *Chinese Political Thought in the Twentieth Century* by Chester Tan, *The Ancient Engineers* by L. Sprague DeCamp, and *Violence in America: Historical and Comparative Perspectives* by Roger Lane, edited by Hugh Davies Graham and Ted Robert Gurr; and scholars consulted by the FBI suggested that he had paraphrased a number of others. Kaczynski had no source of income that we knew of and periodically tapped his brother David for loans of a thousand or so dollars at a time (notably, shortly before the bombings that killed Thomas Mosser and Gilbert Murray). It stood to reason that having very little discretionary income, Kaczynski, if he were indeed the author of the Manifesto, would not be purchasing books but checking them out of the library.

So, armed with a list of books, Phil and I burrowed our way into the Montana library system. My cover story was that I was investigating someone who had written threatening letters to a congressman, citing quotations from various books. But unlike in the old days, when borrowers scrawled their names on cards kept in pockets at the backs of books, in the computer era there was no way to learn who had checked out a book once it was returned. Records were kept only of delinquent borrowers, and Ted Kaczynski was not among them. He may have been a bomber and a murderer, but he was evidently a responsible library patron who returned his books on time. Even to get this far, I needed a subpoena, for what we choose to read is a matter of personal privacy in this country.

But the system would ultimately defeat us—any library in Montana, including the tiny satellite in Lincoln, five miles from Kaczynski's cabin, could order a book for a borrower from any other public or university library in the state. There were no centralized records of these transactions, and we didn't feel we could approach the Lincoln librarian directly, for fear that she might be friendly with her erudite patron (our instincts would prove correct, for we would learn later that the Lincoln librarian was one of Kaczynski's only friends). So, to find out which books Kaczynski might have borrowed from more sophisticated libraries, we would have to visit every library in Montana. The best we could do was a spot check that at least told us that it was entirely possible for Kaczynski to procure most of the books on our list through interlibrary loan and that, further, he could easily get access to the *New York Times* and the *Washington Post,* the newspapers with which the Unabomber had been corresponding.

But we had much better luck with a doctor in Missoula, whom Kaczynski had consulted for a suspected heart ailment. He had written to David about her and seemed somewhat infatuated with her, after one appointment. Before the doctor would talk to us, of course, she asked for a subpoena. On this case, the San Francisco management's commitment to back us up was extraordinary, and much appreciated. We had two agents back in San Francisco who did nothing but crank out subpoenas—thousands of them—and get them to us within hours of a request. We were passing them out like candy on Halloween.

After presenting the subpoena and a cover story, we got Kaczynski's full medical record, including a letter he had written the doctor prior to his first visit in 1991. When I read it in the car, I thought my own heart would stop.

In it, Kaczynski introduced himself to the doctor, describing the way he hoped to work with her. Since he lived in Lincoln, he explained, he would have to travel by bus to Missoula and probably stay overnight, something of a hardship with his limited funds. So he urged her to consider his symptoms and preorder any necessary tests so that they could all be done in one day. Outlining his concerns about his heart, he added that he was having trouble sleeping and suffered occasional bouts of anxiety.

The mention of the bus was an important confirmation for us. John had already been investigating the routes and timetables, and now we knew for sure that we were on the right track. But it was the medical history Kaczynski related that grabbed me. He claimed that he had been under "considerable stress" since 1978—the date of the first bombing—and that he had been under "extreme stress" for the past five years. Nineteen eighty-five, seven years before, had been the Unabomber's most prolific ever, with four bombs planted between May and December; the last one took the life of Hugh Campbell Scrutton, his first murder victim. The Unabomber had then gone underground, surfacing just once in early 1987 to commit the CAAMS bombing. At the time Kaczynski was writing to the doctor in 1991, the Unabomber had been dormant for four-plus years. Something—very possibly "extreme stress"—was keeping him inactive all that time.

Scarcely able to contain myself, I called "Mad Max" on the car phone to read him the letter. "Tell me that again," he kept saying, referring to the line about Kaczynski's five years of extreme stress. The timing had to be more than a coincidence. It seemed too good to be true—a nice, strong, new strand in the web we were weaving around Ted Kaczynski.

Back in Helena, I logged Kaczynski's chart into evidence and then went to meet John and Max, up from San Francisco with some of the other brass, at a watering hole near the FBI office. Max greeted me with hugs and kisses, and I felt like a child showing Daddy a good report card when I placed a photocopy of the letter in his outstretched hands. I knew he would want to see it with his own eyes. Max was thrilled.

We all celebrated with a few rounds of cheap wine and stale beer, blotted up with musty popcorn, before heading out for dinner at the Marysville ski lodge, one of our favorite hangouts. It was about thirty miles outside Helena, a rustic, three-room house, divided into a bar, a dining room, and a kitchen. It was there that I learned that the health-food culture, which had extended tendrils into Chicago and had, like ivy, entwined San Francisco in its green chokehold, had barely floated a seedling over Montana. Man-sized steaks, lobsters, and Alaska king crab legs steeped in butter were the bill of fare, with marshmallows on skewers, toasted over the open stone fireplace, the favored dessert. It was a magical place and a fitting site for a celebration.

But the place that would become our mainstay was the Seven-Up Ranch, a few miles east of Lincoln. It was a huge, warm, Western-style spread, featuring a dining room, a bar with a pool table and jukebox, and a proud display of the stuffed trophies of the region's hunters: bears, mountain wildcats, elk, moose, and deer. It was at the Seven-Up Ranch one night that Jim Freeman, on one of the management's frequent trips to oversee the activities in Lincoln, drew me and John aside. We had been on the job a month and the spring thaw was setting in. Soon, Freeman thought, our quarry might venture out of hibernation and make his way down the mountain from his cabin to Stemple Pass Road, headed for Lincoln. When he did, Freeman wanted us to be on him. It was time for us to go undercover.

I was so excited that I felt like winging my cowboy hat at one of the walls, to catch it, spinning, on an antler. I could sense John's thrill of anticipation too. It was showtime!

"Take the weekend off," Freeman told us. It would be our first break since we had arrived in Montana. "Then go get yourselves set up in Lincoln on Monday."

John and I spent the weekend near Yellowstone National Park, in a tiny hotel over a rushing river. Since it was the dead of winter, we were the only guests. It was like a honeymoon, an intimate, laughing, and loving time. One gate of the park was open to tourists in winter, so we drove the few miles of snowplowed road. The air was crisp and clear and the vistas awesome. We marveled at the animals—bison, coyotes, elk, and moose—that passed within yards of us, undaunted by the car chugging through their winter kingdom. Suddenly I spied a little red fox. "Oh John, look—stop," I said.

We got out of the car, but as I tried to snap his picture, the fox turned to flee. John gave him a whistle, and he spun to a halt. He looked straight at me, and I swear, he winked. "That's Kaczynski," I told John. "He may be sly but he won't get very far."

Having already scouted Lincoln, John and I knew where we would stay, the Sportsmen's Lodge on Stemple Pass Road. Though the town's population was only 500, it had five motels and restaurant/bars—including the Rainbow Café, where we believed Kaczynski had caught the bus to go on his deadly missions—four churches, and even a video store, to cater to the waves of fishermen and hunters who would descend on it

from May to December. The Sportsmen's Lodge overlooked a cluster
of small stores, ringing an intersection on Stemple Pass Road, the thor-
oughfare leading into Lincoln. Kaczynski would pass right by the lodge
if he came down off the mountain. If he did, we would have to track
him and perhaps even pick him up, whether our case was in place or
not. We couldn't take the chance that he would deliver another bomb.

We registered under the names Ralph Grayson, which John chose
because his father's name was Ralph Gray, and Candy Rose, a combination of my dreaded nickname and a truncation of my maiden name,
Rosing. Our cover story was that I was a researcher for *National Geo-
graphic* and that John (who had taken pictures both in the military and
for the Bureau) was a photographer. It turned out to be the perfect ruse,
for the region was littered with abandoned gold and platinum mines. A
group of investors had raised millions to reopen them, with the benefit
of modern technology, and so the town was growing used to strangers
in its midst.

We shared a large room with two double beds and a huge fireplace,
which was always blazing. Its chimney didn't draw well, so smoke hung
in the air, permeating the bedding, the furniture, and our clothes. The
room was the communications base for the Lincoln team and came to
be known as the Wolf Den, for we had picked radio code names to
honor the gray wolf's reintroduction to Yellowstone National Park:
Dave was Lonewolf, John was Gray Wolf, and I was Sweetwolf. Our
aerial reconnaissance pilot, Mike Condon, who was scoping out and
photographing Kaczynski's land and cabin, became Skywolf.

During daylight hours, either John or I was always stationed in the
room, monitoring the radio and watching the road, while the other
gathered intelligence or surveilled the Rainbow Café at the times that
buses were scheduled to stop there. After the buses pulled out, the
watcher would call our two agents in Missoula, Phil Powers* and Jim
Huggins, to report that he hadn't boarded, so they didn't have to cover
the bus station.

One night when I was on duty at the bus stop, I was sure Kaczynski
was on the move. A man who fit his description boarded the bus carrying
a knapsack that, for all I knew, might contain a bomb. I couldn't call in
the troops until I was sure he was Kaczynski, so I had to think up a way

to check him out—and without being made. If Kaczynski got spooked, months of hard work and planning would go right down the drain.

It was too late to rush into the Rainbow to buy a bus ticket, but luck was with me. The driver got off to pick up a cup of coffee. The moment he went inside, I stepped onto the bus, my pulse racing. I scanned the faces of the passengers—women with children, some middle-aged couples, a number of senior citizens—thinking, *If there's a bomb in that bag, these are the lives that are in my hands.*

Lone travelers were scattered throughout the bus. I finally spotted my man sitting close to the back. I made my way down the aisle, feigning distress that was only the faintest shadow of the anxiety I felt. "Excuse me, sir," I said to him. "I was sitting here earlier when I came in from Great Falls, and now I am missing my purse. Have you seen it?"

The man looked me directly in the eyes. He didn't seem at all nervous, and when I smiled at him, he smiled back. He had blue eyes and some teeth missing. "No," he said. "There was nothing here when I sat down."

He helped me look around under the seat, and I came to the conclusion that he wasn't Kaczynski. Thanking him, I got off the bus. I was surprised by how disappointed I felt—that in some corner of my heart I had actually been hoping that it was him. We had been watching and waiting for a long time.

One Sunday morning John went out to grab some breakfast while I stayed in the room watching the road. Because I had the "eye," I had to keep my focus locked on the road, which meant doing everything in front of the window—rolling curlers, without looking, into my half-wet hair; daubing on foundation, powder, and lipstick; applying mascara with only a one-eyed glance into my mirrored compact, which was small enough not to block my view outside. I had become so adept at this ritual that I could have done my hair and put on all my makeup in the dark.

I had all my equipment laid out on the table in front of me: moisturizer, foundation, mascara, powder, lipstick, eyeshadow, makeup sponges; an assortment of combs, brushes, rollers, eyelash curlers, clips, bobby pins—you name it. You'd think a cyclone had hit a cosmetics supply show. I had just picked up the blow-dryer to blast my rolled-up hair when John burst through the door in a state of agitation. "It's Ted," he said. "I just saw him in the restaurant across the road. He's sitting at the bar."

Then he leaned over me to look out the window. "There he goes, he's walking around. We've got to move—now!"

Totally deadpan, I said, "But Ralph—I'm not ready."

I thought John was going to explode. "I'm kidding, I'm kidding," I said, yanking the rollers out of my hair and flinging them to the floor as I grappled with my jacket.

We raced outside just as the man headed into the intersection's small grocery store. Since I looked peculiar with my tangle of wet hair, it was John who followed him in. Within a few minutes John reemerged to tell me that our quarry's purchases were being rung up. "What did he buy? Tell me," I asked excitedly.

The list John rattled off ended with a frozen pizza and instant coffee. My heart sank. In his letter to the cardiologist, Kaczynski said specifically that he never consumed caffeine; and as for the pizza, we knew from David that the only heat source in his brother's cabin was a small wood-burning stove—big enough to boil a pot of water perhaps, but how could he cook a pizza on it?

Now the man came out of the store and started walking in the direction of Missoula. He carried a knapsack, along with his grocery bag, and he was wearing a bright red knit cap. We knew that Ted Kaczynski, whom our reconnaissance team had once seen poke his head out of his cabin, also wore a bright red ski cap. The walker's height, weight, and facial features fit the description of Kaczynski. There was definitely a chance that he could be our man.

But it would be hard to tail him on foot. The rural two-lane road was virtually deserted, and there was nothing but barren land on either side of it. There was nowhere to hide. We were puzzling over the problem when the man stopped walking, turned around, and stuck out his thumb, trying to hitch a ride. A car passed without stopping. Should another come along and pick him up, he could wind up anywhere—and worse, a Good Samaritan driver's life might be in danger. Who knew what the man was carrying in that knapsack? "We've got to pick him up," I told John. "We've got to see if it's him."

We quickly decided that I would be the one to do it—he would be much less suspicious of a woman—while John waited at the beef jerky factory a few miles down the road. If the hitchhiker turned out to be Kaczynski, I was to drive past the factory, and John would raise the alarm. If he wasn't, I would let him out at the factory, claiming that I had reached my turnoff.

I jumped into my rented truck, then let John pass me in his 4×4, as I jammed my semiautomatic Sig Saur pistol under my left thigh. Even if the hitchhiker wasn't our man, I was taking a chance. He could be anyone—a rapist, a sex murderer. As I approached him, I slowed and honked the horn, thinking I'd get a look at him before I let him in the car. If he didn't resemble Kaczynski up close, I could always say that I wasn't heading in his direction. "Hey, where ya going?" I yelled through the slightly lowered window.

But when he bent down to answer, I couldn't see enough of his face straight on to tell if he was Ted Kaczynski. "Oh, just up a ways," he replied.

My throat tight with nervous excitement, I croaked, "Get in."

"Hi, I'm Candy," I said, and he introduced himself as Hans. He had even bluer eyes than the man on the bus—a bright turquoise—and, like him, had a tooth missing. He asked me to let him out at his mother's place a few miles down the road. Knowing that Kaczynski's mother lived back East, I tried to probe a little more. Maybe this was a trick.

"Your mother? That's so nice that you're going to see her, and on such a cold day!" I said.

"No, she won't be there," he told me. He went on to explain that his mother was in the hospital and that he was going over to water her plants. I quizzed him a bit about her medical condition, and what he said sounded wholly credible. It would be hard for just anyone to fabricate enough detail on a recovering patient to fool me, a former nurse.

And a very disappointed one at that. Regretfully, I dropped Hans off at the factory and went to tell John that once again, our suspicions had been misplaced. He didn't want to hear it. He had been absolutely positive.

"Are you a hundred percent sure that wasn't Kaczynski?" he asked, repeatedly.

"Look, I'll bet you a paycheck," I told him. That's what finally convinced him to accept it. He knew that with Seth in college, my finances were so tight that I'd never hazard a bet I wouldn't win.

John had been so convinced that he had already reported to the rest of our team that Kaczynski was on the move. We now had the slightly embarrassing task of calling Max to tell him that it was a false alarm.

Max was very concerned. "Candice, how can you be so sure it wasn't him?"

I started with what I thought was the most solid piece of evidence. "Well, for one thing, he had this missing front tooth . . ."

Max gasped. "Candice, we now believe that Ted has a front tooth missing!"

No one had told us. We were working off the photo and description of Kaczynski that we'd been using all along. The news shook my confidence for a minute, but then I thought about the guy on the bus, with his missing teeth—maybe that wasn't so unusual in this part of the world.

"And his eyes were sort of greenish, more like turquoise than just blue," I went on.

"Candice!" Max exclaimed. "So are Kaczynski's."

Still, I knew I wasn't wrong about Hans. Drawing on the strength of my conviction, I reassured Max, detailing my conversation with the hitchhiker. He then softened, accepting my judgment. But in the background, I could hear Jim Freeman ranting and raving, "You tell her I don't want her ever picking up a suspect again. He's a serial killer, she could get killed! What the hell is she doing?"

As he went on, I held the receiver away from my ear, so John could hear it too. He kept pacing, shaking his head, probably glad that it was my neck on the chopping block and not his. Max, now obligated to assume his managerial role in front of his own boss, grew stern and supervisorly with me.

"Candice, never do anything like that again. I know you used good judgment, but you don't need to take risks like that. We could have deployed the airplane to track him if you two thought he was a solid suspect . . ."

But we hadn't been sure he was solid, and by the time Max got the airplane deployed, the hitchhiker could have been picked up and whisked away by some poor, vulnerable civilian. I didn't argue, however, and told Max, "Okay, I hear you. It won't happen again."

Then with Freeman continuing to rail in the background, I heard Max whisper under his breath, "Hey, Candice—nice goin'!"

The fact there had now been several sightings of Kaczynski, though false, showed the brass that John and I could use a few more pairs of eyes to help keep tabs on him. Shortly after the hitchhiker incident, they brought in two more agents, Chuck and Gerry, installing them at two different motels nearby. When John and I bumped into them in the tiny town, we steadfastly ignored each other. During the day, Chuck and Gerry were dispatched to a perch—a small, unheated shack rented from Kaczynski's neighbor that directly overlooked the dirt road to his cabin. They had to huddle there in the cold keeping watch, unable even to light a fire for fear of drawing attention. One day, they reported that they heard tapping and hammering coming from Ted's cabin. I figured he was making a bomb. *Tick, tock.*

I felt sorry for Chuck and Gerry but also just a shade envious that miserable as they must be, they got to look at a different view than the intersection on Stemple Pass Road. John and I were continuing our surveillance but starting to get stir crazy after weeks trapped in one room, staring at the same sight. We couldn't go out together—even if we had someplace to go—so most of our interactions took place within those four walls.

Since John and I had been living and working together in San Francisco—even on the same case, attending all the same staff meetings and sharing the same friends on the UNABOM squad—I naïvely thought that such close proximity wouldn't prove difficult. But at home we lived in a huge two-bedroom house with a formal dining room and a nice backyard—we weren't on top of each other all the time—and we had constant contact with other people. I was a workout freak, so I could go to the gym or go jogging, neither of which were options in a tiny Montana town in the winter. Sitting all day was making me fat, as well as restless and cranky. Luckily I discovered that one of the local housewives ran a daily aerobics class at five o'clock, so I signed on, and it helped a little. But that alone couldn't solve the problem of being stuck in one room with John, day in and day out, around the clock.

We couldn't even sit and play cards because one of us always had to watch the road. At one point, John, who is a media junkie, went out and bought a small TV for distraction, on the theory that even the one who had the eye could be entertained by the sound. But we soon found out that Lincoln, ringed by mountains, couldn't get television reception—which explained why a minuscule town had such a well-stocked video store. We started renting videos, which John liked to keep blaring all the time, driving me crazy. But in time, I came to welcome any stimulation, even if it was loud and intrusive.

By then John and I were bickering badly. Qualities in him that had merely annoyed me before were growing unbearable—and vice versa, I'm sure. He had a "mother hen" tendency, a need to protect and control everyone around him, which in such close quarters was positively suffocating. He'd ask, "How can you drive around with only half a tank of gas?"

In San Francisco I'd ignore him or needle him back: "Because that's the way I like it!"

But in Lincoln, I found myself shouting, "Get off my back! It's not your problem! There's nowhere to drive to anyway."

We quarreled bitterly one night after I had gone alone to dinner at the Seven-Up Ranch and stumbled smack into a meeting of the San Francisco brass. I had no idea they were in town. "What's she doing here?" someone asked angrily, but Max smoothed it over. I was allowed to grab a quick bite before I got going, so after I ordered I called John to warn him. I didn't want him to make the same mistake.

But he ignored me. When he marched into the Seven-Up Ranch, the managers who had been unhappy to see me were outraged by his intrusion. Maybe John thought—wrongly—that having been in FBI management back in Chicago, he would be more welcome than I was. Whatever the reason, we wound up in a knock-down-drag-out fight, with me yelling, "Why can't you listen to me?" and John yelling back, "Don't try to tell me what to do!"

Somehow nothing was ever the same after that. Our engagement would sputter on for a while once we returned to San Francisco but then it would fizzle out, like some defective device of the Unabomber.

By early April 1996 the Bureau had amassed nearly a hundred pages of circumstantial evidence—insufficient "probable cause" for us to arrest Kaczynski outright but enough to get a search warrant, on the theory that more incriminatory links to the bombings would be found in his home. The plan was to lure Kaczynski outdoors so he couldn't barricade himself in the cabin and destroy evidence while the warrant was being served or, worse, try to shoot or bomb his way out of the situation. The showdown was set for April 4, 1996.

On April 2, however, as San Francisco prosecutors Steve Fraccero and David Cleary were feverishly working the final touches into our affidavit for the search warrant, the press got into the act. Somehow, back in March, Lowell Bergman of CBS's *60 Minutes* had sniffed out the impending arrest in Montana and called George Grotz, the Bureau's media representative, to tell him that he'd gotten hold of the story. At that point our case was still too fragile, so Grotz urged him to hold back. Bergman agreed and sat on it for weeks, in exchange for an exclusive when the time came.

But now ABC and CNN were onto us and even had a name for the suspect, very similar to "Kaczynski." Unwilling to be beaten to their own scoop, especially after showing such forbearance, CBS executives entered into heated negotiations with the FBI. The Bureau bosses managed to buy us two more days but weren't positive that they could trust the guarantee. So it was decided that on April 3, as soon as Freeman, Max, and others emerged from an 8 A.M. meeting with the magistrate in Helena—search warrant in hand—they would "greenlight" the original arrest plan. Everyone was to be in position, waiting for the signal, and then pounce—the arrest would go down a day before the press expected any action.

But there was always a chance that the press would be nosing around and somehow tip off Kaczynski. In case that happened, Max told John and me to stand ready, along with Chuck and Gerry, to move in and make the arrest. We worked out a plan. Since Kaczynski wouldn't be expecting a woman to come after him, I would be the one to approach his cabin and lure him out, by pretending to be lost. Once I got him outside, the men would overpower and cuff him. Part of me hoped that all our hard work wouldn't be undermined—that our hand wouldn't be forced before we had all the right documents and the best chance of winning Kaczynski's conviction. But I have to confess that another part of me longed for the chance get in on the arrest, to pit myself against the monster that I thought of as the Unabeast. I felt thrilled and honored to be chosen.

Fortunately, it never came to that. On April 3 some hundred federal agents, including the San Francisco SWAT team, headed by Tom LaFreniere, and bomb specialists from both the Bureau and the Department of Defense, descended on the Seven-Up Ranch to be briefed on the arrest plan. In the crowd I spied Joyce Seymore, an ATF agent on the San Francisco Task Force, who would be the only other woman from the UNABOM investigation present that day. Later some would claim that the FBI Hostage Rescue Team sent twenty-five highly trained agents to Lincoln to apprehend Kaczynski—which is not true. The Unabomber was brought to justice by the team that had labored so tenaciously and doggedly to make the case, the San Francisco Task Force.

Max was talking to the SWAT Team when he saw me and put his arm around me. He explained that there was a log cabin owned by a local man, Glenn Williams, just downhill from Kaczynski's. John and I were to wait to receive the prisoner, assuming the arrest went according to plan.

Now the SWAT Team moved out in their Gilly suits, camouflage cover against the snow. It would take them three hours to crawl, snake-like, on their bellies, into position in the mountains above Kaczynski's cabin. Meanwhile, Jerry Burns, the local forestry agent, whom Ted knew, and Tom McDaniel of the Helena Bureau waited along with Max at the nearby home of Butch Gehring, the local rancher whose father, some twenty years before, had sold Kaczynski his plot of land. Once they got the signal that all was in readiness, the three of them would move in for the capture.

Finally it came. The trio approached the cabin, speculating loudly about the property line, and Burns called out, "Hey, Ted, can you come out here and show us where it is?"

Slowly the door opened, and a sooty, bearded head popped out. Recognizing Jerry, Kaczynski ventured a little farther out into the cold. "Sure," he said. "Just let me go back in and get my jacket."

At that, the two FBI agents jumped him, before he could get a weapon.

Down the hill, all we heard were a few muffled shouts. Then Kaczynski came into view, handcuffed, being hustled down the road by Max and Tom, who were clutching his arms on either side.

"It must have been quite a struggle," I said to John, for from a distance Kaczynski's clothes looked disheveled and ripped, as if from a scuffle. But as he drew closer I could see that they were not torn but simply rotting off his body. He had been living without running water. He smelled like warm dirt and was so filthy that even his long eyelashes were caked with soot—above the bluest eyes I have ever seen. He was missing a front tooth.

Kaczynski was led into Williams's cabin, where he was seated at the head of a small, handmade pine table, with his hands still cuffed behind him. Max and Paul Wilhelmus of the U.S. Postal Inspection Service took the other two chairs. I went out to the woodpile to get some split logs to stoke the woodstove, thinking that our captive was probably even colder than we were, dressed only in a brown threadbare T-shirt and dark pants, worn paper-thin. It was a beautiful day, the warmest I had seen in my six weeks in Montana, with the early afternoon sun pushing the temperature to 45 degrees. Back inside, I noticed some newly laid insect eggs on the windowsill. Spring was on the way.

As I fiddled around the woodstove, I could feel Kaczynski's eyes tracking my every movement. When I looked back at him, he would avert his gaze, even when I smiled. Max and Paul were making small talk, basically ignoring him, until during a lull he asked them, "What is this about?"

At that point, Kaczynski was not yet under arrest. Max advised him that the FBI had obtained a search warrant on his cabin and that it was currently being executed by federal agents. He explained that they were looking for instrumentalities of some crimes, specifically, bombs, never mentioning the Unabomber to Kaczynski.

Then he looked Kaczynski straight in the eye and addressed the fear that we all shared—that the cabin was booby-trapped. "Ted," Max said, "we have agents about to search your cabin. Agents who have families, wives, and children. Is there any reason for those agents to be concerned, Ted? I mean, is their safety in jeopardy being in your cabin?"

Kaczynski declined to confirm or allay our fears, responding, "Well, this looks pretty serious, and they say if you're ever in serious trouble, you shouldn't talk without an attorney. So I think I'll wait until I have an attorney."

I still remember the look I exchanged with Max, a powerful silent communication of our fervent wish for the searchers' safety.

Kaczynski now asked to see the search warrant, as was his right. When Max placed it before him, he tried to reach for it, forgetting that his hands were cuffed behind his back. That showed me that beneath his impassive façade, he was feeling stressed. Standing beside him, I turned the pages so he could read it, struck by the irony that a man whose bombs had torn and crippled the hands of others was deprived of the use of his own.

After rapidly perusing the warrant, Kaczynski asked, "Am I under arrest?"

"No," Max replied. "You are not."

Kaczynski raised his shaggy head, saying, "Oh, then am I free to go?"

"Well, no," Max told him. "For the safety of others and yourself, you are being detained while we search your cabin."

Now I noticed that the suspect was sweating and trembling, and again reflected on the irony of a killer being detained by armed federal agents for his own protection.

Interestingly, at no time did Kaczynski specifically ask what he would be charged with should the searchers find the materials listed in the warrant. To me this demonstrated "consciousness of guilt"—that he knew we would find what we were looking for, as well as the conclusions we would draw from it. He wasn't confused and indignant, like an innocent man would be. In my heart I felt that he had been preparing for this day for over a decade, expecting to be caught by the very FBI he had described in a letter to the *New York Times* as "a joke."

It seemed that only ten or fifteen minutes had passed when we heard hollers coming from the direction of the cabin. The first whoop startled me so much that I'm sure I jumped. We couldn't tell if the shouts were cries of pain, from someone injured in a booby trap, or expressions of delight at striking pay dirt. Max gestured to me to go outside and investigate the cause of the commotion.

At the door I ran into Chuck Pardee, a former Navy SEAL bearing news that almost brought tears of joy to my eyes. He reported that the bomb techs and the Evidence Response Team (ERT) had discovered three neatly labeled bottles of precursor chemicals, of the kind typically used as catalysts in the devices of the Unabomber.

I felt as if a wave of cool water had washed over me, profound relief that the months upon months of fieldwork, of examining documents with a magnifying glass, of chasing dead-end leads—and finally, the weeks of sitting with my eyes fixed on Stemple Pass Road—were vindicated at last. I could only imagine what veterans like Tony Muljat, who had dedicated years upon years of their lives to the UNABOM investigation, would feel when they got the news.

I had to tell Max. Sticking my head back inside, I rolled my eyes to summon him to the door. He came along, and when we were out of earshot of Kaczynski, I blurted out all I knew, jumping up and down like a kid. We grabbed each other in a bear hug.

Back inside, I noticed that Kaczynski was visibly shivering—from fear, I realized when I saw that his T-shirt was drenched with sweat. So I took off Seth's ski parka and draped it over his shoulders. He smiled and thanked me. I asked him if he was thirsty and he said, "Yes, I am."

Since there was no running water in the cabin, I offered him the soda from the box lunch that I had been issued at the Seven-Up Ranch that morning. His hands were cuffed behind his back, so I held the can up to his mouth so he could sip at it. There was also a candy bar in the box, which I fed to him, thinking that I was showing him far more compassion than he had ever spared for his victims, people who had never personally wronged him, people whom he didn't even know.

When he finished, we made small talk, for he was "lawyered up" and not about to offer me an explanation of his career as a maimer and killer. "What's it like living off the land?" I asked.

He proceeded to tell me how he cooked turnips and carrots in a pot of boiling water on his woodburning stove—making me feel, as he droned on, as if I were on a bad date. I found myself glancing out the window and saw that on the sill, the insect eggs that I had spied earlier were now hatching, warmed by the heat of the stove. It seemed like a sign, a herald of transformation.

It was late in the afternoon when Max and Tom McDaniel returned to the cabin for the last time. They gently but firmly lifted our captive to his feet, announcing, "Ted Kaczynski, you are under arrest for the murder of three people."

The search had turned up not only the precursor chemicals but also the typewriter on which he'd written the Manifesto and various Unabomber letters, dating back to 1978; carbon copies of his correspondence with the *New York Times;* detailed notes on his bomb experiments; his personal diary, describing his bombing forays and expressing frustration when his devices failed; and a half-built pipe bomb as well as a fully assembled, ready-to-be-mailed device that he'd been storing under his bed. We even found his hit list of intended victims. Finally, we discovered his Unabomber "costume," the gray hooded sweatshirt and sunglasses that were featured in the 1987 sketch and had become an inedible image in our popular culture.

Ted Kaczynski didn't offer a word of denial, act surprised, or even blink when Max told him that the FBI suspected him of being the Unabomber. He remained silent as he was placed in shackles and led away.

Back at the cabin, there was a media feeding frenzy going on. Determined to get a scoop, a national TV newsmagazine crew tried to rush the barricades while the technicians were still removing explosive materials. While struggling to keep the crime scene from being trampled by the press, the site supervisor fell and broke his shoulder. Being a registered nurse, I stabilized him for transport to the hospital, leaving the investigation short one bomb expert. The news crew was arrested, and the question of what to do with them went all the way up to Attorney General Janet Reno. Finally, the Bureau was instructed to confiscate the videotape but to release the journalists with a simple reprimand. Being that freedom of the press is a fundamental guarantee of the United States Constitution, which I am sworn to uphold, I certainly believe in the public's "right to know." But where is the media guaranteed the "right to profit" by getting first crack at a sensational story at the expense of people's privacy and dignity or of the integrity of a criminal investigation?

On June 19, 1996, Theodore John Kaczynski would be indicted by a grand jury on ten separate counts of transporting an explosive device with intent to kill or injure, mailing an explosive device with intent to kill or injure, and using an explosive device in a crime of violence: three counts for the death of Gilbert Murray, one for the killing of Hugh Campbell Scrutton, and three apiece for the Epstein and Gelernter attacks. On January 22, 1998, he would plead guilty on all ten counts plus an additional three brought against him in New Jersey, as part of a deal with the government that would let him escape the death penalty. He is now serving life in prison without possibility of parole. The Beast was dead.

17

THE SHARK FENCE

Back in San Francisco, I had a new role, as Head Field Profiling Coordinator, and a new assignment, to the Child Abduction Task Force. One of my first major assignments was the rescue of Joshua. The Bureau also tapped me to be a spokesperson—thanks to my profiling training and all the police education work I'd done—to lecture university and professional law-enforcement groups, as well as the general public, on women's and children's safety. I was even asked to appear as the FBI expert in the nationally distributed educational video *Missing: What to Do If Your Child Disappears*, produced by the Klaas Foundation in 1997.

Of course, a single lecture—or even a few pages—can't really do justice to the subject of safety, which could be a book in itself. But there are some general guidelines that I can offer here, starting with the number one directive I tell my audiences: If you or your child is ever accosted in a place where others might hear you and come to your aid, don't scream "Help!" Instead, yell "Fire!"

A cry of "Help!" tends to confuse people. They often will dismiss it, for it is very common to hear joking or trivial calls for help. Children at play scream "Help!" all the time. It is all too easy to justify ignoring a cry for help by saying, "I didn't understand what was going on," or "I thought it was none of my business." Even if people do recognize that a cry is serious, they will often be paralyzed with indecision, reluctant, or afraid to intervene personally but uncertain whether the situation warrants a call to the police. But we all know exactly what to do some-one yells "Fire!"—pick up the phone and call 911.

Obviously, I am not advocating yelling "Fire!" in a crowded theater or for frivolous reasons. But if your life or safety is truly in danger, don't be embarrassed to use this stratagem. I have been giving this advice for years and have been assured by many fire departments that they are more than willing to thwart a rape, abduction, or violent assault. Yelling "Fire!" in these situations is not at all the same as giving a false alarm.

The time to plan what to do if you or your child is accosted is right now, not when the attack is under way, when most people will be too panicky to think straight. Mentally rehearsing ahead of time or coaching your child on what to do in various situations will not only build confidence but help you recognize that you may have options for repelling the attacker. God willing you will never have to implement these strategies, but if you do, planning ahead and keeping your wits about you might well save your life.

Women often ask me whether they should sign up for self-defense classes. My answer is yes, certainly, for you may well pick up some useful tips, but with a caveat—even if you hold a black belt in karate, you can't count on being able to overpower a determined assailant. Remember that even female FBI agents, with months of physical training by the experts at Quantico, are warned against overreliance on their defensive skills. Nor do I recommend that you keep a gun in the house for protection, unless you are very well trained to use it; and even then, don't let it make you cocky, for there is a sizable risk that it will be turned on you. Your brains will be as valuable as your brawn or your Beretta when it comes to handling a sexual assault.

The first place to think about protecting yourself is at home, where some 37 percent of rapes and sexual assaults of adults occur. The best way to foil a home invasion is to prevent it from happening in the first place, by keeping your doors and windows locked. Your doors should have sturdy deadbolt locks, and you can easily secure double-hung windows by pounding a nail halfway into each side of the upper window's sash so that the bottom window can be raised only a few inches. Don't leave your shades up and your curtains open—both burglars and sex offenders target the homes of women living alone or with young children. If a criminal encounters a house that is well secured and where there is the possibility of a male in residence, he will pass it by in hopes of finding an easier mark.

Don't open your door unless you are expecting the person on the other side, and never let a would-be visitor know that you or your children are home alone. Jeanine Nicarico's killer broke down the door to get at her after she revealed that her mother wasn't home. But these rules do not apply only to strangers. Remember that virtually every rapist, killer, and child molester is somebody's neighbor; and plenty of them reside in ordinary suburban neighborhoods. Some 22 percent of those convicted of rape and sexual assault are married at the time of their arrest, and more than a third are divorced or separated. If their own spouses and children don't know that they are sex offenders, how can you?

Don't assume that such factors as your size, age, or visible pregnancy will make you less of a target. More than one of the Burlington rapist's victims was a hundred pounds overweight, just to cite one example. There are close to twice as many sexual assault murders of women over sixty—an astonishing 14 percent of the annual total—than of women aged forty to forty-nine (8.3 percent) or fifty to fifty-nine (6.3 percent). Certain killers deliberately seek out older women in order to act out their anger against authoritative females in their lives and because the elderly are more vulnerable and easier to control.

Prepare yourself for every woman's worst nightmare—waking to find an intruder in the house—by keeping a cell phone by your bed. Fix some possible escape routes in your mind, as well as your likeliest sources of aid. If you live in an apartment building with thin walls, yelling "Fire!"—not "Help!"—may rouse your neighbors to action, but if your house is too isolated for others to hear you, screaming may do you no good and it may panic your attacker into harming you more than he intended.

There is no one best or safest way to handle a sexual assault. Every situation is different, but your goal will always be the same—to survive the attack. Most rapists, fortunately, fall into the "power reassurance" category and will use force more to ensure your compliance than because they enjoy inflicting pain. If you are very angry or physically aggressive with them, they may respond in kind. So keep your head—do your best to find a way out—but if you can't find one, consider the fact that in some cases compliance may be your best or only option. Compliance is by no means the same as consent. I am not advocating immediate submission but pointing out that you are going to have to determine the difference between productive struggling, which may help you escape, and provocation. Be aware that you may be walking a thin line.

If you can't get away and it seems appropriate, persuasion may be worth a try, but watch your words. Don't patronize a sexual assailant—remember that this is a man who has problems with women. Don't lie to him, for if he's in your house he may already know your name, among other things about you, and lying may give him a reason to hurt you. A backhanded compliment—"You're such a good-looking guy that you don't need to do this to get sex"—will very likely backfire on you; as will saying things like "I'm a doctor" or "I'm a virgin" that seem to elevate you above him. Strategies like throwing up, urinating, defecating, or acting crazy are very risky, for women have paid with their lives for disgusting rapists by losing bowel control out of fear. I shiver when I hear women advised to forestall rape by claiming to have AIDS or a venereal disease, thereby establishing themselves as "whores," deserving of punishment, in their assailants' minds. I wouldn't try it. For the same reason, don't make the mistake of getting sexual with a rapist, taking the initiative to arouse him or feigning enjoyment, on the theory that showing him a good time will get you off easy. It could be fatal. Rape is all about power, not sex.

A rapist who is abusive from the outset, physically or verbally, should be regarded as very dangerous. Do whatever you can to mitigate his rage. Don't cry. Try twisting rather than pulling to get out of his grip. If he gets his hands around your throat, don't waste time trying to pry them off. Assume that you are fighting for your life, and go straight for his eyeballs with your fingers, jamming them into his head as hard as you can—don't be squeamish—with no letup.

The second most common place for sexual assaults to occur is in the residence of someone other than the victim (about 19 percent), which brings up the issue of date or acquaintance rape. About 41 percent of all rapes and sexual assaults are committed by acquaintances of the victim. Prudence is the key here. Until you know a person well, dates should be in public places, not at home, and always let someone know who you'll be with and where you're going. Make sure you have cab fare, a cell phone, and change for a pay phone. If something makes you uneasy, don't hesitate to call a taxi or a friend to pick you up and present it to your date as a fait accompli. Don't fight about it—just make a polite excuse and get away.

During the dating period of a relationship, both parties should be on their best behavior. That means that you should not drink too much and make yourself vulnerable to an attack, and if your date seems intent on getting high, consider it as a warning sign. Other signals that trouble may be brewing are aggressive behavior, such as rough touching and hard poking to make a point, or derogatory remarks about women. Many date rape victims later report that they ignored such cues, to their regret.

Date rapists count on their victims' silence and, because they so often move in the same social circles, especially in campus settings, can effectively intimidate them with threats of denunciations to peers ("I'll tell everyone you were so stoned that you don't remember how you came on to me") or denials. Some victims won't report assaults that stop short of frank violence or forcible intercourse ("Nothing really horrible happened, so it's not worth it"). But whether or not you choose to prosecute, it is always worth reporting such incidents to the authorities so that there's a record when the creep pulls the same stunt with someone else—which he will definitely do, possibly with greater force.

A word on drinking: Unfair as it may seem, women should not go to bars alone. Sex offenders don't think like normal men and are always on the alert for what they perceive as "provocative" behavior. I once heard a silver-haired child molester in his fifties explain that an eight-year-old was "flirting" with him. If you give a sex offender the hint that you may be available—through your presence in a rowdy bar or in the park at 2 A.M., your behavior, or your dress—he will project his own desires onto you and may well try to take you up on your supposed invitation. It's not right and it's unjust, but that's the way it is.

Should you be accosted in a public place, scream "Fire!" and fight hard to escape. Don't go along meekly because an assailant has a weapon, but seize any opportunity to sound the alarm or twist out of his grasp. Your priority in this situation is to stop the assailant from dragging you away from other people or, worst yet, into his car. Once you get into his personal environment, your options will be much more limited and you are not likely to escape unscathed.

Most of us spend so much time driving that car safety is an issue unto itself. Don't drive a ratty car that is likely to break down, and don't attract the interest of a potential assailant with vanity plates bearing your name, your profession, personal data ("MAMA II," "BIGSIS," "WIFEY") or—God forbid—such teasers as "QTPIE," "LUVBUG," or "GOTCHA." Always make sure that you have enough gas so that you can be picky about where you stop to fill up, avoiding bad neighborhoods and deserted areas. At a gas station, check for suspicious characters lurking around before you get out to work the pump, then turn off the motor, take your keys, and lock the car doors. Never leave children in an unlocked car if you have to go inside to pay the attendant. When you return, don't sit in your parked car, checking your makeup in the mirror and calling attention to the fact that you are a woman alone (or with young children) on the road. Get going.

If your car does break down, don't accept help from strangers. I tell my audiences that a cell or car phone is not a luxury but as essential as gasoline for a woman driver. If you can't get to an exit on the freeway, turn your flashers on and keep your doors locked. If a man tries to come to your aid, even if it's not true, tell him—with your window cracked, not open—"I've already called the police, but would you please call again?" Never get out of the car.

The same rules hold true when any stranger approaches your car. Keep the motor running, the doors locked, and the windows up, and don't get out even if he pulls a gun and threatens to shoot you through the glass. Step on the gas and hightail it out of there—forward, backward, any way you can. Blast the horn to summon help. Remember that your car is a one-ton weapon in itself. Use it if you have to.

If you are bumped from behind while driving by a male driver or a group of men, don't assume that it's an accident. Don't get out of your car or open your window more than a crack; and if something looks fishy in the situation, speed away. Dents are easy to fix. Approach red lights with caution, staying well back of the car ahead of you and alert to who is alongside you. Don't be so busy chatting on the phone or fiddling with the radio that you can get caught in a menacing situation. If you have reason to feel nervous, honk your horn and get out of there. If you have to—and can do so safely—run the light.

Exercise care in parking lots and garages, which is where a surprising 7 percent of adult sexual assaults occur. Never park or even walk alongside a van—the sex offender's vehicle of choice—which can also block an assault or a kidnapping from view. If you return to your car and find a van parked beside it, enter your car from the door farthest away from it. Don't get close to it. Never park in a slot next to a wall, where you might be boxed in on both sides. Pay attention to what's happening around you when you put packages or children in the car. At night or any other time when a lot is deserted or feels threatening, have a legitimate security guard, not just some guy who looks official and offers to help, walk you to your car. There's no need to feel embarrassed—you won't be the first woman to ask.

Finally, keep a flashlight that works in your trunk, and have a mechanic show you how to trip the latch from the inside. You may even want to practice getting yourself out of the trunk (with someone you trust standing by, of course). Should you somehow wind up inside an attacker's trunk that you can't open, remember the story of the woman who was wise enough not to panic, as most of us would, but to root around for a weapon. She found a sharp object, and the minute the attacker opened the trunk, she sprung at him and disabled him with it. No matter what is happening to you, it pays to keep your wits about you and think through your best course of action. Ideally, decent luck, reasonably good judgment, and the precautions we've been discussing will keep you from ever finding yourself in such a dire situation. But just in case, it only makes sense to maximize your chances of surviving an assault by being prepared.

Being prepared is even more important for your child, who will not have the same defensive and strategic capabilities that you might in a threatening situation. Prevention is the absolute best protection against molestation or abduction. Many parents worry that repeated warnings about these issues will frighten their children and rob them of their innocence, but the sad fact is that if you don't address these possibilities head on you may leave your child more vulnerable to a predator and without resources, forced to figure out what to do on his or her own, should a dangerous situation arise. A onetime discussion isn't going to do the trick either. I recommend that parents consult their children's teachers and librarians to find out the best guidebooks and other re-sources currently available; and then, armed with good advice, give the child an updated age-appropriate talk each year. Make it as matter of fact as a "Don't cross on the red light" lecture rather than an embar-rassing ordeal—it's just as much a part of life. Remember that a shocking 78 percent of the sexual assaults committed every year have victims under age eighteen. Some 45 percent of these victims are under the age of twelve.

Obviously a thoroughgoing discussion of child safety is beyond the scope of this book, but again, I can offer a few guidelines. First of all, your child's safety begins with you and how alert you are to adults in his or her life who may be showing too much interest. The vast majority of sexual assaults against young children are committed by family mem-bers (about 49 percent for children under five and about 42 percent for children aged six to eleven) or acquaintances (some 48 percent for those under five and about 53 percent in the six to eleven range). Strangers are responsible for only 3.1 and 4.7 percent, respectively, of the sexual assaults in these age groups, as opposed to roughly 30 percent for adults.

Girls represent about 70 percent of the victims in the under-five group and about 75 percent among those ages six to eleven. For both sexes, there is a peak around age four. After that, girls' risk will decline slightly until around age eleven, when it will start shooting way up to reach a lifetime high at age fourteen. For boys, age four remains the time of life when they are most likely to be victimized.

The message here is clear: Parents must be very careful about the adults to whom they entrust their children and must keep close tabs on relatives, friends, and neighbors, as well as the adults, such as nannies and teachers, who play a role in their children's lives. Don't permit sleepovers unless you know the other parents well, or else host your own. Be leery of weekends away, scouting and camping trips, and any outing for which the adult in charge turns you down if you volunteer to come along. Any leader who is on the level will be thrilled to have extra help.

Be specific with your children about what constitutes inappropriate attention, even from people they know. I find it helpful to speak of "the bathing suit area" as the expanse of unclothed body no one is allowed to see or touch and that they are not to look at or touch on an adult, if asked. If someone transgresses this rule, a child should remember the three-word formula "No, Go, Tell."

"No" means that the child should say firmly, "No, don't touch me there."

"Go" means to get away from the offender immediately and head for a place of safety, where there are other adults.

"Tell" means that as soon as it is safe—stress this—the child should tell an adult about the incident. Sex offenders very often threaten to punish children for disclosure or to harm their families, so I advise parents to explain that this is one situation in which it is not only okay but imperative for children to lie. The child should promise the attacker silence, but then reveal the truth as soon as he or she gets away to a safe place. As for the threats, it can be helpful to reassure children that bad adults will sometimes try to "trick" them and they should not believe the offender.

When a child tells you about inappropriate touching, above all, take it seriously. Give children permission to confide in you by assuring them that they have done nothing wrong, that the offending adult is solely to blame. Get as much detail as you can without putting words in a child's mouth by asking, "So what did Uncle Bob say?" or saying, "Show me where he put his hand." Don't get emotional or you may frighten or shame the child, who is already upset, into silence.

A child may be too young or, for whatever reason, unable to bring him- or herself to tell you about an offense, so you should familiarize yourself with the signs of trouble. When you are changing diapers, check the child's anal and genital areas for redness or irritation. Though about 95 percent of sex offenders who target children are male (77 percent of

whom are adults), children under six had the highest proportion of female victimizers (12 percent), followed by children of ages six through
twelve (6 percent) and teenagers (3 percent). Just 1 percent of sexual
assaults on adults are committed by women. These figures certainly make
a persuasive case for "nanny-cams," secret video cameras planted to observe caretakers' interactions with young children; and because they re-
flect only reported assaults, suggest that female childcare providers may
constitute an even larger, undetected category of child abusers.

In older children, the physical signs of abuse may be painful bowel
movements; redness, pain, swelling, or bruising in the anal and genital
areas; and vaginitis and urinary tract infections. A child may complain
of stomachaches or headaches, have fitful sleep, or develop signs of emotional upset such as bedwetting, a new fear of adults, or reluctance to
leave home. Sexualized behavior—having an age-inappropriate knowledge of sex, excessively touching the genitals, exhibitionistic actions like
skirt raising in little girls—may also be a tip-off.

Listen to what children say and read between the lines. If a child says,
"I don't like Uncle Billy" or "I hate to go to Mary's house," ask why.
If the answer doesn't perfectly satisfy you, keep your child away from
the person or the place and do your best to get to the bottom of the
problem. Don't endanger your child by letting him or her return to an
environment of abuse—or worse.

The foregoing discussion does not mean to imply that your child has
little to fear from strangers. On the contrary, it is essential that you instill
a healthy fear of strangers in your children, giving them concrete trouble
signs to watch for and clear images of what to do in a crisis situation.
Obviously, the advice you will give a five-year-old will be vastly different from what you will tell a ten-year-old, but here are a few sketchy
principles.

First of all, explain clearly to your child what stranger means. What
I give parents as a working definition to tell children is, "A stranger is
someone who has never eaten dinner in your home." That means that
neighbors, casual acquaintances, and anyone else on the periphery of
your child's world, whom you haven't had a chance to evaluate personally, should be regarded with roughly the same degree of caution as those
completely unknown.

Establish a secret password with your child, never to be divulged to anyone, so that if a stranger claims to have been sent by you to get him, he can apply a concrete test. Seth and I used the word "Garfield," the name of the famous cartoon cat.

Teach your child never to go anywhere alone, but with the warning that there isn't much safety in numbers unless one of the parties is an approved adult. Two or three nine-year-olds are no match for a grown man. Unless properly chaperoned, your child should never be beyond hailing distance of help—so there are no forays to a fishing hole or a secret clubhouse in the woods (which may be no secret to a sex offender).

But even in public places, your children must use good judgment. Among other things, teach children of both sexes to check for lone lurkers before they enter public restrooms, which are perfect hiding places for offenders. Don't let your young son use a public men's room alone. Open the door and yell, "Anybody in there?" Wait till it clears out before you let him go in and wait for him right outside the door. When he gets to be eight or nine, make sure your son knows the "zip and split" rule—that if anyone ogles him for more than a few seconds, he should simply leave, whether or not he has concluded his business.

Be as explicit as possible with your child when describing danger signs and possible solutions rather than offering vague, confusing generalities. For example, list the kinds of things adults don't normally ask children for: directions, help carrying packages out to a car, aid in finding a lost puppy. Most children are overeager to please adults, so it is wise to encourage a natural wariness in them. Tell them what to do if a stranger approaches them for help: Say no and run away!

Underscore these lessons by enacting them with your children. Role-play what to do should they be grabbed by a stranger: Kick, bite, twist away, and yell "Fire!" I know of a child who managed to save himself when accosted in a movie theater bathroom by a bold assailant who had already killed three other children. As he was being carried away through the crowded lobby, where people ignored his plight, assuming that he was just another child having a tantrum, he screamed: "Help me, he's not my daddy! He's going to kill me!" The killer dropped him and fled.

You may also want to tell children that there may be situations when no one is around to help them and they may have to wait and watch for the right moment to break free—that they are not to give up or be paralyzed by fear of an attacker who has threatened to kill them if they try to escape. In one recent case in Vallejo, California, a trucker driving down the road was hailed by a little girl, who had a strange story to tell. She had been abducted two days earlier while waiting for the school bus. After two days of abuse, she was left tied up in the backseat of the offender's car while he stopped into a store—to buy garbage bags, as it turned out—and managed to get free. She pointed out the car she had escaped from to the trucker, who summoned the police, and the man was caught. Thanks to her courage, self-possession, and patience, the little girl had watched for her opportunity, seized it, and saved herself.

Inevitably someone in each of my lectures will ask, "What should I do if I am—or worse, my child is—the victim of a sexual assault?" My answer is: "Call the police immediately." Don't go home to call a friend or to nurse your psychic and emotional pain privately, waiting until the next morning or until a time when you feel strong enough to face the ordeal of an investigation. Don't bathe, for there may be evidence on your clothing or on your person, such as the assailant's hair or DNA. You may have bruises, which the police should photograph. All these things can put your assailant behind bars if and when he is apprehended. Don't compromise your own case.

Many rape victims fear coming forward because of the horror stories they've heard about vicious defense lawyers, who drag victims through the dirt and put their personal lives on trial. I'm not saying that never happens, but today it is less common than in the unenlightened past. In the words of New York prosecutor and victims' rights crusader Linda Fairstein (cited in *Obsession* by John Douglas): "The stranger-rape defense nowadays is generally very gentle on the victim . . . It doesn't have to impugn her reliability, her personality, or her lifestyle at all."

Speaking of the recovery process, Fairstein, who has prosecuted countless sexual assault cases, goes on to say, "Getting control back is the first step. I am a big believer in the fact that most rape victims recover from the crime. They don't forget that the crime has occurred, but they recover very well."

So don't be defeated by shame, guilt, fear, "dirtiness," unworthiness, and all the other torments that rape victims feel. If you are and your attacker goes unpunished, he will have succeeded in violating your sense of self, just as he has your person. He will be "winning" again.

Should you discover that a child has been victimized—I hate the word *molest* because it sounds so benign, when in fact what child molesters do is shatter lives—take action. Especially when the sexual assailant is a member of their immediate circle, a close friend, or a family member, maybe even a spouse, people often want to retreat into denial, loath to destroy their own relationships and families. Even the child him- or herself may be torn with ambivalence, confused by newly aroused sexual feelings, ashamed and guilty, fearful of being blamed for the dissolution of a family and, sometimes, even of losing the attacker whom he continues to love. But if you fail to act, you are not only imperiling your child's ability ever to achieve a satisfying emotional and sexual adjustment in life but you are leaving him or her with a terrible burden—a sense of being not worthy of protection, of being the one at fault. If you prosecute, you will show your child unequivocally that it is the adult who has done wrong and deserves punishment. The child may hate you now if you act, but if you don't you may risk losing his or her love for the rest of your life.

Then too, very few sexual predators, whether of children or adults, can ever be content with a single victim. These are obsession-fueled acts, by their very nature self-perpetuating, with each new assault whetting the offender's appetite for more. As Douglas writes in *Obsession*, "Unlike burglars or bank robbers or even drug dealers, who do not necessarily enjoy what they do for a living—who merely want the money it brings them—sexual predators and child molesters do enjoy their crimes; in fact, many of them do not even consider them crimes. They don't want to change . . . In the vast majority of cases, once someone has developed the obsession to commit rape, child molestation, and other heinous sexual crimes, it is going to be very difficult, if not impossible to turn him around."

By not reporting such crimes, you are virtually assuring that the offender will prey on others. In the case of child molestation by a relative
or friend, chances are that the other victims will be within your own
family.

As I remind my audiences, public safety is not the sole responsibility
of the FBI or even the police. Law enforcement bodies are only nets.
The legislature determines where the nets are dropped and how big their
holes can be; and the legal system sorts the catch—harmless minnows,
stingrays, swordfish—with the medical profession picking through the
haul for exotic species. But it is up to us as citizens, as a society—an
ecosystem, if you will—to decide who should be swimming freely in
our midst. How many voracious sharks, parasitic lampreys, and other
predators can be allowed to infest our waters before we are overrun?

In the year 2000 I reached the twenty-year mark in my FBI career, the
point at which most agents retire. Working for the FBI has been more
thrilling and challenging (and often heartbreaking) than I ever could have
imagined when I slipped through the doors just cracking open for
women at Quantico and accepted my father's gift of a "lady's" gun.
Now, as I look back, I marvel at how much the perception of women
in the Bureau has changed in the course of my own life—from barely
tolerated gate-crashers to "priority recruits" today. We represent 15 percent of the agent force, and given the Bureau's current hiring policies,
stand to become, along with minority group members, an even more
significant constituency in the future. The face of the FBI is no longer
white and male.

We are already making a significant contribution. Today there are
women in every field of service—on the technical squads, performing
acts of derring-do and engineering wizardry, such as break-ins to plant
court-ordered bugs; on the aviation squad, even on SWAT teams. Two
of us of have sacrificed our lives in the line of duty. The first, Robin
Ahrens, died in 1985, the victim of "friendly fire" in a massive shoot-
out. The second, Martha Martinez, died a hero in 1994. She was sitting
at a desk in a Washington, D.C., police station when a gang member
suspected of a double homicide came looking for the cop who was

working his case. The suspect opened fire, killing a male agent and a cop, then wounding three others before Martha got to him. She shot his gun, jamming it, but when one of his rounds caught her in the arm, it broke her grip on her weapon. He sprang for the gun, and she fought him but lost—he managed to grab it and shoot her in the head. Then he turned the gun on himself. What courage she had! She sacrificed her own life that day to save others.

As I become a private citizen, I salute the esteemed colleagues, female and male—for I have known many fine, even heroic men too—with whom I have had the privilege to work as a public servant. To me and to the colleagues I respect, male and female, the "duties" of a special agent that Hoover referred to in his directive barring women—ensnaring terrorists like the FALN or the Unabomber, routing corrupt racketeers, vanquishing serial rapists and murderers, among the other predators who inhabit the murky social, psychological, and moral depths of our society—have felt less like an onus than a mission, the fulfillment of a sacred public trust. We have been part of the net of protection, the shark fence.

SOURCES

The statistics cited in this book derive from various reports issued by the U.S. Department of Justice, Office of Justice Programs, Bureau of Justice Statistics, notably: *Sex Offenses and Offenders: An Analysis of Data on Rape and Sexual Assault; Child Victimizers: Violent Offenders and Their Victims; Sexual Assault of Young Children as Reported to Law Enforcement: Victim, Incident and Offender Characteristics; Urban, Suburban, and Rural Victimization, 1993–1998; Female Victims of Violent Crime and Violence Against Women: Estimates from the Redesigned Survey;* as well as from the FBI's *Uniform Crime Report* (1998/1999).

Other publications referred to in the book include:

Douglas, John, and Olshaker, Mark, *Mindhunter* (New York: Scribner, 1995).

Douglas, John, and Olshaker, Mark, *Journey Into Darkness* (New York: Scribner, 1997).

Douglas, John, and Olshaker, Mark, *Obsession* (New York: Scribner, 1998).

Douglas, John, and Olshaker, Mark, *The Anatomy of Motive* (New York: Scribner, 1999).

Dubner, Stephen, article in *Time* magazine, October 18, 1999.

Graysmith, Robert, *Unabomber: A Desire to Kill* (Washington, D.C.: Regnery, 1997).

Hazelwood, Roy, and Burgess, Ann Wolbert, editors, *Practical Aspects of Rape Investigation: A Multidisciplinary Approach* (Boca Raton: CRC Press, 1995).

Michaud, Stephen G., and Hazelwood, Roy, *The Evil That Men Do* (New York: St. Martin's Press, 1998).

Ressler, Robert, and Shachtman, Tom, *Whoever Fights Monsters* (New York: St. Martin's Press, 1992).

INDEX

Note: Names followed by asterisks (*) are pseudonyms.